I am naturally proud of this
Boy from Adel!
He was certainly an incredible
Journalist

Hope you will find time to
read it for yourself
Mother

The Changing South
of Gene Patterson

Southern Dissent

Florida A&M University, Tallahassee
Florida Atlantic University, Boca Raton
Florida Gulf Coast University, Ft. Myers
Florida International University, Miami
Florida State University, Tallahassee
University of Central Florida, Orlando
University of Florida, Gainesville
University of North Florida, Jacksonville
University of South Florida, Tampa
University of West Florida, Pensacola

Southern Dissent
Edited by Stanley Harrold and Randall M. Miller

The Other South: Southern Dissenters in the Nineteenth Century,
by Carl N. Degler with a new preface (2000)

*Crowds and Soldiers in Revolutionary North Carolina: The Culture
of Violence in Riot and War,* by Wayne E. Lee (2001)

*"Lord, We're Just Trying to Save Your Water": Environmental Activism and Dissent in
the Appalachian South,* by Suzanne Marshall (2002)

The Changing South of Gene Patterson: Journalism and Civil Rights, 1960–1968,
edited by Roy Peter Clark and Raymond Arsenault (2002)

University Press of Florida

Gainesville | Tallahassee | Tampa | Boca Raton
Pensacola | Orlando | Miami | Jacksonville | Ft. Myers

Edited by
Roy Peter Clark and
Raymond Arsenault

Foreword by
Stanley Harrold
and Randall M. Miller

The
Changing
South
of
Gene
Patterson

Journalism and Civil Rights,
1960–1968

07 06 05 04 03 02   6 5 4 3 2 1

Library of Congress Cataloging-in-Publication Data
The changing South of Gene Patterson: journalism and civil rights,
1960–1968 / edited by Roy Peter Clark and Raymond Arsenault; foreword
by Stanley Harrold and Randall M. Miller
p. cm. — (Southern dissent)
Includes bibliographical references (p.) and index.
ISBN 0-8130-2574-5 (c.: alk. paper)
1. African Americans—Civil rights—Southern States—History—
20th century. 2. African Americans—Civil rights—Georgia—Atlanta—
History—20th century. 3. Southern States—Race relations. 4. Atlanta
(Ga.)—Race relations. 5. Patterson, Eugene C. (Eugene Corbett), 1923–.
6. Journalists—Georgia—Atlanta—Biography. 7. Civil rights workers—
Georgia—Atlanta—Biography. I. Clark, Roy Peter. II. Arsenault, Raymond.
III. Patterson, Eugene C. (Eugene Corbett), 1923–. IV. Series.
E185.61 .C535 2002
305.896'073075—dc21 2002071463

The University Press of Florida is the scholarly publishing agency
for the State University System of Florida, comprising Florida A&M
University, Florida Atlantic University, Florida Gulf Coast University,
Florida International University, Florida State University, University of
Central Florida, University of Florida, University of North Florida,
University of South Florida, and University of West Florida.

University Press of Florida
15 Northwest 15th Street
Gainesville, FL 32611–2079
http://www.upf.com

We dedicate this book as a legacy to our daughters
Amelia Hardee Arsenault
Anne Hardee Arsenault
Alison Clark Hastings
Emily Faith Clark
Lauren Elizabeth Clark

Contents

Series Foreword   xi

Acknowledgments   xv

Part One. Introduction

1. A Journalist's View: How Gene Patterson Persuaded His White
   Southern Kinfolk to Do What Was Right   3
   Roy Peter Clark

2. A Historian's View: Gene Patterson, Southern Liberalism, and the
   Vise of History   17
   Raymond Arsenault

Part Two. The Atlanta Columns of Eugene Patterson, 1960–1968

3. 1960: A Rising Wind   45
4. 1961: The Rock and the Anchor   61
5. 1962: Acts of Honor   89
6. 1963: One Small Shoe   121
7. 1964: How Do You Reach Them?   153
8. 1965: Thumping the Melon   181
9. 1966: The Savage Difference   199
10. 1967: Hooked on a Log   219
11. 1968: A Thousand Times Unafraid   231

Part Three. Reflections

12. Forged in Battle: The Formative Experience of War   245
    Eugene Patterson

13. The Long Road Back to Georgia   255
    Eugene Patterson
14. Gene Patterson: An Appreciation   277
    Howell Raines
15. The Legacy of Gene Patterson:
    An Interview with Cynthia Tucker   281

Cast of Characters   287
Selected Bibliography   295
Notes on Editors and Contributors   301
Index   303

Photo section follows page 263.

Series
Foreword

The famous Louisville newspaperman Henry Watterson once remarked that a great newspaper editor must have undaunted courage, unmatched scholarship, and 51 percent of the company's stock. Eugene Patterson had his share of the first two and enough of the last, in his friendship with and support from *Atlanta Constitution* publisher and editor Ralph McGill, to emerge as one of the South's most persistent editorial voices calling for an end to segregation and the beginning of a new South based on mutual respect and common decency among all citizens. From 1960 to 1968 he occupied the most important editorial citadel in southern journalism, writing a daily column for the *Atlanta Constitution*. He wrote at the height of the civil rights movement, amid real and threatened violence to anyone who bucked Jim Crow. He wrote when southerners wanting to make sense of the civil rights movement looked to one another for courage and leadership, for a moral compass in a world seemingly coming apart. He wrote when newspapers mattered much in "making" news by what they reported, or ignored, and what they encouraged people to do. As a daily columnist, he had to write whether he had anything to say or not. He found plenty to say. This collection of 122 of Patterson's columns attests to that.

Patterson wrote at a time when newspapers were the principal news source and public opinion forum in the South and when many southern newspapers were reluctant to cover civil rights issues and activity. He also wrote for the South's most widely read newspaper. The reach of the *Atlanta Constitution* extended far beyond the immediate metropolitan area. Although many of Patterson's columns focused on Atlanta and environs, his and his newspaper's drumbeat of the need to address matters of race and civil rights and to accord all people basic civility echoed across the South, emboldening some newspapers to join in the refrain and evoking condemnation from others. Whatever the effect, by making civil rights a matter of daily consideration, Patterson and the *Atlanta Constitution* reminded people that the issue was central to their identity and interest as southerners, black and white. By treating blacks and whites as equal subjects of honest and candid observation and rendering in print, and by such simple courtesies as referring to married black women as "Mrs.," Patterson and the *Atlanta Constitution* subtly changed the character of conversation about race.

Patterson's appeal was one of attitude and attention rather than obligation to any program or policy. He professed no certain answers to the difficult questions of the day, save the need to think openly and honestly and not to look away from injustice. He sought to affect people's perspective on civil rights—on how they saw themselves and others and might interact respectfully as citizens in a democratic society. He argued for common sense and common decency. To Atlantans, who boasted that they lived in the "city too busy to hate," Patterson said slow down to see what was really going on around them. To others across the region and the nation, he pointed to the possibility of a "southern" way toward racial "progress" and renewal. Patterson argued for a pragmatic progressivism. He insisted that people accept the new facts of civil rights after the *Brown* decision on school desegregation and during the 1960s, especially the federal government's growing willingness to intervene in local affairs to protect blacks and others in their efforts to gain equal access to public accommodations, transportation, education, the courts, and the ballot box; and he urged southerners to act responsibly within that context. To do less, he argued, was to concede to others control over the character and direction of civil rights. Like Ralph McGill and other white southern liberal newspapermen, Patterson also asked for understanding and patience from the North and other critics of the southern way.

As such, Patterson revealed the contradictions that marked so much of white southern liberal thought, especially among the second generation of southern journalists who had come of age during, and because of, World War II and the postwar era of "the American dream," Gunnar

Myrdal's *American Dilemma*, the *Brown* decision, and the Cold War. Even as Patterson and other white southern liberals decried crimes and outrages against black people and spoke out for basic rights, they too often thought more in terms of desegregation than of full integration of blacks into all areas of social, cultural, and political life. And they never fully grasped the anger of the "freedom now" chants of black protesters who took to the streets and took over public attention on civil rights. Patterson called for an honest confrontation with the problems of race, but he balked at the confrontational tactics and style of an increasingly militant civil rights movement. By the mid-1960s the civil rights movement threatened to rush over and past the Gene Pattersons of the southern liberal stripe. Patterson adapted better, and sooner, than many others, though he later confessed that too many of his columns in the 1960s were akin to "pale tea" that went down easily at a time when events called for stronger stuff.

For all the regional and national attention Patterson received, including winning the Pulitzer Prize for standing up for Julian Bond's right to be seated in the Georgia legislature, even though Patterson found Bond's antiwar stance and civil rights style obnoxious, few blacks likely either read or heeded his cautionary approach to civil rights and social change. Patterson's real audience was white. He wrote for them and about them because he was unabashedly one of them. He never forgot his own roots in rural Georgia, following behind mules plowing the fields and worrying about getting by during the Depression. He found much good in the old ways of straight talk and the simple pleasures of hunting, fishing, and passing time on the porch. Throughout his career he used homespun stories of southerners at work and play as a template for many of his columns. He wrote always as a southerner—but one who had fought against Nazism and cruelty during World War II and had lived long enough outside the South to know that it had to change lest it lose its soul. He wrote knowing the "loneliness" of being a southerner in the national mind, because northerners knew southerners only as one-note no-counts who yipped when the band played "Dixie." He opened his editorial career by noting that while he thought "Dixie" an honorable song and wanted to keep it, it was time to "write some new songs for the South." Balancing the old and the new was the special talent of white southern liberals like Patterson, though doing so sometimes muted calls for change.

Patterson balanced criticism of racism with accounts of individual whites' compassion and common decency. By showing what some good whites did, he showed what good all whites might do—how, as he wrote in 1963, the true southerner was or could become "a better man than his condemnors think, a better man than he himself knows." Such an approach no doubt made Patterson palatable to many white readers, but it hardly recommended him to angry black activists and others impatient with words and distrustful of established authority, including white-owned newspapers.

It is not easy to measure the effects of an editorial or column, and less so a life of such work. Patterson's writings were quoted and reprinted inside and outside the South. His column "A Flower for the Graves" (September 16, 1963), an angry indictment of all southern whites as complicit in the Birmingham church bombing that killed four girls, was read on the national nightly news. But the extent to which his columns changed people's thinking and behavior can never be known with any precision. Still, it is significant what people did say about Patterson in his day and still say today. What they say suggests why having this large sample of his writing is important both as a historical source, a measure of white southern liberal thinking during the last turbulent days of Jim Crow, and as an inspiration to human agency.

If white journalists gained courage from Patterson's example, so too, in time, did some black journalists. Cynthia Tucker, the award-winning African-American journalist who now sits in Patterson's editorial chair at the *Atlanta Constitution*, recently said just that. She concluded her own assessment of Gene Patterson (published herein) by noting that his daily columns not only helped make Atlanta a better place, and likewise the South; when read chronologically, as they are arranged in this book, they also reveal whites' inner struggles with race. Patterson's courage was facing his own history while facing down segregationists at a time when they insisted you were either with them or against them. Patterson, Tucker observed, kept "moving" toward progressivism. By pointing a direction, on a daily basis, he helped southerners imagine changing the South and helped will it to be. Therein lies the measure of Patterson's columns.

Stanley Harrold and Randall M. Miller
Series Editors

Acknowledgments

The idea for this collection began one day at lunch in St. Petersburg, Florida, when Roy Peter Clark asked his friend and mentor, Gene Patterson, the whereabouts of his collection of columns from the *Atlanta Constitution*. Roy had always wanted to read them. Patterson said he had boxed them up, along with the rest of his literary effects, for delivery to Duke University, which plans to house them. "If you want to take a look at them," he said in that soulful Southern voice, "you can come on over to the house."

He led Roy to his office and threw open a closet door. There they were in a box, nine crusty old albums, one for each year from 1960 through 1968, in which clippings of his original columns had been glued. The stain of the mucilage had bled through the newsprint, making some columns almost unreadable.

Roy loaded them in the trunk of his car before Patterson could change his mind, ferried them to the Poynter Institute, the school for journalists where Roy works, and handed them over to historian/archivist/librarian David Shedden, who acted as if he had just received the tablets from Sinai. Roy did not see them again for six months. During that time, Dave and his colleague Jean Wood tenderly photocopied the columns, stored them in protective boxes, saved one set for the archives, and turned another back to us for study and selection. Thanks to David and Jean for doing the hard work of restoration.

We would also like to express our gratitude to Larry Larsen and Priscilla Ely, both of the Poynter Institute, for preparing a collection of old photographs for reproduction in this book, and to Rita Estrada, Gene's former secretary at the *St. Petersburg Times*, who retyped and formatted the columns with special care. Thanks to the *Times* for granting permission to reprint Gene's memoir of World War II.

We considered a number of possible publishers but quickly settled on the University Press of Florida, impressed as we were by the professionalism of its editors and staff and the care and attention they offer their authors. Series editors Randall Miller and Stan Harrold added their scholarly advice from beginning to end. Susan Fernandez surrounded us with encouragement and led us gracefully through the process. Judy Goffman, as always, was an anchor of calm efficiency throughout production.

Special thanks go to Ron Martin, the editor of the *Atlanta Journal and Constitution*. When we apprised him of our intention to republish the Patterson columns, it took Ron about three seconds to give his blessing. In ten minutes we had a fax granting us formal permission to reprint them. And many thanks to Robert Cauvel of the *Atlanta Journal and Constitution* for helping procure photos of the era from the archives of that newspaper.

We are also grateful for the advice and encouragement provided by the staffs of the Poynter Institute, the Nelson Poynter Memorial Library at the University of South Florida, St. Petersburg, and the *St. Petersburg Times*. Kathleen Arsenault, director of the Nelson Poynter Memorial Library, and James Schnur, Special Collections librarian at the Poynter Memorial Library, were especially helpful, providing indispensable research assistance. To Howell Raines and Cynthia Tucker, thanks for expressing, in their words and in their work, the enduring legacy of Gene Patterson. To Geneva Overholser and Robert Schmuhl, thanks for the encouragement they brought to the earliest reviews of the book.

And finally, to Gene Patterson himself, to his daughter, Mary, and his granddaughters, and to the memory of his dear wife, Sue, we say thank you for your generosity and courage and for reminding us all that we can be better than we are.

* * *

Portions of chapter 2 have been adapted from two previously published essays by Raymond Arsenault, "The Folklore of Southern Demagoguery," in *Is There a Southern Political Tradition?* edited by Charles Eagles (Jackson: University Press of Mississippi, 1996), 79–132, and "Civil Rights Movement," in *The Oxford Companion to United States History* (New York: Oxford University Press, 2001), 126–28.

* * *

Editors' note: In fewer than a dozen cases, we have changed the punctuation in Gene Patterson's columns for reasons of clarity. Except for a few longer pieces, we have deleted the lines of asterisks that once served to break up columns of gray type in the newspaper. In all other respects, the columns and headlines read as they first appeared in the 1960s. The ellipses in the columns were placed there originally by Patterson and do not indicate material deleted by the editors. Readers can consult the Cast of Characters, beginning on page 287, to identify key figures who appear in Patterson's writing.

One

Introduction

1

A Journalist's View

How Gene Patterson
Persuaded His White
Southern Kinfolk to
Do What Was Right

Roy Peter Clark

From 1960 to 1968, Eugene C. Patterson held one of the most important jobs in American journalism: editor of the *Atlanta Constitution*. He
inherited this job from his good friend and mentor Ralph McGill, who
was elevated to publisher. Both titles were misleading because both men
were writers and opinion shapers. McGill was "Babe Ruth," as his boss
Jack Tarver called him, with his picture and column appearing on page
one; and Patterson was Lou Gehrig, his image and daily column an-
choring the editorial page.

In the year 2002, the idea of a daily newspaper column is unthinkable. These days, three times a week looks heroic. Like the good soldier
he was, Patterson met the challenge every day—for eight years. The
columns averaged about 750 words, with occasional longer pieces mixed
in. Grounded in the craft of wire service reporting, Patterson's work
carried him across the nation and around the world, including a 1964

journey to Vietnam, where he confirmed his opinions about the war and produced a ten-day series for the *Constitution*.

To read these columns sequentially, more than three thousand in all, is to experience one of the most impressive bodies of work in the journalism of the twentieth century. To find something comparable, one would have to reach into the treasure box, such as the World War II correspondence of Ernie Pyle.

A claim that Patterson's work ranks so high is a bold one and requires evidence. Perhaps a contrast with Pyle is a place to begin, for the beloved war reporter gave his life to the effort of bringing home to Americans the stories of common soldiers engaged in an uncommon struggle. Once Pyle avoided the filters of officialdom, his rhetorical task was easy, although it required front-line access. His readers back home were hungry for every tidbit of news about their children and sweethearts.

Patterson had a much tougher task: to converse each day with his white southern kinfolk and persuade them to climb aboard the train of racial change in America—or get out of the way. And to assure them that the sky would not fall if they did change.

Given the tumult of the sixties, the murders, assassinations, bombings, social protest, and war, his was a job fraught with danger. Southern whites faced personal attack for speaking out against the prevailing segregationist attitudes. In a real sense, Patterson was on the front lines and as vulnerable as Ernie Pyle, who caught a fatal bullet at the end of World War II.

Patterson's goals were both humanitarian and democratic: to keep people from getting hurt, to preserve the peace, to discourage extremism in any form, to build community, to prefer voluntary adherence to the good over coercion. Toward these ends, Patterson spoke to his kinfolk in ways that called upon their higher nature. "I see what you're doing," one reader accused. "You're trying to make us think we're better than we are."

All of this was possible only because Patterson never wrote down to his readers. He was one of them, striving with them toward a collective conversion that would create a more tolerant South. The earlier columns are tentative and probing, skeptical about the acts of civil disobedience that he thought might hurt the "Negro" cause. Looking back, Patterson borrows the words of Ralph McGill to criticize himself. Some of those columns, he says now, are "pale tea."

Patterson never claims to have escaped the prejudices of his own time and place. In the language of these columns are vestiges of an older South, not just the commonly used "Negro" but an occasional reference to a young black man as a "boy." The context, as always, is crucial. His reference honors a college student who has performed at the highest levels.

Clearly, Patterson is being carried along by the momentum of the movement. Dr. Martin Luther King Jr. and his followers are climbing toward the mountaintop to catch a glimpse of the promised land. Patterson and McGill wanted to climb that mountain too, even as too many of the South's political opportunists preferred to hold people down in the ditch—and to stay down there with them.

Despite his powerful drumbeat against segregation, Patterson was no one-note-Gene. He wrote extensively about local and national politics, foreign policy, mental health, economics, Communism, and Vietnam. At the age of twenty-one, Patterson had been a tank commander in Patton's army. His vision of war and American leadership in the world was forged by the battles against Nazi aggression. It was almost unthinkable to him that America's role in Vietnam was less than just, that the government of the United States was less than honorable. His personal journey to Vietnam in 1964 told him that good soldiers were fighting for a good cause. He was a most reluctant convert to the idea that we needed to get out.

In a way, Patterson's editorial legacy is not unlike Lyndon Johnson's political one: a shining inheritance on civil rights, shadowed by a war that could not be won. To his credit, Patterson was willing to write against his own biases when it came to constitutional issues and the rule of law. He encouraged the Georgia House to seat Julian Bond, in spite of the young black man's equating racial progress with the Vietnam peace movement. The columns cannot veil Patterson's disdain for Bond's antiwar rhetoric, but by God, he was elected by the people and should be seated in the House.

A Southern Life

For Eugene Patterson to persuade his Georgia kinfolk to change their ways, he needed to be one of them. He had the advantage of impeccable credentials.

Patterson was born on October 15, 1923, in a little town north of the Florida border named Adel. This hamlet in the piney woods is said to have gotten its name from the central syllables of "Philadelphia," which some founding citizen saw printed on a feed sack. Adel was also down the road from the town of Sparks, inspiring one of Patterson's favorite expressions: "Adel is so close to hell, you can see Sparks."

Patterson's father, William C. Patterson, was a bank cashier who kept losing his jobs during the Depression. His mother, Annabel (Corbett) Patterson, spent almost forty years as a schoolteacher and superintendent of the family farm. With only thirty-six dollars in cash, they moved in 1930 into a small frame farmhouse that had been built for tenants.

"I toiled as a boy," wrote Patterson, "behind a plow drawn by two mules across 50 acres of isolation. . . . My older brother, Bill, and my younger sister, Anne, and I grew up hard there. We milked cows, butchered hogs and steers, hoed peanuts and pulled corn and picked cotton and cropped tobacco." School, fishing, and literature provided the only means of escape.

Patterson remembers, "My mother . . . told me I appeared to have some writing talent, but that newspapermen were drinkers. So I started thinking journalism school." He wrote for his high school newspaper and knocked on the door of the *Adel News*, a country weekly in the county seat, where he was permitted to read proofs.

His interest in journalism carried him to the University of Georgia, where he received his degree in 1943. "What skills I actually learned came in the evenings when I worked with my peers to get out the school newspaper. The curriculum didn't teach me much about writing and reporting. The newspaper—and reading—taught me everything" (Patterson 1988, 46).

He enlisted in the army at nineteen and landed in Normandy at twenty. As a decorated tank platoon leader in Patton's Third Army, he fired his rifle reluctantly and suffered the deaths of his friends and comrades deeply. The experience of the war in Europe was powerfully formative for Patterson. He once told *Editor & Publisher* magazine, "My mother was a country school teacher and . . . taught me a tolerance that increased during World War II as I traveled the world and observed tyranny and oppression" (Hill 1977, 17).

He considered making the military a career and after the war earned his wings in Texas as an army aircraft pilot. But without a good war to fight, Patterson's interest in a military career flagged. He resigned a regular army commission in 1947 with the rank of captain.

He walked into the nearest newspaper office, landing a cub reporting job at the *Temple Daily Telegram* in Texas. Soon he would head back home to Georgia, taking a job at the *Macon Telegraph* and then at the Atlanta bureau of United Press (UP). Over the next decade, his career at UP took off as he became bureau manager in South Carolina (1948), night bureau manager in New York City (1949), and bureau chief in London (1953). It was from London that Patterson issued his most famous news lead after a noted American author crashed his plane in Uganda and was feared dead: "Ernest Hemingway came out of the jungle today carrying a bunch of bananas and a bottle of gin."

Patterson joined the staff of the *Atlanta Constitution* in 1956, where he stood at Ralph McGill's shoulder, became his closest friend, and succeeded him as editor in 1960. It was then that Patterson began to write his daily column. In *Ralph McGill, Reporter*, Harold Martin observes: "The appointment of Patterson to succeed [McGill] as editor could not have pleased him more. . . . [Patterson] had become the closest thing to a soul-brother McGill had in the business. He had that quality which Ralph admired above all else—courage, both physical and moral. He could not be bullied or bought and he wrote like an angel" (167).

Joseph Cumming described the transition for *Newsweek*: "McGill, that grave, vexed, playful, wheezy-voiced, square-faced, weight-plagued and rumpled old editor who for thirty years was like a tabernacle, destined to carry forward the simple and unradical message that black people, too, are human beings . . . continues his column and is given the title of publisher. Patterson, who succeeds him as editor, is just right for the image; a young man, thirty-six, a native Georgian, a liberal on race with compassion for the white agony, a tough, jaunty figure with a do-right jut to his jaw and a tight prose style that shone like a suit of armor" (Martin 1973, 167).

Friends and foes alike tended to comment on Patterson's physical presence, which reinforced his image as courageous leader or tough opponent. He was compared to Jimmy Cagney. His hair was as red as a stump on fire; his eyes blue and piercing; his jaw jutting; his chest a barrel; his strut determined. Then there was the matter of his height, which Georgian Joe Parham described as "sawed off, standing five feet, seven inches, with all hackles raised."

Patterson and McGill, who both won Pulitzer Prizes at the *Constitution*, kept up their one-two punch until 1968, a few months after the death of Dr. Martin Luther King. In an oral history of the civil rights movement, *My Soul Is Rested*, edited by Howell Raines, Patterson describes how the FBI tried to use the *Atlanta Constitution* to besmirch King's reputation: "What [the FBI agent] offered me was the name of the Florida airport and the time of day that an airplane would be leaving there on a coming weekend when Dr. King was supposedly leaving for a tryst with some girlfriend—perhaps in the Caribbean. He put it to me, 'Why don't you have a reporter and a photographer there? Get a picture of this as well as a story on this man and expose him to the South and to the world.' And I just said, 'Well, that's pretty dangerous stuff, and it's not our kind of journalism.' Interestingly enough, that agent called . . . he came to see me a second time. Obviously, he'd checked it back to Washington, and they'd said, 'Go back and lean on him.' And I showed him the door a second time" (369).

In 1968, Patterson got worn down by conflicts with Jack Tarver, president of the Atlanta newspapers, a man whose attitude toward him Gene came to find unacceptable.

For the next three years, Patterson served under Ben Bradlee as managing editor of the *Washington Post*, where he was a central figure in the publication of the Pentagon Papers, but the two could not harmonize. Patterson was quoted as saying that the dominating Bradlee needed a managing editor "like a boar needs tits" (Pratte 1993, 238). Bradlee offered, more generously, that any editor needed Patterson, "if only to tell him that the South will rise again, that Agnew had something when he carped about Eastern effetes, and that we Northern boys can't sing worth a goddamn." Bradlee was referring to another expression of the Patterson persona, a crystal clear tenor voice that sang "Danny Boy" at the drop of an arpeggio. "The one I remember best," said Harold Martin, "was 'Git Along Little Dogies'—with that line, 'Whoopee ti-yi-yo, get along little dogie for you know Wyoming will be your new home.' When we got to that line everybody would hush, and Gene would rare back and take a deep breath and shut his eyes and the muscles in his neck would swell and his vocal cords would quiver and when he hit that 'ti-yi-yo' crescendo, steers miles away on the west side of town would head for Wyoming" (Black 1977, 24).

After a year as a professor of public policy at Duke University in 1971–72, Patterson would get what most of his friends thought he needed: his own paper. In 1971, he was invited by Nelson Poynter to become editor of the *St. Petersburg Times*. Poynter owned the *Times* and had founded *Congressional Quarterly*. During his sixteen years at the helm, Patterson turned the *Times* into one of the world's most highly regarded metropolitan newspapers, famous for its young talent, enterprise, political coverage, color, design, and writing.

Upon Poynter's death in 1978, Patterson rose from editor and president to succeed him for the next ten years as chairman and CEO of the Times Publishing Company, part of an unprecedented legacy by a newspaper owner. Poynter wanted to leave his company in the hands of a news professional, and Patterson fit the bill. Part of the job required Patterson to chair the board of trustees of what would become the Poynter Institute, a nonprofit school for journalists that would one day own all of the company stock. It would take Patterson's personally selected successor, Andrew Barnes, to seal the deal by buying in troublesome minority shares.

Patterson's stature rubbed off on the *Times* like ink on a newspaper reader's hands. In 1977 he was elected by his peers to become president of the American Society of Newspaper Editors. Under his leadership a movement to improve the quality of newspaper writing in America took form, along with a sustained initiative to multiply the presence of minorities in American newsrooms. He became an advocate of what he called explanatory journalism, which would become a Pulitzer Prize category.

Patterson also became known for his ethical standards. After a DWI arrest, he insisted that the *St. Petersburg Times* play it prominently on page one. He became an outspoken opponent of "undercover" journalism, in which journalists disguised their identities. He was the only member of the Pulitzer board who did not vote to give a prize to Janet Cooke for a *Washington Post* story that turned out to be a hoax. "It just didn't smell right," he said at the time.

Patterson retired from the *Times* in 1988 but continued to receive honors and awards and to speak out on issues such as editorial independence, the quality of journalism, great newspaper writing, and racial justice in the South. He holds honorary degrees from fifteen institutions, including Harvard, Duke, Emory, Indiana, and Tuskegee universities.

In 1998 his wife of forty-nine years, the former Sue Carter, died. She was born in Virginia and met Gene while she too was a reporter in the South. She knew the ways of journalists and hosted parties for hundreds of them. A generation of them ate her food and drank her wine and sang around her piano. The stories told at those parties built camaraderie among the troops. The standards at the Patterson house were high: No political windbags or journalistic mountebanks allowed. Beyond that, any rogue found welcome. Sue and Gene produced one daughter, Mary Patterson Fausch, who gave them three granddaughters, Laura, Molly, and Emily Fausch, of Raleigh, North Carolina.

The Context of Dissent

Eugene Patterson was not the first white southern editorialist to wield a pen against the evils of racism, segregation, and social injustice. In fact, by 1967 when Patterson won his Pulitzer, a string of southern "liberals" had blazed a trail: Hodding Carter in 1946 for the *Delta Democrat Times* (Greenville, Mississippi); Virginius Dabney in 1948 for the *Richmond Times-Dispatch*; Buford Boone in 1957 for the *Tuscaloosa News*; Harry S. Ashmore in 1958 for the *Arkansas Gazette*; Ralph McGill in 1959 for the *Atlanta Constitution*; Lenoir Chambers in 1960 for the *Virginian-Pilot* (Norfolk, Virginia); Ira B. Harkey Jr. in 1963 for the *Pascagoula Chronicle* (Mississippi); and Hazel Brannon Smith in 1964 for the *Lexington Advertiser* (Mississippi). As this list demonstrates, when it came to the Pulitzer Prize for editorial writing, the winners' circle was dominated by southern journalists writing about race. The Pulitzer board recognized the power of their arguments, the urgency of their commentary, and the personal dangers that confronted them.

While Patterson followed footprints in the sand, his went deeper, a journalistic pathway distinctive for its quotidian quality, quantity, rhetorical power, and timely connection to some of the most important events in the history of American civil rights.

Three of these historical moments preceded Patterson's eight years as editor of the *Atlanta Constitution*. The first came in 1954 when the Supreme Court concluded, in the case of *Brown v. Board of Education of Topeka*, that "in the field of public education the doctrine of 'separate but equal' has no place." The public schools would be desegregated "with all deliberate speed," an intended oxymoron that created a great social tug-of-war persisting today. In 1955 Rosa Parks refused to give up her seat, and the Montgomery Bus Boycott heated up the civil rights movement under the determined leadership of a young preacher named Martin King. By 1957, nine African-American students faced white mobs in an attempt to desegregate Central High School in Little Rock, Arkansas. Governor Orval Faubus predicted that "blood will run in the streets," drawing a pattern of defiance and violence that would repeat itself again and again across the South.

Southern news coverage of such events ranged from white racist propaganda to looking the other way to grudging acknowledgment that something important was in process, a narrow spectrum that made Patterson's rhetorical candor all the more persuasive.

During Patterson's tenure as editor, events such as these captured the nation's attention: the student sit-ins at lunch counters and the development of the Student Nonviolent Coordinating Committee (SNCC); the arrests and imprisonments of Dr. King; the Freedom Rides led by the Congress of Racial Equality (CORE); the attempts to desegregate public universities throughout the South; demonstrations and police violence in Birmingham; the Birmingham church bombing; the March on Washington; the Freedom Summer of 1964; the signing into law of federal civil rights legislation; the Selma Voting Rights March and "Bloody Sunday"; the honoring of the Nobel Peace Prize to Dr. King; and his assassination.

As these columns reveal, Patterson confronted the issues surrounding these events, and many more, with a passionate determination and consistency that dissented from the standard white argument on race. To locate his rhetorical distance from that argument, one has only to flip through the pages of Patterson's own newspaper. There, readers could find the "Pickrick Papers," paid advertisements for the Pickrick restaurant and furniture store written by Lester Maddox, whose stubborn refusal (enforced by ax handle) to desegregate his establishments made him a folk hero for reactionary whites. They would elect him governor.

The newspaper ads occupied a full wide column of type. One on February 6, 1965, contained this typical message: "The KKK was almost forgotten until some of our public officials and others started the Communist-inspired race-mixing program for America. So the more race mixing you people force upon Americans, the more the KKK grows. . . . You race mixers are not fighting the KKK . . . you are supporting it." In the middle of such tirades, Maddox stuck the ad for the dinner special: "Order of Lester's Skillet Fried Chicken . . . Drumstick and Thigh . . . 25c . . . Breast and Wing . . . 50c . . . Please, no carry-out orders at these special prices."

The mix of demagoguery and gastronomy seems grotesque or parodic by contemporary standards, but it reinforces the ordinariness of the racist argument. Although Patterson and McGill came to regret allowing Maddox to "denigrate a whole race" on the pages of the *Constitution*, their decision reflected their confidence that their own arguments would prevail and were more likely to do so if all points of view could be exposed to the light of day.

A more respectable, but in some ways more insidious, example of white media rhetoric on race came from the likes of James Gray, the owner of the only television station and dominant newspaper in Albany, Georgia. In the wake of black civil rights protests there, Gray delivered a formal televised speech in which he blamed the unrest on "cells of professional agitators" that smacked "more of Lenin and Stalin than of George Washington, Thomas Jefferson, and Abraham Lincoln." He targeted the NAACP as the chief instigator and attacked Dr. King as an opportunist: "He has learned that martyrdom can be a highly productive practice for the acquisition of a buck." Gray describes segregation as "a system that has proved over the years to be peaceful and reward-ing" (Branch 1988, 554).

Similar arguments came from William D. Workman Jr. of the *Colum-bia State* in South Carolina: "What the moderates cannot understand is that hosts of white Southerners are not in the least willing to accept integration as inevitable, or 'to relax and enjoy it'" (1960, 274). The *Richmond News-Leader*'s James J. Kilpatrick, whose career as a syndicated columnist survived his segregationist past, wrote in 1962 that "the South will maintain what I have termed essential separation of the races for years to come. This means very nearly total segregation" (1962, 192).

If such rhetoric was the koine of the white southern realm, it pro-vided the basis for the dissent of McGill and Patterson. One description of their political evolution is "from moderate to liberal," but it proved to be an important distinction, especially from the point of view of the civil rights movement. In his letter from the Birmingham jail in 1963, Dr. King wrote that he had "almost reached the regrettable conclusion that the Negro's greatest stumbling block in his stride toward freedom is not the White Citizens Counciler or the Ku Klux Klan, but the white mod-erate" who had not "recognized the urgency of the moment and sensed the need for powerful 'action' antidotes to combat the disease of segre-gation" (Mullane 1993, 638).

There can be no denying that the "powerful action" of nonviolent resistance, which provoked horrific countermeasures, attracted the at-tention of the northern media, galvanizing the nation against southern violence and the values that produced it. From a strategic standpoint alone, Dr. King's dismissal of the southern moderate was understand-able.

But when the itinerant revival preacher leaves town, the pastor is left to guide the flock. In that sense it was left to Patterson to shepherd white opinion toward change, to nudge, cajole, confirm, console, push, persuade, reprimand, and reward. No black man, however charismatic, could speak directly to the intransigent South. No carpetbagging white liberal from the North could undertake the mission and hope to suc-ceed. It took writers of the southern soil. Gene Patterson was one of them.

This collection passes on the enduring legacy of Patterson's work. For journalists working their craft, Patterson is an exemplar of courage, hard work, literary excellence, and endurance. He is the kind of writer George Orwell hoped for in his condemnation of the nexus of political and linguistic corruption. Patterson used the language the way only a lover could, with hope, care, and passion, and for the higher purposes of democracy and justice.

The conversation he inspired on race in the 1960s must continue today if America is ever to exorcise the ghosts of racism that continue to haunt us. Because of work like Patterson's, Atlanta is a different city than the one for which he wrote. The South and the nation are different. But issues of race persist, from hostility between police and the African-American community to an organized retreat from integration, a bias against new immigrants, and debates over affirmative action, political correctness, the welfare state, the drug culture, and the prison system.

Gene Patterson's columns are an invitation to struggle on, a notification that things have changed and the sky did not fall, and a daily reminder that at that last ding-dong of doom, we will have proven ourselves to be better than we are.

Better Than We Are

In this introduction I have tried to define Gene Patterson's work within the context of the journalism of the twentieth century, but to understand its full meaning we need a historical frame as well. In the following essay southern historian Raymond Arsenault creates that frame, helping us understand the forces that shaped the moment of Patterson's dissent. Arsenault also contributes historical headnotes for the year-by-year chapters.

To capture the rhythms of history and Gene Patterson's personal journey, 122 of his columns are printed in chronological order, with representative pieces from each year from 1960 through 1968. Each column reveals at least one of the three interlocking themes that Patterson used to make his case to Atlanta and the South.

The first theme concerns the need for the community to confront all the issues related to desegregation, civil rights, race, and social justice.

Patterson knew that social and political progress required courageous leadership, so he developed a second theme by holding up for the South powerful models of leadership, some discovered in surprising places. To be heard at all, Gene needed a third theme, establishing his credentials as a southerner, which he does in funny and tender essays on the sweetness of Georgian culture and the power of being rooted in the soil. Atlanta is becoming the city too busy to hate. In the face of such change, Patterson takes time to remember the good in southern people and beauty in their old ways.

Patterson grew up reading Dreiser and Sherwood Anderson and found a model in the muscular prose of Hemingway, flavored by a Faulknerian sense of place. McGill hired Patterson knowing that Gene could write "like an angel"—but an angel carrying a harp in one hand and a sword in the other.

He swings that sword most powerfully in his most famous column, "A Flower for the Graves" (chapter 6), a passionate challenge to the conscience of southerners after the dynamite bombing of a Birmingham church and the murder of four little girls. He says he wrote it with tears in his eyes, and those tears burn with every word. In its time, the piece was considered so important that Patterson was invited by Walter Cronkite to read it on the *CBS Evening News*. It is worth the reader's special attention, as is Patterson's brief unsigned editorial written in shock and sorrow after the assassination of Dr. Martin Luther King Jr. (chapter 11).

Two essays by Patterson serve as prequel and sequel to the collection of columns. "Forged in Battle: The Formative Experience of War" first appeared in the *St. Petersburg Times* (1994), a memoir of D-Day and Patterson's journeys through Europe (chapter 12). He reflects upon his early years and explores the forces that toned his muscle for the civil rights fight of the 1960s. Patterson was an American liberator in Europe, but in a real sense the experience of war helped liberate him.

At the age of seventy-seven, Gene Patterson has written his own sequel to his columns. With the enthusiasm of a cub, he reports on an event early in 2001: a reunion of the key figures involved in the desegregation of the University of Georgia. Patterson uses the occasion to reflect on the legacy of his generation of southern leaders.

The collection concludes with two brief contemporary pieces on the Patterson legacy. The first is by Howell Raines, who, inspired by Patterson, has risen to the position of executive editor of the *New York Times*. A final appreciation comes from Cynthia Tucker, the most recent successor to Patterson at the *Atlanta Constitution*. As an award-winning journalist and African-American woman, she exemplifies the powerful nature of the change that Gene Patterson helped bring about.

A Historian's View

Gene Patterson,
Southern Liberalism,
and the Vise of
History

Raymond Arsenault

Gene Patterson wrote as a southern liberal, which means that he frequently found himself at odds with friends and neighbors and sometimes even with himself. Surrounded by conservative and reactionary defenders of "the southern way of life," he wrote about his native region with passion and restraint, a curious but necessary combination for a journalist who preferred continued engagement to noble exile.

Part critic, part native son, he wrote with a light touch and a heavy heart. While he loved the South, he could not abide its cultural hypocrisies and racial demons. How could he remain silent or complacent in a history-haunted land that, for all its claims of moral righteousness, denied the full humanity of one-third of its citizens and maintained a blind eye toward the poverty and ignorance of so many others? He knew enough about the complexity of southern history—about Jeffersonian liberalism, Civil War Unionism, Populism, and other strains of dissent—to know that the region possessed cultural reserves that transcended the limitations of neo-Confederate mythology. But he also knew enough about the mood of the contemporary South to realize that it was not going to be easy to tap these reserves.

Patterson wrote his columns during the turbulent 1960s, in the midst of radical social change spawned by urbanization, industrialization, the Cold War, and the black freedom struggle. To some degree, this "revolutionary" context set him apart from the reform-minded southern journalists who came before him. At the same time, his struggle to bring editorial enlightenment to the region represented a continuation of a half-century-long tradition. Patterson himself was well aware of both the achievements and the limitations of this tradition and tried to learn from the mistakes of his predecessors. Like William Faulkner, he always kept at least one eye on the past as he looked for solutions to the region's social, political, and racial dilemmas. Thus it seems fitting that we spend at least a few moments revisiting the liberal southern journalists of the first half of the twentieth century before plunging into the dizzying world that Gene Patterson wrote about during the 1960s. To understand the full significance of his words, we need to explore the origins and evolution of the liberal tradition that Patterson came to embody.

It would be misleading to suggest that there has been a strong or consistent tradition of dissent among twentieth-century southern journalists. But beginning in the 1920s each generation has produced a handful of editors who cut across the grain of regional conformity. In many cases, their critique of the social and political status quo was gentle and halting, full of backsliding contradictions. In the hidebound white South, this was enough to earn them the "liberal" label. What might pass as moderate or even conservative today appeared reformist and liberal in the early twentieth-century South. Maintaining consistency in the use of political or ideological terminology is always a slippery matter, but in the southern context the term *liberal* is especially elusive. In his classic 1944 study *An American Dilemma*, Gunnar Myrdal suggested that the term *Southern liberal* was almost an oxymoron and that "Southern liberalism is not liberalism as it is found elsewhere in America or in the world" (456).

Few scholars have challenged Myrdal's caveat, but several have tried to come up with at least a working definition of the prototypical southern liberal. Perhaps the most useful definition, for our purposes, is the one offered by Morton Sosna, the author of *In Search of the Silent South: Southern Liberals and the Race Issue* (1977). After admitting that "'liberal' can mean anything from John Locke's philosophical tenets to Franklin D. Roosevelt's New Deal programs," Sosna simplified the problem by restricting his definition to racial liberalism. "My test of the white Southern liberal lies in his stance on the race issue," he wrote in 1977. "I use the term broadly, classifying as 'liberal' those white Southerners who perceived that there was a serious maladjustment of race relations in the South, who recognized that the existing system resulted in grave injustices for blacks, and who either actively endorsed or engaged in programs to aid Southern blacks in their fight against lynching, disfranchisement, segregation, and blatant discrimination in such areas as education, employment, and law enforcement. Though issues other than race could be used to determine one's disagreement with the Southern status quo during the Jim Crow era—advocacy of popular education, promotion of child labor reform, and support for labor unions, to name a few—the ultimate test of the white Southern liberal was his willingness or unwillingness to criticize racial mores" (viii). To reinforce his point, Sosna offered Ralph McGill of the *Atlanta Constitution*, Gene Patterson's friend and mentor, as a concrete example of "a white racial liberal, a man who deeply loved his native region, who recognized its more glaring shortcomings, and who devoted much energy toward solving its problems" (vii).

The first southern journalists to fit this model emerged in the years following World War I. During the first two decades of the twentieth century, reform-minded journalism and white supremacist orthodoxy went hand in hand, following the lead of Bryanist and later Wilsonian progressivism. The progressive editors who agitated for good government and good roads and against child labor and the trusts were often among the most militant proponents of disfranchisement and Jim Crow. Searching for order and a "reconciliation of progress and tradition," they saw no contradiction between social reformism and racial discrimination (Grantham 1993). For the vast majority of southern journalists, this calculus of race and reform remained an article of faith during the 1920s and beyond. But for a small minority, a more inclusive notion of social justice began to take hold. Prodded by several factors—the revelations of wartime experience, the racial turmoil that plagued many communities after the war, postwar restlessness and disillusionment, the popularity of H. L. Mencken and other iconoclastic social critics, and the influence of "regionalist" social scientists, particularly those at the University of North Carolina—these liberal pioneers began to question the shibboleths of sectionalism and white supremacist ideology. In the mid-twenties the excesses of the Ku Klux Klan and Negrophobic southern demagogues, and the evangelical and antimodernist enthusiasms inspired by the 1925 Scopes Trial, reinforced their alienation from the regional mainstream.

The first generation of liberal southern journalists included George Fort Milton Jr. (1894–1955) of Tennessee; Louis Jaffe (1888–1950) of Virginia; Julian Harris (1896–1988) of Georgia; John Temple Graves II (1892–1961) and Grover C. Hall (1888–1941) of Alabama; and Gerald W. Johnson (1890–1980) of North Carolina. All were born in the 1880s or 1890s and grew up under the spell of a dark and ascendant racism, but each managed to find a way to transcend at least some of the limitations of family and regional background. Harris, the son of the romantic folklorist Joel Chandler Harris, attacked the Klan and lynching and won a Pulitzer Prize as editor of the *Columbus Enquirer-Sun* in 1926. Hall, who grew up in the rural isolation of northern Alabama and never went to college, also won a Pulitzer (1928), as did Jaffe a year later. Graves, the son of an Atlanta editor who helped incite the 1906 Atlanta race riot, did his best to infuse the *Birmingham Age-Herald* with a measure of racial tolerance during the 1920s and 1930s, though he turned sharply to the right from the 1940s onward. Milton's father, the editor of the *Knoxville Sentinel* and the *Chattanooga News*, was a crusading progressive and prohibitionist who nonetheless maintained a hard-line approach to the segregation and subjugation of blacks, whom he termed "the lowest order of mankind" (Kneebone 1985, 11). While the son, who assumed control of the *Chattanooga News* in 1924, retained his father's passion for Prohibition, he eventually jettisoned most of the white supremacist baggage.

A committed regionalist, he believed, somewhat naively, that Jim Crow laws would vanish with the elimination of the South's grinding poverty. Like Jaffe and Johnson, Milton spent time in Europe during and after World War I, encountering "new sets of values and behaviors" and gaining "an awareness of alternatives to the southern way of life" (Kneebone, 19), a liberation that Gene Patterson would experience in a later world war. None of these men, with the possible exception of Johnson, broke completely free from the segregationist mind-set, but they all made important strides in the right direction.

The most liberal member of the group, Gerald Johnson, was also the most influential. A native of Riverton, North Carolina, where his father was a small-town editor, he studied at Wake Forest College before joining the staff of the *Greensboro Daily News* in 1913. At the *Daily News*, he developed a reputation for graceful writing and unblinking honesty, prompting H. L. Mencken to praise him as the best editorial writer in the South. Following a two-year stint (1924–26) as a journalism professor at the University of North Carolina, he became an editorial writer and Mencken's colleague at the *Baltimore Sun*. Under Mencken's tutelage, he wrote hundreds of editorials and iconoclastic essays attacking southern backwardness, especially religious and racial intolerance and the economic exploitation of poor whites—and blacks. After 1930, he focused more on national political affairs, and from the mid-1940s on he worked as a free-lance journalist and even wrote several novels and works of popular history. But his most important legacy was the clear and consistent editorial voice that he unleashed in the 1920s.

Johnson's success helped spawn a second generation of liberal southern journalists, most of whom entered the profession in the mid- or late 1920s and rose to prominence during the 1930s. But the expansion of the South's liberal journalistic fraternity had more to do with the broad social and economic forces that gripped the nation following the onset of the Great Depression in 1929. With the emergence of the New Deal four years later, the focus on the social and economic ills of the South sharpened, inspiring a new round of journalistic insurgency. The collapse of the southern economy and the intrusions of New Deal agencies forced subtle but significant adjustments in the region's time-honored system of racial control, and a number of southern journalists wondered aloud why the rules of racial etiquette could not be stretched a bit further.

The roster of journalists who fit this description includes Mark Ethridge (1896–1981), the editor of the *Macon Telegraph* who ended his career at the *Louisville Courier-Journal*; Clarence Cason (1898–1935), an Alabama-born *Birmingham News* and *New York Times* reporter who became a professor of journalism at the University of Alabama; Ralph McGill (1898–1969), a native of Tennessee who worked at the *Nashville Banner* before moving to the *Atlanta Constitution* in 1929; Wilbur J. Cash (1900–1941), a native of Gaffney, South Carolina, and a Mencken protégé who wrote for the *Charlotte News* before devoting the last decade of his life to the completion of the magnum opus *The Mind of the South*; Virginius Dabney (1901–95), editor in chief of the *Richmond Times-Dispatch* from 1936 to 1969 and the son of a University of Virginia professor; Jonathan Daniels (1902–81) (son of Josephus Daniels, Secretary of the Navy during World War II), who replaced his father as owner and editor of the *Raleigh News and Observer*; and Hodding Carter (1907–72), the Louisiana native who battled Huey Long's political machine before becoming the publisher and editor of the *Delta Democrat Times* (Greenville, Mississippi) in 1938.

For the most part, the liberal southern journalists of the 1930s were somewhat bolder than their predecessors and more insistent that regional progress depended on fundamental change, including the gradual abandonment of Jim Crow. The word *gradual* is key here. None of them called for an immediate end to racial separation; nor did they expect to see such a fundamental shift in the foreseeable future. Indeed, most of those who adopted the liberal label continued to search for social justice within the confines of a segregationist society, sustaining the vain hope that the "separate but equal" doctrine enunciated by the United States Supreme Court in 1896 could still become a reality. Nevertheless, by the end of the decade, several—at least in private—were beginning to question the moral and social viability of racial separation.

Paralleling and drawing upon the southern literary renaissance—the regional flowering of elemental prose led by William Faulkner and Thomas Wolfe—the liberals of the 1930s probed and poked at the weaknesses of the South, both past and present. As the historian Richard

King has observed in *A Southern Renaissance*, journalists played an integral part in this renaissance, which "was more than 'just' a literary movement." The result of considerable cross-fertilization, "it also represented an outpouring of history, sociology, political analysis, autobiography, and innovative forms of journalism" (5). For some liberal journalists, an awareness of the Harlem Renaissance and the culture and literature of black liberation also was part of the mix. But in general, the intellectual underpinning of southern liberal commentary was limited to white sources, which helps explain why it almost always stopped short of radical or revolutionary prescriptions. For better or worse, the liberals of the 1930s drew most of their inspiration and ideas from regionalist social scientists such as Howard Odum, Rupert Vance, and Arthur Raper. Immersed in the flesh-and-blood realities of a region in crisis, social scientists gathered and analyzed a mountain of data on southern shortcomings, much of which appeared in *Social Forces* and other academic journals. After digesting this sociological material, liberal editors assumed the responsibility of putting it in a form that politicians, community leaders, and ordinary readers could understand.

There was plenty to write about during these difficult years, from FDR and Huey Long to the plight of sharecroppers and the Scottsboro boys—the nine young black men sentenced to death in Alabama in 1931 for a rape they did not commit. Considering the social and political turmoil at home and abroad, including the rising power of totalitarianism in Europe, it is not surprising that the region's best journalists tried their hand at redefining the limits of journalistic inquiry or that they did so in a self-consciously liberal mode. As they wrote about race and class, religious and political demagoguery, and social pathology, they sought historical models of moderation and tolerance with which they could identify.

With this in mind, Virginius Dabney, the self-appointed dean of Dixie liberalism, published *Liberalism in the South* in 1932. Reaching back to Jefferson and beyond and uncovering a long tradition of dissent that did not square with the conservative mythology of the southern mainstream, Dabney provided a historical framework for internal criticism of the region. Much of his historical analysis was little more than wishful thinking, and since his goal was reform, not revolution, he seldom strayed from conventional wisdom, especially on matters of race. But his early excavation of southern liberalism proved useful, if only because it inspired others to turn their talents to book-length studies of the southern scene. From the mid-1930s on, liberal southern journalists produced a series of books that extended their influence far beyond the confines of weekly columns and editorials. Books such as Clarence Cason's *90 Degrees in the Shade* (1935), Jonathan Daniels's *A Southerner Discovers the South* (1938), Wilbur J. Cash's *The Mind of the South* (1941), Hodding Carter's *Southern Legacy* (1950), and Ralph McGill's *The South and the Southerner* (1963) became essential volumes in the liberal southern canon, and their authors became regional, as opposed to merely local, figures.

Unfortunately, with the notable exceptions of those by Cash and McGill, these liberal tracts have not worn well. Notwithstanding their literary and autobiographical skills, the liberal southern journalists who came to maturity prior to World War II were seriously constrained by racial taboos and other cultural conventions. They often fell victim to the same feelings of regional defensiveness that obscured the vision of their conservative counterparts. To quote Richard King, "They were men of considerable intelligence, decency, and often courage, a credit to any region or community. And yet they were quite traditional southerners finally, unwilling to cut loose from the strong constraints of their ethos. Perhaps it was their position as newspaper editors, as partial 'insiders,' which held them back. They had to stay 'in touch' and couldn't get too far ahead of their constituencies. Like Clarence Cason in *90 Degrees in the Shade* (1935), they held that lynching for example, was an aberration, somehow not central to the Southern experience. This being so, they . . . felt that the South they represented could solve the region's problems without outside interference. 'Just give us time; don't rush us' was their constant plea" (150–51).

Written in 1980, King's rebuke reflects a post–Civil Rights Act sensibility that would have puzzled Cason and his colleagues of the 1930s. They lived on the other side of a great historical divide, before the civil rights movement and the Second Reconstruction brought deep and irrevocable change to the South. In their world, the opinions of black militants and northern intellectuals were of little consequence. Although vaguely aware of the NAACP (National Association for the Advancement of Colored People) and the political left, liberal southerners such as Cason focused almost all their attention on the mind of the white South. Indeed, when Cason committed suicide on the eve of his book's publication—apparently because he feared that he would be ostracized by his fellow white Alabamians—he gave testament not only to his own personal insecurities but also to the parochial preoccupations of his type. When Hodding Carter titled his 1953 memoir *Where Main Street Meets River,* he captured the essence not only of Greenville, Mississippi, but also of the circumscribed world in which he lived. Despite its pretensions of social control and stability, it was a world that could not survive the Second World War. The river, as Carter and others discovered during the 1940s, intersected with a wider world, one that would engulf the South in the years to come.

All of this had profound implications for liberal southern journalists. As the debate over the South's destiny became biracial and national in the 1940s, the region underwent a dramatic polarization that left white liberals in an increasingly untenable position. For a time they saw themselves as occupying the "vital center," to use Arthur Schlesinger's apt phrase, but by the mid-1950s it was clear that the center would not hold. In effect, they were caught in the vise of history, pressed between two powerful and irreconcilable forces: the black civil rights struggle and the massive white resistance that came to dominate southern politics in the 1950s and 1960s. Unable to satisfy either side, southern liberals either redefined themselves as moderates or withdrew into an uneasy silence on matters of racial justice. As the external pressure on the white South increased, the tradition of internal criticism lost its viability, repeating the pattern that pushed the region into a self-destructive orthodoxy prior to the Civil War.

*   *   *

The quickening of the civil rights movement caught most liberal southern journalists off guard. With few exceptions, they were unprepared for the challenges of racial adjustment that became commonplace during and after World War II, even though there were warning signs dating back to the beginning of the century. During the early years of the progressive era, the accommodationist philosophy of Booker T. Washington dominated discussions of racial progress. But as the numbers of mass lynchings and other incidents of white supremacist violence mounted—belying Washington's faith in racial accommodation—an alternative philosophy emerged, rooted in racial pride and the protest traditions of nineteenth-century abolitionism. Following the 1906 Atlanta race riot and a similar racial massacre in Springfield, Illinois, in 1908, a group of liberal white intellectuals founded the NAACP; two years later a somewhat more conservative group formed the National Urban League (NUL). Although it would be several decades before these organizations became effective instruments of social change, the NAACP and the NUL provided an embryonic organizational base for the modern civil rights movement. The NAACP was especially influential in this regard, primarily through the activities of W.E.B. DuBois, the outspoken editor of *Crisis* magazine from 1910 to 1932, and James Weldon Johnson, the NAACP's first black executive secretary and the guiding force behind the proliferation of NAACP branches in the South after World War I. Despite Johnson's efforts, the organizational center of the civil rights struggle remained in the North, where the post-1914 Great Migration had created a critical mass of black activists. But the seeds of a southern movement were germinating, especially among sleeping-car porters and other black union members, black teachers and professionals, and ministers.

During the 1920s, a medley of voices joined the chorus of civil rights advocacy, including the black nationalist Marcus Garvey, writers and artists associated with the Harlem Renaissance, socialist and communist politicians, and black labor leaders such A. Philip Randolph. But the disparate activities of these individuals did not constitute an organized civil rights movement. Despite continued fragmentation and few tangible signs of progress, the civil rights struggle entered a new phase during the Great Depression of the 1930s, setting the stage for the development of a high-profile national movement. President Roosevelt's political dependence on white southern Democrats and his single-minded determination to end the depression left little room for a forthright assault on racial discrimination. But the social justice orientation of Roosevelt's New Deal offered a measure of hope to civil rights activists, who for the first time since Reconstruction regarded the federal government as a potential ally. Though strapped for funds, the NAACP decided to devote almost all of its limited resources to judicial and legislative reform. While Charles Houston, Thurgood Marshall, and other NAACP attorneys waged an extended effort to dismantle the legal structure of racial segregation and discrimination, Executive Secretary Walter White led a campaign to enact federal antilynching legislation. Although the antilynching campaign ended in failure and the legal assault on the Jim Crow system made little headway prior to World War II, the NAACP's public advocacy of civil rights during the 1930s set an important precedent for future efforts.

The 1940s proved to be a pivotal decade for the civil rights struggle. As the disappointments of depression-era politics gave way to the opportunities and challenges of World War II, many civil rights activists sensed that the prospects for fundamental change were brightening. By threatening a mass march on Washington in 1941, black labor leader A. Philip Randolph forced President Roosevelt to create the Fair Employment Practices Commission (FEPC), an agency empowered to combat racial discrimination in wartime employment. Black experiences on the battlefield and on the home front after America's entry into the war brought new hopes and expectations. As the contributions of black servicemen and industrial workers became critical to the war effort, Randolph and others promoted the Double V campaign—the determination to win twin victories over foreign enemies on the battlefield and racial discrimination at home.

The Double V campaign yielded mixed results: despite widespread black participation in the war effort, the American armed forces remained rigidly segregated throughout the war; episodes of interracial violence became commonplace in northern cities such as Detroit, where black in-migration exacerbated racial tensions; and many white southern politicians continued to wallow in the politics of racial demagoguery. Nevertheless, there were clear signs of progress: a government propaganda campaign to discredit the racial theories of Nazi ideologues; a noticeable softening of racial attitudes among intellectuals, some of whom were inspired by Gunnar Myrdal's epic study of American race relations, *An American Dilemma* (1944); *Smith v. Allright*, a 1944 Supreme Court decision outlawing white primaries. The full impact of the white primary decision would not be felt for many years, but the reversal of the black South's half-century-long slide toward disfranchisement gave black leaders renewed hope that a Second Reconstruction was in the offing.

For most civil rights advocates, the court's increasingly liberal trajectory confirmed the wisdom of the NAACP's legalistic approach to the struggle. For a small but vocal minority, however, the rising expectations of wartime led to more militant tactics, such as sit-ins, economic boycotts, and protest marches. The war years witnessed the birth of direct action as a significant component of the civil rights struggle. The NAACP's Youth Councils and the American Communist Party fostered some of this activity, but the most important source of direct action was the Congress of Racial Equality (CORE), an interracial band of northern pacifists, labor activists, and left-wing intellectuals. Founded in Chicago in 1942 as an offshoot of the pacifist Fellowship of Reconciliation (FOR), CORE drew inspiration from the success of nonviolent resistance in Gandhi's India and from the first stirrings of decolonization in Asia and Africa. Although the organization remained small and its most ambitious effort, a 1947 freedom ride through the upper South, met with limited success, CORE symbolized the growing resolve among black Americans to enjoy the full rights of citizenship.

In the immediate postwar era, the civil rights cause continued to advance with the breaking of the Major League Baseball color line by Jackie Robinson, desegregation of the armed services, the convening of a presidential commission on civil rights in 1947, and a series of encouraging Supreme Court rulings. The NAACP expanded its legal assault on Jim Crow, which culminated in the May 1954 *Brown v. Board of Education* school desegregation decision.

By striking down the *Plessy v. Ferguson* doctrine of "separate but equal," the *Brown* decision signaled an impending revolution in American race relations. But to the dismay of Thurgood Marshall and other civil rights advocates, the pace of the civil rights revolution was soon slowed by legal backsliding and political demagoguery. In the implementation, or second *Brown* decision of May 1955, the Supreme Court created an ambiguous standard of enforcement, allowing southern school districts to desegregate "with all deliberate speed." At the time, the NAACP saw *Brown* II as an unmitigated defeat, a backward step that needlessly complicated the process of school desegregation by steeling the resistance of white segregationists. Some activists later recognized the hidden benefits of a decision that forced the civil rights movement to draw upon and mobilize its nonlegal resources, redirecting its attention to civil rights concerns other than school desegregation. Most important, the stalemate on school desegregation created an opening for civil rights activists willing to use direct action tactics that transcended the NAACP's legalistic approach.

In the months following the second *Brown* decision, the prospects for civil rights seemed to fade as White Citizens Councils spread across the South and as the brutal lynching of Emmett Till, a thirteen-year-old black boy from Chicago visiting relatives in Money, Mississippi, dominated the headlines. The movement gained new strength in early December 1955, when an act of courage galvanized an entire black community. In Montgomery, Alabama, the arrest of Rosa Parks, a forty-three-year-old seamstress and NAACP activist who violated a local segregation ordinance by refusing to move to the "Negro" section of a city bus, sparked a thirteen-month bus boycott that attracted national and international attention.

Led by the charismatic and articulate twenty-six-year-old Atlanta Baptist minister Martin Luther King Jr., who promoted a Gandhian strategy of nonviolent resistance, the Montgomery Improvement Association (MIA) became the touchstone of the modern civil rights movement. Following a mass indictment of boycott leaders in February 1956, national civil rights leaders began to realize that more than bus desegregation was at stake in Montgomery. Scores of organizations contributed money and other resources to the MIA, and a national support network became a critical factor in the boycotters' success, magnifying the impact of the boycott. By donating funds, dispensing advice, or passing resolutions of support, blacks and whites who lived far from Montgomery were drawn into a social protest that directly challenged the myth of American equality. Moreover, confronting an unexpected mass movement in the Deep South forced many civil rights advocates to reconsider the traditional reliance on northern-directed legal challenges. In effect,

Montgomery became a testing ground for contesting theories of racial adjustment and social change. What civil rights activists observed there—the economic and moral vulnerability of segregation, the inability of even moderate segregationists to compromise, the resolute courage of many southern blacks, the political salience and emotional power of African-American religious belief, and the viability of nonviolent direct action—ultimately reshaped the organizational and philosophical contours of the entire civil rights movement.

In 1957, the year following the boycott, the movement seemed to be gaining momentum with the formation of the Southern Christian Leadership Conference (SCLC) by Dr. King, President Eisenhower's use of federal troops in the desegregation of Little Rock's Central High School, and the passage of the first federal Civil Rights Act in eight decades. But the final years of the decade proved disappointing; the pace of school desegregation slowed and the symbolic nature of the Civil Rights Act became apparent. Cold War politics dominated American public life, frustrating NAACP and SCLC leaders who sought to refocus national attention on civil rights issues. Hampered by organizational and personal rivalries, their hopes languished until four young college students staged an impromptu sit-in at a Woolworth's lunch counter in Greensboro, North Carolina, in February 1960. The youth-led sit-in movement soon spread to more than a hundred southern cities, prompting the founding of the Student Nonviolent Coordinating Committee (SNCC) in April 1960—only a few weeks before Gene Patterson took over as editor of the *Constitution* and began writing his daily column.

SNCC's youthful exuberance reenergized the civil rights movement, recapturing the mass-movement spirit of Montgomery. Although many NAACP and SCLC leaders were wary of SNCC's confrontational style and ultrademocratic organizing principles, King's endorsement and the wise counsel of longtime activist Ella Baker helped sustain the new organization, which drew strong support from black college and high school students in cities such as Nashville, Tennessee, and Albany, Georgia. In Nashville, SNCC activists forced the desegregation of the downtown business district in early 1961, and later in the year they played a critical role in a CORE-sponsored Freedom Ride designed to test a recent Supreme Court decision prohibiting segregation on inter-state buses. When white supremacist violence in Anniston and Birming-ham forced CORE to suspend the Freedom Ride, Nashville's student activists vowed to complete the ride. Dramatic confrontations with state officials and other white supremacists in Alabama and Mississippi en-sued, prompting additional Freedom Rides, a full-scale mobilization of the civil rights movement, and the belated intervention of the Kennedy Administration, which provided the riders with safe passage into Missis-sippi but not protection from imprisonment. During the summer of 1961, as hundreds of Freedom Riders languished in Mississippi jails and CORE and SNCC chapters sprouted up across the Deep South, an irre-pressible "movement culture" began to take shape, setting the stage for the rising expectations and escalating demands of the mid-1960s civil rights struggle. In November 1961, an Interstate Commerce Commis-sion ruling effectively desegregated interstate transit facilities, but this success merely whetted the appetite of a movement on the rise.

The Freedom Rider crisis forced the Kennedy Administration to pay attention to the emerging civil rights coalition, but it also deepened ad-ministration fears of an uncontrolled mass movement. Uncomfortable with direct action tactics that inevitably elicited intemperate and some-times violent responses from southern segregationists, Attorney Gen-eral Robert Kennedy urged civil rights leaders to redirect their efforts toward voter registration. Offering logistical and financial support as incentives, he convinced some activists that a quiet campaign for black suffrage was the best option for a movement facing massive resistance. But most civil rights leaders, including King, were unwilling to abandon an approach that greatly enhanced the movement's emotional energy and moral power, while providing a dramatic focus that maximized me-dia attention.

Unfortunately for King and SCLC, the viability of mass protest in the Deep South was called into question in 1962, when advocates of nonviolent direct action suffered a serious setback in Albany, Georgia. Not only did Albany officials confound the movement's efforts to fill the jails with civil rights protesters, but persistent tensions between SCLC leaders and local activists eventually convinced King and others that his presence in the city was doing more harm than good. Later in the year,

James Meredith's attempt to desegregate the University of Mississippi provoked such a violent response from white supremacists that some observers feared the South was moving toward civil war. While civil rights advocates applauded the Kennedy Administration's decision to enforce the law at the University of Mississippi, they worried about the increasingly violent nature of massive resistance in the Deep South.

Opposition to civil rights reached a fever pitch in 1963, with the murder of NAACP leader Medgar Evers in Mississippi, Alabama Governor George Wallace's celebrated stand in the schoolhouse door, Birmingham public safety commissioner Bull Connor's use of attack dogs and fire hoses to quell SCLC-sponsored demonstrations, and the fatal bombing of four black children at a Birmingham church. But such excesses served only to strengthen a movement that relied on the public perception that civil rights demonstrators possessed the courage and moral integrity to outlast their opponents. The rising power of the movement was confirmed by a successful mass march on Washington in August, the breaking of the color line and a major public relations victory in Birmingham, and the Kennedy Administration's long-awaited endorsement of a comprehensive civil rights bill. Following President Kennedy's assassination in November, Lyndon Johnson used his considerable legislative skills and the image of a martyred president to push through a Civil Rights Act that outlawed state-supported racial discrimination.

The passage of the 1964 Civil Rights Act was a milestone in the history of the movement, but King and other leaders continued to press for an end to the remaining vestiges of Jim Crow, especially black disfranchisement. In the summer of 1964, a "Freedom Summer" voter registration campaign that involved hundreds of college students and other volunteers revealed continued opposition to black suffrage and civil rights in Mississippi, a harsh reality highlighted by the murder of three civil rights workers in Philadelphia, Mississippi, and by the disillusioning experience of the Mississippi Freedom Democratic Party's delegation to the 1964 Democratic National Convention. After continued agitation, including the march from Selma to Montgomery of March 1965, Congress approved a voting rights act that brought an end to legally sanctioned disfranchisement and voter intimidation.

The Voting Rights Act of 1965 marked the high point of the civil rights movement. But the euphoria did not last long. Among African Americans, the culmination of the struggle for civic equality brought a revolution of rising expectations that inevitably gave way to frustration and disillusionment. The growing realization that civil rights legislation had done little to alter the intractable problem of racial prejudice or the structural realities of race and class in the United States exacerbated tensions within the movement. The limitations of the civil rights revolution became painfully clear in 1966 and 1967 when the focus of the movement moved north to cities such as Chicago and Detroit, where poverty, urban blight, and de facto segregation bred despair and anger. The movement's failure to make much headway in the North contributed to confusion and fragmentation among African Americans, many of whom found the politics of racial pride and Black Power increasingly attractive. Between 1965 and 1968, a series of inner-city riots fueled the fires of racial polarization and white backlash.

As the commitment to nonviolence waned, the politics of law and order displaced the white liberalism that had been an important element of the civil rights coalition. At the same time, movement leaders were sharply divided over King's efforts to broaden the scope of the civil rights movement to include antipoverty campaigns, opposition to the Vietnam War, and international agitation for human rights. The movement was in serious disarray by 1968. During that tumultuous year, a combination of factors—including King's assassination, the public's growing preoccupation with the Vietnam War, and the passage of civil rights legislation that put the finishing touches on the legal structure of civic equality—brought the classic phase of the civil rights movement to a close.

*   *   *

During the 1960s, liberal southern journalists found it almost impossible to keep pace with the escalating expectations, not to mention the organizational twists and turns, of the civil rights struggle. The perplexing nature of the movement was only part of the problem. Journalists also faced a daunting political landscape in a region fixated on external threats to its traditions and beliefs. For the better part of two decades, the center of southern politics had been moving to the right, inhibiting open expressions of liberal sentiment south of the Mason-Dixon line. The trend began as early as 1946, when a wave of southern demagoguery swelled from the rising tide of the Cold War and the first ripples of reaction to the Second Reconstruction. Employing a superheated mixture of racism, anti-communism, and anti-unionism to crush their more liberal opponents, Gene Talmadge of Georgia, Theodore Bilbo of Mississippi, and several other pyrotechnic politicians set the tone of postwar southern politics. Two years later, during the presidential campaign of 1948, the region produced the Dixiecrat revolt. Outraged by President Harry Truman's unexpected endorsement of civil rights and unnerved by the perceived threat of domestic and international communism—not to mention an increasingly liberal Supreme Court, which had already struck down the white primary system, segregation on interstate buses, and even some forms of school segregation—South Carolina Governor Strom Thurmond and other militant Dixiecrats bolted the Democratic National Convention and formed a third party. Although Thurmond's presidential candidacy failed to prevent Truman's reelection and the Dixiecrat Party soon faded from view, the animating spirit of the revolt persisted, inspiring a new generation of politicians to mount the battlements in defense of the vaunted "southern way of life."

During the late 1940s and early 1950s, this new generation of conservatives shared the regional spotlight with a cadre of Fair Deal moderates—pragmatic politicians who were open to evolutionary change and who were generally willing to put sectionalism aside in the interests of economic growth or national Democratic solidarity. Led by Senators Lyndon Johnson and Ralph Yarborough of Texas, Albert Gore and Estes Kefauver of Tennessee, and J. William Fulbright of Arkansas, the Fair Dealers generally represented rim-South states that had managed to sidestep the 1948 Dixiecrat revolt. Yet even in Deep South states such as Alabama (where the voters put the folksy neopopulist "Big Jim" Folsom in the governor's mansion in 1947 and the liberal Carl Elliott in the House of Representatives in 1949, and where moderates such as Lister Hill and John Sparkman held United States Senate seats), there was a countercurrent of moderation and nascent liberalism. For a time, all of this led some observers to predict that the long-awaited New South was about to become a reality. But such optimism soon proved to be unfounded.

By the mid-1950s, the New South countercurrent had been reduced to a trickle as a tidal wave of racial demagoguery and massive resistance engulfed the region. Following the *Brown* school desegregation decisions of 1954 and 1955, demagogic politicians, abetted by the White Citizens Councils and a resurgent Ku Klux Klan, mounted a frenzied attack against the forces of change. Targeting Chief Justice Earl Warren, the NAACP, communist agents, left-wing union organizers, and a whole cast of meddling "outside agitators," white supremacist stalwarts such as Senators Herman Talmadge of Georgia and James Eastland of Mississippi had a field day. As anxiety turned into hysteria, southern moderates and liberals retreated into silence, particularly after the Little Rock crisis of 1957 forced the hand of a national Republican administration that had been extremely reluctant to implement court-ordered school desegregation. When Arkansas Governor Orval Faubus, once considered to be a racial moderate, turned himself into a white supremacist folk hero by defying President Eisenhower and a battalion of paratroopers, he established a pattern that other southern politicians, including Alabama's George Wallace and Mississippi's Ross Barnett, were eager to follow.

In the early 1960s, the sit-ins, freedom rides, and civil rights marches organized by the SCLC, SNCC, and CORE added fuel to the fire, as did the stiffening resolve of Attorney General Robert Kennedy and the Justice Department. By 1963—the year of the celebrated march on Washington, Medgar Evers's assassination in Jackson and John Kennedy's assassination in Dallas, Bull Connor's fire-hose defense of segregation in Birmingham, and George Wallace's brief but symbolic stand in the schoolhouse door—southern politics was on the verge of a complete meltdown, or so it seemed.

Knocked off balance by President Lyndon Johnson's determined defense of the sweeping 1964 Civil Rights Act, the champions of segregation soon became entangled in the politics of Goldwater Republicanism, a development that destroyed the partisan solidarity that had traditionally constricted southern politics. Barry Goldwater's fervent opposition to the Civil Rights Act—set against a backdrop of escalating white supremacist violence in Mississippi and Alabama—split the white South, encouraging some southern voters and politicians to consummate a flirtation with presidential Republicanism that had begun in 1952, while encouraging others to draw back from the politics of race and sectionalism. Although Goldwater carried five Deep South states— Georgia, Louisiana, Mississippi, Alabama, and South Carolina—the rest of the South voted Democratic, albeit by a narrow margin. Most important, for the first time in nearly a decade, a loose coalition of southern moderates raised their voices on behalf of reason and compromise. Following the passage of the Voting Rights Act of 1965, this moderate coalition expanded, as a surge in black voter registration forced white politicians into a pragmatic and often grudging acceptance of civic equality.

At the same time, the politics of demagoguery was gaining even greater momentum as the Jim Crow South searched for and found new allies in its preservationist struggle. Despite Goldwater's defeat, suburban Republicanism and right-wing populism continued to gain strength, both inside and outside the South, and by 1968 a transregional conservative movement had taken shape. By joining hands with western and northern conservatives, unreconstructed southerners once again became a powerful force in national politics. However, in the process they inevitably lost much of their regional identity. As the White Citizens Councils gave way to the John Birch Society and the National Rifle Association, the regional focus of southern dissent became blurred, especially after George Wallace's run for the presidency in 1968. Taking advantage of a national and partly generational backlash against black assertiveness, urban rioting, antiwar demonstrations, sexual permissiveness, feminism, and an ascendant counterculture, Wallace became the first southern demagogue since Huey Long to develop a national constituency. Wallace's strong showing among blue-collar workers and other northern conservatives marked a turning point, not only because he took southern demagoguery north of the Mason-Dixon line but also because he forced Richard Nixon and other northern politicians to return the favor. Nixon's successful southern strategy in the elections of

1968 and 1972 sealed the merger between Yankee and Dixie conservatism, an ominous development that had profound implications for the South and the nation.

*   *   *

Gene Patterson's Georgia passed through all of this: the emergence and maturation of the modern civil rights movement; the rise and fall of massive resistance; and the breakup of the Solid South. But it did so in a unique way. Perhaps more than any other southern state, Georgia during these years exhibited a divided mind. In the rural hinterland and in small towns and cities, Georgia was pure Deep South, a land of rigid segregation and rock-ribbed tradition. But the metropolis of Atlanta was a complicated blend of Old South nostalgia and New South boosterism, reflecting a city that aspired to be a center of regional renewal and cosmopolitan civility. From the 1930s onward, the struggle between the two Georgias dominated state politics, as rural Georgia produced a hardy strain of agrarian demagoguery—featuring the father and son political team of Eugene and Herman Talmadge—and Atlanta nurtured a style of political pragmatism symbolized by Mayor William Hartsfield's characterization of his city in the 1950s as the city too busy to hate.

White Atlantans did not always live up to this noble aphorism, and Hartsfield himself began his career as a strict segregationist. But the general trajectory of Atlanta politics was toward moderation, even during the tense decade following the *Brown* decision. In the early 1960s, the growing influence of the SCLC and SNCC—both headquartered in Atlanta—and the challenge of the sit-ins and other forms of nonviolent direct action sorely tested the local white elite's openness to change. However, the leadership of Mayor Ivan Allen Jr.—and the determination of local civil rights leaders to keep the pressure on—prevented the city from sliding backward into the politics of fear. Atlanta did, of course, produce Lester Maddox, the ultrasegregationist demagogue who swept to the governorship in 1966. But Maddox, who did not represent himself as an Atlanta-based candidate, received relatively few metropolitan votes. As Allen put it, "Although Maddox was an Atlantan in fact, he was not an Atlantan in spirit. His heart was in the small

Southern Baptist churches out in the flat stretches of segregated south Georgia rather than in the board rooms of Atlanta corporations" (Bartley 1983, 206).

Ironically, in a limited way, the same could be said of Gene Patterson. Born in the small south Georgia town of Adel in 1923, he was rooted in the populist folkways of rural life. While his adult experiences as a student at the University of Georgia, as a tank commander in World War II, and as a well-traveled journalist allowed him to transcend the cultural limitations that encased so many rural Georgians in self-destructive parochialism, at least part of his heart remained in the countryside. Like his close friend Ralph McGill, who hailed from Igou's Ferry, a small farming community in east Tennessee, he was a rural transplant who never felt entirely comfortable in the corporate culture of metropolitan Atlanta. For both Patterson and McGill, a lingering attachment to what the historian Jack Temple Kirby has called "rural worlds lost" inspired an empathetic concern for the angry and often bewildered white southerners caught in the throes of a wrenching social and economic transformation. At times, this empathy may have obscured their vision and unduly tempered their critiques of southern foot-dragging, but it also gave their words an enhanced credibility among the region's lost souls.

Following McGill's lead, Patterson tried to strike a balance between ideology and practicality, between an intellectual commitment to liberalism and a largely emotional attachment to regional identity. He wanted to be a southern liberal, but he also wanted to avoid both condescension and the atavistic excesses that had bedeviled so many well-meaning southern journalists. He wanted to open the minds of his readers with a fresh look at their past and present circumstances, but he did not want to frighten them with a vision of the future that left them powerless to affect the pace and character of change. In effect, he wanted to readjust their moral sensibilities without indulging in moral censure, to teach rather than preach. In the 1920s and 1930s, as we have seen, liberal southern journalists were invariably more southern than liberal, and this had a lot to do with their understanding of the past. As John Kneebone noted in *Southern Liberal Journalists and the Issue of Race*, "In the end, definition of southern liberalism must emphasize the adjective.

Downplaying the southernness of these people tends to identify them with a national racial liberalism that takes its tradition from a history emphasizing the ideals of Jefferson's Declaration, the abolitionist movement, the Radical Republicans during Reconstruction, and Negro protest in the twentieth century. Southern liberals, however, shared a different interpretation of that American history" (xviii).

Kneebone's point is well taken if we consider only those journalists who came to maturity before World War II. But if we look carefully at the words of Patterson and others who appeared on the journalistic scene in the postwar era, we can detect a new strain of southern liberalism. Grounded in national ideals and informed by a more expansive and humanistic sense of history than the neo-Confederate mythology that dominated the prewar era, this new liberalism tended to be less parochial than that of earlier generations. For Patterson, and perhaps for several others, the origins of this new sensibility can be traced to the historical watershed of World War II. By leaving the South during the war to fight Nazism—an enemy that blended history and racial hatred in a manner that was disturbingly familiar to many southerners—he caught more than a glimpse of a wider world, an experience that challenged the received truths of regional orthodoxy. As we have seen, the war also quickened the pulse of a worldwide struggle for decolonization and human rights, altering intellectual and political conceptions of freedom. And this was only the beginning of a reordering of the world that inevitably prompted new ideas of social organization.

Trying to make sense of totalitarianism, the Holocaust, the Cold War, and nuclear technology created intellectual ferment and debate, much of which was disseminated by expanding networks of education, communication, and popular culture—even in the Deep South. On the regional level, the postwar intellectual paradigm became manifest in a fresh look at the southern past. C. Vann Woodward, a native Arkansan who published such classics as *Origins of the New South, 1877–1913* (1951) and *The Strange Career of Jim Crow* (1956), led a new generation of southern historians who abandoned the neo-Confederate orthodoxies that had sanctioned sectionalist outrage for nearly a century. And black intellectuals such as James Baldwin offered new insights into the human costs of white privilege in the South. Prior to the mid-1960s, many white southern journalists were either ignorant of or unimpressed by these developments, and more than a few reinvested in the mythic certainties of a social stability based on racial identity. But for some there was no going back to the insulated world of Jim Crow.

The trick, of course, was to leave the mythic South behind without actually leaving the front lines of southern journalism. In the wake of the Little Rock crisis, *Arkansas Gazette* editor Harry Ashmore (1916–98) wrote *An Epitaph for Dixie* (1958), a searing indictment of southern segregationists, and won two Pulitzer Prizes for his efforts. But he soon left his Arkansas editorship for a position at the Center for Democratic Institutions in Santa Barbara, California. In the age of massive resistance, few liberal editors were able to withstand what Patterson once called "the conflicts that beat in on any editor in the South in that period who offended and differed with the majority of his readers" (Raines 1977, 367).

McGill, with Patterson's help, was one who did stick it out, sustaining the reputation of the *Atlanta Constitution* as the most controversial—and most important—newspaper in the South until his death in 1969. Of the half-dozen prewar liberal journalists who continued to write in the 1950s and 1960s, McGill was almost certainly the boldest on matters of race—and perhaps the only one to embrace the civil rights movement with enthusiasm. But his greatest achievement, according to Patterson, "was to start a conversation." As Patterson explained to Howell Raines in the 1970s: "To know that period of the South is to know that it was frozen in silence. People were not discussing the issue. Neighbor and neighbor were afraid of each other. Conformity was established by precedent. And for a man who might doubt the wisdom of segregation to sit down with his neighbor and say, 'Hey, I'm not sure we're right,' could have ruined that man in most Southern states. . . . Therefore nobody discussed the issue. Only the politicians, who were aggravating emotions, were discussing it. McGill suddenly and boldly on the front page of the *Constitution* began to talk openly about the rights and wrongs of segregation, and this led people to be emboldened to talk about it, even if all they did was cuss McGill" (Raines 1977, 368).

Patterson's admiration for his risk-taking mentor is understandable. More than any other southern journalist of his day, McGill assumed the responsibility of facilitating a local and regional conversation on civil rights. He shouldered this responsibility in a number of ways—by writing provocative weekly editorials and by authoring a remarkable book-length exposition of regional identity, *The South and the Southerner*, published in 1963. But one of his most important contributions to the conversation was his decision in 1960 to ask Patterson to write a daily column on southern life.

Over the next eight years—as Atlanta and the South experienced a series of remarkable social and political transformations—Patterson's words served as a touchstone for thought and debate, sustaining and deepening the all-important conversation that McGill had initiated years earlier. Day after day, his carefully crafted columns prompted reflection and reconsideration, puzzlement, and even wonder. Although he ranged across a wide spectrum of topics—from matters of race and class to those of leadership and literary inspiration—he never strayed too far from the pressing concerns of a region in dire need of honest self-assessment. Combining folk wisdom with sophisticated journalistic scrutiny, he maintained a persistent call for human decency and moral responsibility. Even during the decade's darkest moments, he neither let up nor gave up, refusing to sink into a disabling despair or to give his readers an easy way out. Here, at long last, was an indefatigable liberal southern journalist who would not allow the vise of history to crush the hopes and dreams of a better tomorrow.

Two

The Atlanta Columns of Eugene Patterson, 1960–1968

Richard M. Nixon questioned by Ralph McGill and Gene Patterson as he campaigned unsuccessfully against John Kennedy in 1960. Gene described Nixon as "morally barren." By permission of the *Atlanta Journal and Constitution*.

3

1960

A Rising Wind

January   The United States and Japan sign a mutual defense treaty, prompting
          protest demonstrations in Tokyo. Fidel Castro gains firm control of
          Cuba.

February A sit-in by four black college students in Greensboro, North Carolina,
          initiates a regionwide movement challenging racially segregated pub-
          lic accommodations in scores of southern cities, including Atlanta.
          The Reverend Martin Luther King Jr. joins his father as co-pastor of
          the Ebenezer Baptist Church and moves the headquarters of the
          Southern Christian Leadership Conference from Montgomery, Ala-
          bama, to Atlanta. Governor Ernest Vandiver and the Georgia legisla-
          ture create the Sibley Commission, a nineteen-member body autho-
          rized to conduct public hearings on school desegregation across the
          state.

March   A ten-nation nuclear disarmament conference convenes in Geneva,
          Switzerland.

April   At a meeting in Raleigh, North Carolina, black student activists create
          the Student Nonviolent Coordinating Committee. Senegal becomes
          the first of fourteen former African colonies to gain independence in
          1960, among them the Congo (August 15) and Nigeria (October 1).

May   The Cold War intensifies after a U-2 spy plane piloted by Francis
          Gary Powers is shot down over the Soviet Union. The Civil Rights Act
          of 1960 modifies the Civil Rights Act of 1957, providing a modest ba-
          sis for federal supervision of voting rights.

June   Eugene Patterson becomes editor of the *Atlanta Constitution* and be-
          gins publication of his daily column.

July   Senator John F. Kennedy of Massachusetts wins the Democratic Party nomination for president on the first ballot. He selects Senate Majority Leader Lyndon B. Johnson of Texas to be his running mate. Vice President Richard Nixon wins the Republican nomination and chooses Henry Cabot Lodge of Massachusetts as his running mate.

September–
October   Four televised presidential debates highlight a hotly contested election. Following his arrest during an Atlanta sit-in, the Reverend Martin Luther King Jr. is sentenced to four months' hard labor. John Kennedy gains favor among black voters after calling King's wife to express his concern and after Attorney General Robert Kennedy intervenes to secure King's release on bond.

November John F. Kennedy narrowly defeats Richard Nixon. The electoral college vote: 303 to 219.

June 3, 1960
When Wind Rises a Mind Changes

A week ago a little windstorm ruffled middle Georgia. It is widely forgotten now. But it left a mark on the mind.

The car radio had mentioned tornado conditions. But my mind was on the general problems that ride with a man on a trip. Between Cochsran and Eastman the wind rose and the problems dwindled.

It was just a little blow. But for a while it took my attention.

A curtain of dust moved across the earth. Headlights were needed in places to drive. Clouds as gray as the dust moved low. Grit got in the teeth.

The wind combed the knee-high corn nearly flat in the fields and turned up the whites of leaves. Tops of the pecan trees and oaks leaned east like a bob-haired woman in a west wind.

Here and there, as the car moved south, a tree limb tore and dropped. In fields where dust devils swirled and eddied the cattle stood, not grazing, heads high.

The wind rocked the car as it moved. It whipped fishponds into surf. A barn waved a strip of its tin roof at passersby.

A few hundred yards ahead a pine tree snapped off and thumped to the ground by the road. There were power lines overhead and no place to hide if it had been a tornado. All you could do was drive on. The gusts rose and struck the side of the car with odd booms and shook it.

School zone signs in the twig-littered streets of Eastman lay flat. "Can't sell you any gas," the man at the filling station said. "Power's off in the pumps. Tree must have hit a line." The no-sale didn't seem to bother him. "Some wind," he said, and looked off down the street.

Going on toward McRae you noticed again how the noise of nature put a hush on the beasts in the fields. And in farm yards men stood with the uncertain, listening stance of those who are waiting for something they can't do anything about.

On one porch a farm wife stooped quietly and picked up her baby from a pallet and put him in her lap.

Then it was over. The wind died, the dust settled and the scud lifted to its ordinary place in a high, bruise-purple sky. When I got to McRae the man at the filling station was picking up his blown-over sign. He was back in business. He wanted to sell me an oil filter.

The problems of the day came back to ride along the road with me.

Yet for one hushed hour a mightier force had chastened the earth. It cleansed the forest of weaker trees and the trees of weaker limbs and, for a little while, anyway, it made a man feel how really frail his petty power to run things is.

July 14, 1960
Issue Is Honest, Treatment Wasn't

LOS ANGELES [site of the 1960 Democratic National Convention]—The floor fight on civil rights was ugly on its surface. But in its depths it had the ache of wrenching sadness. Here before the nation lay an honest issue—the wrongs suffered by the Negro.

And it was treated dishonestly by inarticulate Southerner and glib liberal alike. This is not new. But it was so profoundly sad this time because most of the Southerners were old and lost and groping with the hoarse cries of the cornered to find a way that isn't there.

Pity is less for the liberals because victors don't need it or brook it.

But it is sad all the same to see the precious mechanism of the human mind so stifled in righteousness that it ceases to function as a critical instrument. If this is the way of politics, Democratic politics needs a good shaking. The American spirit needs a bath.

For a responsible political party to advocate solemnly that every school start the desegregation process by the arbitrary date of 1963, neatly meeting the anniversary of the Emancipation Proclamation, is so flip an approach to a massive problem that one questions not the party's wisdom but its honesty.

And to see the governor of Mississippi shout that 99 percent of the whites and Negroes of his state are happy with things as they are, when he knows quite well their silence is rooted in fear, is to judge him by the same measurement.

Where are these people taking this nation?

It is said that nobody listens unless one takes "a position." What this country has got are royal doses of "positions" that blot out the simple, clean beauty of balanced thought.

Because the only direction from up is down, it is the people who voted uncritically for the faulty plank who must increasingly examine their intellectual honesty in the time ahead. If certain of the Negro demonstrations of the sort they encouraged in this plank are ruled un-constitutional—and their platform chairman blithely said this point is as yet unsettled but doesn't matter—let them explain to the Negro youth what sort of faith they kept with him by hieing him on. While Sen. Kennedy's own privately expressed position is to approve legal but not illegal sit-ins, the platform committee members pondered and rejected such distinction. Let the Negro, on some cooler day, ask them why this was. And why they thought he wanted friends not to be frank with him.

As for the poor gray Southerners who spoke, their day is almost done. I watched moderate Southern leaders here try manfully to get a dignified presentation prepared and presented by someone impressive. They failed. The presentations were self-defeating. Some of the men were embarrassments, giving the convention and the nation a din of fumbles and shouts.

The younger men who will succeed these older ones will, lacking the prestige of age, do worse instead of better unless they face the basic flaw that makes the Southern presentation unacceptable. This flaw is their insistent effort to justify instead of rectify Southern wrongs. Until the dignity of all men is accepted and advocated as a goal, not even Demosthenes could make a completely honest speech for Dixie.

Surely the lessons that sprang from the television screen will get into the consciousness of America and make this night of sadness a start toward something a little worthier.

August 1, 1960
A Southerner Can Get Very Lonely

It is very lonely to be a Southerner in a national gathering. We are treated as pawns, not powers, in the political conventions. The band plays *Dixie* and we yip. The others smile and look at each other.

It is the only song they know us by.

Dixie is a song we love. We will go on with it even though it ushers no nominees to the winner's circle. The band plays *California Here I Come* or *Happy Days are Here Again* when the payoff comes. It usually gets around to *Dixie* as a sort of novelty number, an amiable salute to the also-rans.

Dixie is an honorable song. Let us keep it. But who will write some new songs for the South?

This is not a suggestion that Tin Pan Alley can settle the civil rights issue. It is a piece about the South's loneliness.

At Los Angeles one afternoon a room full of Georgia delegates sat looking bewildered. The delegates, all of them men of experience, had sat in on a platform committee session and come back to their hotel. They had heard liberals testify on civil rights. The gulf between the things they heard there and the things they believed here was so enormous as to leave them stunned.

"I feel a little sick," one of the Georgians said quietly.

It does traumatize many a Southerner to go to a national gathering and discover the poverty of understanding between regions and race, the differences in social vocabulary, the literal disbelief in each other's decency and common sense. Americans are strangers.

At Chicago [site of the 1960 Republican National Convention] the Southern delegates simply did not matter.

The South served both parties chiefly by just being there so liberals could vie to see which one could give us the widest berth. The vote of the urban East depends substantially on our being treated as social undesirables. There is too much cynicism in this.

Anger rises in the Southerner as it always has and his reaction—to defend, deny and denounce—is precisely the reaction that is politically expected and desired. It is not the right reaction.

The right reaction is not to lament the obvious—that we are whipping boys—but to examine why it is that we can be used as whipping boys. Then we can repair the wrongs that make us vulnerable instead of claiming they are right.

Coming home this time to the gentle South, where people do not speak roughly to each other, and do not think they have to act hard-boiled, and do not put gouging among their first motivations, I felt a special love for this place of trees and soft voices, and a faith that such a people is going to face up to society's changes in good time.

Certainly the South has been lonely long enough.

September 9, 1960
Hit Child Forgets but Driver Can't

School is starting. And four little children were hit by cars in Atlanta Tuesday. One is dead at the age of 6. And the anguish that will weight the hearts of these drivers for the rest of their lives is a punishment that comes even to the faultless.

Police Superintendent J. F. Brown said something that struck home. He asked drivers to "watch for children who aren't old enough to know better than to cross streets at the wrong places."

This really is the important thing. A parent will always do his best to teach a child safety. But there always will be children who are too young or too forgetful, to "know better."

The burden is on us to drive watchfully. These are our children. The very innocence that gives them their sweetness also places their lives in our trust when they are on their way to school.

The cold type of an accident report is bare. It does not describe the look on the face of a man I saw once in the emergency room of Macon Hospital . . .

The man drove rapidly up the ambulance ramp and stopped his car, which had ice cream sprayed across the hood. He lifted out a little girl he had hit. She still held a crumpled ice cream cone. There was blood on her face.

The man's face was more terrible to see as he carried the child he had injured to an intern and said, "Please."

He repeated the word. "Please."

He went into the operating room and stood beside the child on the table. Her mother had arrived but could not compose herself to come in. She was walking up and down the ambulance ramp, screaming. The intern asked the man whose car had hit the child to leave the room.

"Let me stay," the man said. It was a minor cut over the eye. The child was not injured otherwise. The doctor let him stay. He stood there beside the table, with his hand on the child's arm and tears standing in his eyes, until the doctor had closed the cut and bandaged the little head.

When it was over the man, his face still dead white, lifted the girl and carried her out and handed her to her mother. "I am so sorry," he said to the woman. She was now weeping with relief and the child began to cry for the first time.

The little girl was well in a week.

But the good, decent man whose car had struck her stopped me on the street six months later and said he did not think time would ever relieve his mind of the sick terror he felt that afternoon.

September 13, 1960
She Paid $7.75 and Sent Thanks

This is a word for people, policemen and Thomaston, Georgia. When a policeman shoves people around it frequently makes news. This is not that kind of story. Lt. W. D. McDaniel, nine years on the Thomaston force, does not shove people who don't shove him.

"I will treat any person just like the next one," he says. "If people are courteous to me, I am going to be courteous to them. Besides, a lot of people are upset when they have an accident, and there wasn't any point in making this woman feel any worse than she did . . ."

The woman was Mrs. Anne W. Smith of Bainbridge, Ga. She is a high school mathematics teacher there. She was driving home from Nashville, Tenn., with her grandbaby in the car and it was raining in Thomaston. Most of us have experienced her feeling at what happened next. In front of the hotel, she said, a truck forced her too far over and she hit a parked car.

"The baby fell on the floor and started to cry. I didn't have my mind about me and didn't get the truck's number," she said.

Lt. McDaniel went to the scene of the crash. "It wasn't much of a wreck," he said in a telephone interview. "She was just as nice as she could be. I treated her like I treat anybody who is courteous."

"He didn't make me get out of the car in the rain," Mrs. Smith said by telephone from Bainbridge. "He told me to stay there and he went to his car in the rain and radioed for a filling station man to come move my car for me."

Lt. McDaniel said the man who owned the parked car was nice about it. Mrs. Smith's insurance covered the damage. "She couldn't describe the truck that she said forced her over," Lt. McDaniel said, "so I had to write a ticket for reckless driving. I just got her in out of the rain and sat her down in a chair and wrote out the charge right there."

"He had to make a case against me, I know," Mrs. Smith said. "But the fine was only $7.75. The main thing was, he didn't act mean. Four or five years ago I was stopped in Georgia near the South Carolina line for a much smaller offense. The fine was $75. But, worse than the fine, the state patrolman who stopped me was very nasty. He frightened me and humiliated me. That's why I wrote the officer in Thomaston."

What Mrs. Smith wrote to Lt. McDaniel after she got home to Bainbridge, was this: "Dear Sir: As a child, seeing the way people were treated by officers, I grew up with a fear of ever having to come in contact with one. How much better the feeling for law enforcement officers would be if there were more like you."

She sent a copy of the letter to the *Constitution* because "the kind of consideration given me by Officer McDaniel needs to be made known to the people of Georgia who, in many instances, have lost faith in our law enforcement officers. I would like the citizens of Georgia to know that a man like this represents our division of law enforcement."

Only incidentally do we mention that Mrs. Smith is Negro.

October 4, 1960
Two Routes and One Vehicle

John Greer of Lanier County is one of those unhurried South Georgians who will be pleasant to all but will do his own thinking. He practices the courtesy that marks men of good quality in the pine and palmetto country: He respects those who disagree with him, but he, too, has the courage to differ.

Calmly, Sen. Greer stated the facts on school desegregation Monday in a Macon speech. He did not argue and fuss. He simply gave his reasons for wanting Georgians to accept the majority report of the Sibley Commission, of which he was a member, and thus keep our schools open.

Every commission member, he said, was a segregationist. None represented "voluntary integration." "There has been nothing voluntary about any move we may make to preserve our public segregated education," he said.

"If it were not for the court orders we would not be here talking about it . . . Anybody that says anything about voluntary integration has either lost his mind or has been asleep as long as Rip Van Winkle."

What the Sibley Commission wanted to do was the opposite of destroying segregation, he said: the aim was to keep "our system of equal but segregated education from being completely destroyed."

Mr. Greer's approach may shake those who want something more than a reluctant and legalistic approach to desegregation. But he was at least plain in stating his own view that "utter chaos will follow any mass integration of the schools in this state" and that "we must maintain every bit of segregation that is possible . . . or we will face a catastrophe."

Therefore, he said, "we should turn to another battleground where we certainly can win over 90 percent of the battles instead of losing them all."

According to Greer, adoption of pupil placement and local choice laws as recommended by the Sibley Commission would place the state in this new battle position.

"So we must not fool ourselves," he said. "We . . . are right up to the licklog. Some people argue that we could keep the Atlanta case in court another year . . . What if we can? The ultimate result would be the same . . . We now face not only a federal court opinion but direct court decisions with a date on them."

The Legislature and the people ought to listen to Mr. Greer's speech. The January session is not preparing to adopt the Sibley report. It may take up the constitutional amendment portion, in an effort to delay, since an amendment vote would have to wait until 1962. But it is unlikely the courts will allow such a delay. And Georgia's children are threatened with a shut-out from education.

It is time for the people to wake up, as Mr. Greer said. Both those who doubt the justice of forced segregation and those who, like Mr. Greer, want to maintain it, are led by differing paths to the same conclusion, if order and education are to continue in Georgia. The answer is the Sibley Commission's majority report.

October 10, 1960
Old South Fitted into New Dress

ADEL—From boll weevil to Benson, except for wartime, the small farmer in Cook County has had to scratch hard to make a living. But he had a good town here to lean on.

Intelligent businessmen saw they couldn't go on simply making sales in town to fewer and fewer farmers. So they began making jobs.

As a result Adel's population has nearly doubled in 10 years.

The factories are diverse. A sawmill makes lumber from pine. A veneer crate plant makes boxes from black gum. One plant mills feed. Another sews shirts. A third manufactures fertilizer. And a metal products plant fabricates auto parts while a next door factory applies the plating in boiling vats of chemicals.

With such a spread no single industrial misfortune could wipe out the town. But the businessmen are hunting for more industry to broaden the base. The labor and the will are here and so are many problems.

For instance, fabrication of headlight brackets, ashtrays, chrome molding and fittings for the new cars is seasonal. But the light employment period here coincides with the heavy period of farm work. And when the farmers' work lightens after tobacco is sold, the metal products plant needs them to meet its rush period. It is an intelligent and fortunate arrangement of timing. The plant employs some 400 people. Georgia needs more such self-sustaining plants in specialty industries such as electronics and plastics.

At the Del-Cook Company, lumber stacks cover 40 acres. The planks season in the sun and await shipment. The big Florida market is off abruptly, perhaps reflecting over-building. But President Jim Paulk was on the phone trying for a military contract for 5,000,000 feet. And the mill is working a night shift, skinning whole pines and conveying them end-first into a combwork of circular saws that dice the trees into planks at one whining cut. The pines are coming from as far as 150 miles away. But reforestation promises a resupply.

At Bill Talley's box factory, sweet gums and black gum, snaked out of swamps, also come from far away. Nearby swamps as well as pine lands have been cut over. A blade deals off the thin moist sheets of veneer like a card dealer. Oven-dried, the sheets go clacking down an assembly line to be stapled and wired into crates for packing poultry in Georgia, Delaware and Maine (New England likes the whiter black gum best; Georgia buyers go for the sweet gum).

And the problem here is that in the frenzy to plant pines nobody has reforested the swamps with the gum hardwoods. Talley and other veneer men are going into action on this score. A current University of Georgia program for hardwood forestry is crucially important if hardwood industries are to avoid running themselves out of raw materials.

New problems, new products, new jobs. This is the new shape the old South is taking.

November 12, 1960
The Whirlpool Is Tightening

The whirlpool is tightening toward finality. Georgians can let their schools be sucked under. Or they can order the January legislature to act. John Sibley, who commands respect, explained the facts again Thursday. He told how school closings may turn the present hesitation in the state's development into stagnation. He repeated the law—to shut one school in Atlanta will be to shut them all over Georgia. He re-emphasized the Sibley Commission finding—we should scrap our void laws before they damage us, and adopt valid laws to accord with what is coming.

All Georgians know this. If they are told what must be done, they will support it now.

Their politicians are not sure this is so, however. They are being too cautious.

The governor apparently plans no action in January beyond an effort to delay again. He will urge passage of a constitutional amendment on the subject, maybe, hoping for delay until 1962 when the people would have their first chance to vote on such an amendment. If the delay were possible, Georgians would support it.

But what if the courts refuse to grant the delay? Such a refusal seems likely.

Then desegregation of an Atlanta school would be ordered next September. And if the Atlanta school is shut, schools everywhere in Georgia may be shut. Then what?

The governor's position would be clear. Gov. Vandiver, a sensible man, would have to call a special session of the legislature to repeal and enact as Mr. Sibley now recommends.

But he would have to do it in the storm of another's making instead of in the calm of our own judgment. Gov. Almond did it in Virginia. But he did it as a new governor with his years of power ahead of him. By this time next year, Vandiver will be a lame duck. If the people, and therefore the legislature, have not been prepared to accept the shock, a declining governor may not be able to convince and move the legislature. Then a disaster greater than prophesied can strike Georgia, retard her children, revolutionize her politics, and dash her hopes of growth into the pit with Arkansas [site of the desegregation crisis in 1957 at Little Rock's Central High School].

To chance such damage is really pretty silly. Georgia is a magnificent and mature state—one of the original 13. She can do better than this.

She must say to Gov. Vandiver, "Ernie, your campaign promise of absolute segregation was made under laws that have changed since you made the promise. Your own position therefore may change and be accepted by all reasonable Georgians. They expect you now to frame new laws to care for their children. Frame them in January, while you have the power, and submit them to a newly elected legislature, which has heard from us, and which therefore will keep our schools open."

If we do not say this now to the governor and our legislators, then our state and our children may be terribly hurt.

November 18, 1960
Why Men Jeer at a 6-Year-Old

The pictures from New Orleans are not the ones to place in the national album. Most people in Louisiana are heartsick at these happenings. The screamers and egg-throwers are few. They are the flotsam left on the beach by a tide that went out without warning. Yet this driftwood of the South is being pictured to the nation as the timber of Louisiana. America is intelligent enough to know the truth, and should bear enough love to understand.

If the pictures are not fair to Louisiana, neither has Louisiana been fair to herself. She has let her state leaders mislead. This will not happen in Georgia. Our leaders may not be leading adequately yet. But they have ceased to mislead. They have not blinded Georgians to the coming tide. They desire understanding, not abuse, now that they seek a way.

One prediction: No Georgian of our acquaintance will direct abuse in Atlanta at a frightened first-grade child whose first day in a strange school is spent sitting in a chair outside the principal's office—sitting with a ribbon in her hair, alone and 6 years old.

It wouldn't have happened in Louisiana either if the people had been better led. Shock and surprise struck that state blind. Blame her leadership. Even as grown men turned fury on 6-year-olds, the Louisiana Legislature egged the men on. While these few men and women carried their hateful signs and spat into the microphones, soiling the face of a great city, state leaders gave bravos to the disorderly few instead of giving leadership to the humiliated many.

Georgia's Legislature will do better than this. But the state administration wants to wait until the moment of crisis to do it. Louisiana waited. What is happening in New Orleans shows it was not a good idea. And Louisiana even had a pupil-placement law on the books, ready to control the crisis. Georgia does not even have that. She needs it. She needs to arm herself with the Sibley Commission safeguards in the coolness of this coming January, not in the heat of next September. To wait for the September crisis is to gamble.

It is a gamble to encourage the people to expect another delay; a heavy shock may fall if they do not get it. It is a gamble for the governor to expect that his power to control and influence will remain intact indefinitely; his time in office is shortening. The Georgia Baptist Convention spoke for the state's majority; the people want the schools kept open. The state's political leaders have given the welcome answer that they will keep them open. But they are tempted to wait until the crisis crashes down upon Georgia, then improvise.

Louisiana waited.

This is Georgia. She can do better than that. Without changing her position of reluctance, which is politically understandable, she can and ought to prepare laws now to cope with the crisis when it comes—to control it with dignity and a manliness that will mark this state as a shrine of Southern honor, not scar it as a place where unprepared, unled men react by jeering at a 6-year-old.

December 20, 1960
Shall We Choose Vengeance?

There comes a time in every deadlock of management and labor, in every contention between friends, in every life, when the fever of force and pressure must break, to be replaced by the faith and forbearance Christ preached. The alternative is vengeance.

So much is wrong with the present racial deadlock in Atlanta. It seems not only dangerous but wrong to celebrate Christ's birth in a spirit that his condemned. Atlanta lies hurt and passing men look the other way. The city's condition can become serious indeed unless she is helped.

Still nobody acts. It is true that a Negro group, with force still applied, has proposed talks, and the Chamber of Commerce, engaged against the force, has declined them. This is not because reason and understanding are absent on either side. It is because the faith and forbearance needed to apply them are not present.

It would speak well for the Christian profession of the Negro movement if it withdrew its force as an expression of faith before asking for talks. If it chooses to keep tension on the crowbar, it appears to want only to dictate terms.

And those white men who have disapproved of, as I have, the law-breaking part of the Negro method, must not use that disapproval as a comforter to relax their consciences to the legitimate ends sought by the Negro. "I have not taught my children that they must go to the back window to get a sandwich," a Negro seminary student said. "I hope that by the time they are big enough, it won't be necessary, so they will never have to know."

Atlanta has a choice of settlements—by faith or by vengeance. There are many who would choose the latter. They will tell you that forbearance gets you hurt in this dog-eat-dog world. That is not, of course, what Christ was preaching 20 centuries ago. It is not the First Commandment. But it is true.

So in talking this week with a group of ministers, I asked the question: How can a man practice Christianity in this world without being run over by a truck; doesn't a soft answer to wrath get you clobbered?

Every one of them gave the same response, which is a Christmas message to both races in Georgia: If a man is going to be a Christian, he has missed the message of his faith unless he accepts, as secondary, the risk at times that he will get clobbered.

Isn't it about that time?

Or shall we salute the birth of Jesus with a raised fist?

Hamilton Holmes and Charlayne Hunter, the first two students to desegregate the University of Georgia. By permission of the *Atlanta Journal and Constitution.*

1961

The Rock
and the Anchor

January The United States severs diplomatic relations with Cuba. John F.
Kennedy of Massachusetts becomes president of the United
States. Despite opposition from Roy V. Harris and other arch-
segregationists, Charlayne Hunter and Hamilton Holmes desegregate the University of Georgia.

February The Georgia legislature adopts the recommendations of the Sibley
Commission.

March President Kennedy creates the Alliance for Progress and the
Peace Corps.

April Soviet cosmonaut Yuri Gagarin becomes the first human to travel
in space. Hoping to topple the Castro regime, the Kennedy Administration authorizes but later abandons the ill-fated Bay of Pigs
invasion. The centennial celebration of the Civil War begins.

May Navy commander Alan Shepard becomes the first American in
space. Freedom Riders—an interracial band of civil rights activists
sponsored by the Congress of Racial Equality—test compliance
with two U.S. Supreme Court decisions prohibiting racial segregation of interstate bus passengers.

June President Kennedy and Soviet Premier Nikita Khrushchev hold a
two-day summit meeting in Vienna, Austria.

July–August East Germany completes construction of the Berlin Wall. The Soviet Union resumes nuclear testing following a three-year hiatus.

September The United States resumes underground nuclear testing. Following a summer of Freedom Rides, the Interstate Commerce Com-

mission issues an order implementing the desegregation of interstate transit, to go into effect on December 1.

November   Local civil rights activists organize the Albany Movement in the
south Georgia city of Albany.

December   The Reverend Martin Luther King Jr. is arrested in Albany.

January 12, 1961
Let the Means of Force Now Die

Georgia has faced its moment of truth on desegregation and the sky has
not fallen down. There is even a sense of relief in it. Parents know now
that their children will have schools. The people know that their leaders
are responsible men. The nation knows that Georgia is worthy.

Thousands of university students showed good breeding under
stress. The few who felt no shame in dogging and goading two less comfortable beings did, of course, provide photographs which displayed
their bullying across the country. Some of them even made page one of
the *New York Times*, with their mouths open. But the insensitive few did
not dominate the campus. The body of the students behaved with grace.

A nation appalled by the performance of Faubus in Arkansas and
Davis in Louisiana discovered Vandiver of Georgia to be a Southern
governor who obeys the law and puts the education of the young ahead
of an old politics when it wears out. The bloodthirsty liberal may deny
him credit, but history won't.

The people of the state found their legislature suffering their own
torn emotions but also manifesting their own traditional maturity when
tested. Louisiana's people did not receive such respect from their legislature.

And in the hours of crisis, when men had to stand forward for Georgia or stand back in trembling, two leaders in particular stood firmly,
regardless of political risk, to do what had to be done to preserve education. They were Sen. Carl Sanders of Augusta and Rep. Frank Twitty of

Camilla. Let the voters of the state mark this by their names: They had guts when it took guts to have guts. Other men in the present leadership may try to take the peacetime bows, but these men, and Vandiver, faced the combat. For a few tense hours they were the custodians of Georgia's good name, and of a good part of her future.

While the state had the leadership, and her people had the character, to meet the crisis, Georgia also had the good fortune to have time— time to think, to prepare, to observe and to learn from the errors of other states. The time was not used well; but the learning was. This knowledge of the facts, coupled with leadership and character in the people, caused the inevitable to be met with dignity.

And the sky has not fallen down. My mind goes back two years to a conversation with the president of a Negro college in Atlanta. "If Georgia's colleges were desegregated tomorrow," he said, "I do not think more than a handful of my students would transfer to the white schools. But when you tell us we are barred by law from going to those schools, we will not rest until that law is taken from the books. We do not want to be forced to a course of action any more than you do."

January 14, 1961
Federal versus State Power

Gov. Vandiver had the majority of Georgians behind him when he made the basic decisions of his governorship last Monday—decisions to keep the University of Georgia open, and to obey the law.

His Monday decision was not enforced on Wednesday. The Monday decision still stands, however, as fine and right. The Wednesday collapse of authority in the face of a mob cannot be erased. But on second chance it can be corrected.

It is a lasting blot on the name of the University of Georgia that some of its students cannot be trusted to act like men. But they placed that tag upon themselves Wednesday night. They ought to go home and grow up. But they are still in Athens enjoying rights they denied to others by mob action.

Therefore, Gov. Vandiver is forced to make one more basic decision, the saddest of the lot: what kind of police are to be used to teach some University of Georgia students to act like men?

Federal marshals can always be sent if the state wishes to align itself with the Roy Harris–Peter Zack Geer position that the student mob demonstrated character and courage.

But if the governor takes his stand with that pair, and abdicates state responsibility for the safety of women in university dormitories, we will be surprised.

To be able to say federal tyranny forced us is one thing: to say state troopers stood aside while a mob broke the windows in the bedrooms of young Georgia women is quite another.

If the safeguarding of Georgia students in peril is not the duty of Georgia's own police, then state's rights have come to a poor pass indeed.

The question was one of law and order. The governor, the legislature, and the people of Georgia have faced the law. The question now is solely one of order. It is the governor's job to keep order. And we do not have the slightest doubt that Ernest Vandiver is going to snatch a knot in the arm of the first aide, underling or unfriendly kibitzer who presumes to discourage or short-circuit his power to keep the order in the state, with state forces, and by state decision, next time.

We have seen that the federal power acts only when we do not. Political leaders have denounced the way it acted in the university crisis; they can forestall it in the public school crisis by heading it off with valid state laws enacted now.

But the immediate question is one of order in Athens. We believe it will clearly pit the runted faith of Roy Harris against the decency of Ernest Vandiver. We believe the people are behind Vandiver's decency.

And as a footnote, we believe that never in the history of our alma mater has the University of Georgia been so shamed by any sons of hers as these who made this melancholy issue.

January 24, 1961
A Certain, Simple Understanding

Only John A. Sibley can answer why he left the insulated comfort of his wealth and quiet position to open the door of the racial firebox in Georgia and take the heat full on. But he did.

Because he did this, this generation of Georgians and ones to come owe thanks to him. His Sibley Commission was the pivotal force that created the climate in which politicians could act to save public education in the state.

He seemed at first an unlikely man to head an unlikely mission. He was a conservative financier-lawyer from the city. He presumed to barnstorm into country gymnasium and small-town courthouse with a committee of men bent on the nebulous assignment of hearing the voice of the people on the school desegregation prospect.

Yet these hearings, remarkable in Georgia history, broke a freeze of fear and silence. The commission produced a report that formed the basis of the new laws now recommended. But its great act was the opening of a steamcock in the boiler of emotion. And the character of the unlikely chairman, John Sibley, was the force that drove the relieving valve into the pressure chamber.

He sat like a firm, sympathetic father and invited all to bring him their troubles. They testified, denounced, protested, confessed, and to all of the troubled ones the courtly elder with the plain face gave respect; to the angry ones he gave humor. Always, though, he seemed to understand.

For he was of the South, and a conservative and a conservative proud to be Southern. Some might try to call him a Bourbon. He was less pretentious than that. But he did understand. He declined to believe adherents to a legitimate past were unworthy illegitimates because the future had suddenly changed. He traced that future with gentle reason and not rancor. He took men as they were and not as he wanted them to be. He did not go out to deal with perfection; he went out to deal with life.

And the people who came to testify under his benign eye sensed this. The people of Georgia sensed it. The pressure dropped like a hot wind sighing and the climate cooled to reason. This week we see the result. But no eyes are on John Sibley.

He has dropped back quietly into his own world from which he stepped only briefly when Georgia needed a man of understanding. Why did he make his emergence? Noblesse oblige? A Bourbon paying his debt when the challenge was worthy of his steel? That isn't entirely right.

He has a farm across the Chattahoochee, and a cabin there where he goes on weekends. The place is unmanicured. In worn clothes he rides his horse, counts his cattle—and his children and grandchildren, the latter being more easily counted by fives. And when he takes one end of a five-foot log, and his son Jimmy takes the other, and they swing it one-two-three before pitching it into the rough fireplace on the third swing, they do not count out loud. They know the cadence of one another.

The man who contributed so powerfully to the future of Georgia's children has a certain, simple understanding with children and grandchildren.

February 11, 1961
Santayana and the Sit-Ins

For many years the Southern Negro has drawn his chief strength from a dignity of which George Santayana said, "If you have it, what need have you of parading it? The base and sordid side of life must be confessed and endured humbly; the confession and the endurance will raise you enough above it."

Steadily since Christ, the humble have so raised themselves. The naked power of unarmed truth which Pasternak celebrated has been the only certain softener of the hard conscience. And the grace of the Negro's endurance, and the painstaking rectitude of his petitions for relief of pain, have left even the most hardened consciences no comfortable way to assail him.

The Negro has been the offended man, not the offender, and strength born of this endurance has raised him step by unarguable step from the cellar of segregation, through unassailable court actions when force of law was required.

Now the youthful militants of the sit-in movement are pressing into a realm where the offended do not endure, but rather return offense; where unarguable pressure to change offending law is displaced by disobedience to the law. And because of the change from endurance to parade, the consciences that would assail the Negro's rise have found the comfort they have lacked before. And this is the weakness of what the young Negroes are doing, as they fill up the jails.

Their opponents are given an argument at last. They can say with accuracy that the Negro has gone outside the law; has chosen not to test, but to break, a law that he, not the courts, has judged.

The Negro's reply is strong with moral fervor: If the law brings indignity to us, then why must we endure it? If we break the law in moral protest, we have asked no immunity from that law, but have readily paid in full for our offense by going to jail and serving the penalty for what we have done. We ask no mercy; we offend and we pay. Why should we wait for our rights to be meted out to us one by one? If we are denied human dignity, then why are we denied a human response of outraged action? If our life is base and sordid, why must we as free men endure it?

And the white man knows full well that these questions are legitimate; that he would be outraged himself if he were forced to take his children to a back window to get their supper. No human being can truly justify treating another human being in such a way. The Negro's aim of changing it is unarguably just.

But the method he has chosen is new. It goes outside the law. To many who sympathize with his aim, this is all right. To many, however, it is not; and that is the weakness the Negro might as well weigh: regardless of whether he is right or wrong, he is giving cause for comfort to some white consciences, where none have been comfortable before. In this important respect, Santayana was wiser than the sitters. It is questionable whether the gains the Negro has made through the new militance can offset the effect he has lost.

April 22, 1961
King Becomes a Granddaddy

Oglethorpe County once had 15 cotton gins. It had one left, until last Saturday. Then a bolt of lightning burst from the heavens and struck it down in fire.

The owners of the last gin in Oglethorpe County looked at the ruin of the 50-year-old plant—its scorched conveyor belts twisted, its tin and metal sprung—and said they might not build it back.

It was the only industry in the village of Vesta. It employed three men. Only 5,000 acres of cotton still are grown in the county, anyway. Farmers have switched to dairies and poultry.

It's the same all over Georgia. Old gins rusting and still, with a little lint clinging to their cobwebs, stand sentinel at forgotten fields. And they guard memories . . . of a boy riding to town in the sunshine on a wagonload of cotton that smelled a little like warm milk and felt good to lie on and to sink the bare feet in, except for the sticky burrs here and there . . . and when he parted the fluff and took out a cottonseed and bit down on it the taste was not unpleasant . . . and when the team started through town he might be allowed to take the reins and drive along in case his girl saw him . . . and when he got to the gin, he watched the wagon backed under the great tin pipe which sucked up the cotton like a tornado, flung it through machinery and churned it out free of seed and burrs, a magic white, to be pressed into the great bales, wrapped in burlap and strapped with blue shiny metal, negotiable. And he watered the mules at the town trough, listening to the noise they make sipping with a bit in their mouth, and went on home.

But the memories are bad, too. The anguish of a father leading his wife and children, stooped in the heat, down the rows to pick all day for a few hundred pounds at a price—do you remember—of a nickel a pound. And the wry song that the guitar player picked at the frolics—

Said the farmer to the boll weevil
I wish you very well.
Said the boll weevil to the farmer
I wish you was in - - - -.

Well, old boll weevil had his way, and the mechanical cotton pickers made it so that only one Southern Negro in 10 now works as a field hand, and the guitar player began to sing at night while cooking tobacco, not worrying about cotton, and in red-dirt Georgia the farmers began to look at the chicken and the cow.

Cotton averaged 9 cents a pound in 1930 and rose only to 32 cents in 30 years. But tobacco brought a dime in 1930 and is up to 60 cents. And people in Egypt and Texas began to grow cotton while the last 20 years halved the market, anyway, for their natural fiber of cotton, wool, flax and silk because the synthetic fibers came in.

So get along, old king. We still need you around and we're proud of you and we still grow a third as much of you as we did 30 years ago. But you don't erode our soil and shackle our men and control our credit like you once did. You're just one of the boys now, king. And since you aren't the big boss now, we love you like a reformed granddaddy.

May 31, 1961
"What Can We Say to a Child?"

Dear Editor: As a classroom teacher I hear many remarks from my students which lead me to believe that the teacher's task in the integration crisis is stupendous.

We need help. What can we say when a child blurts out, "But teacher, Daddy says the governor won't speak to an integrated group!" Who has the time and understanding and influence to help the teacher?

Name Withheld
Atlanta

Dear Teacher: Everybody can help you, including the governor, if they will simply pause and put themselves in your shoes for a moment.

You are faced with implementing a court decision you did not seek.

You are told to do it in a state where some political leaders continue to say it ought not to be done, despite the fact that it must be done.

You are trying to calm the anxiety of children and create respect for order while many adults still inject anxiety into them and question the process they are expected to honor.

You are expected to shield the children from spiritual and physical injury at the moment of crisis. Yet you will suffer the animosity instead of receiving the help of some parents.

You face a stupendous job indeed.

And only because the public has come to trust the judgment and rely on the common sense of the schoolteacher can it face September with any equanimity.

You, trained for tranquil rooms of learning, have learned to nurse stubbed toes on the playground and to ease broken hearts at the prom as well as you instruct in arithmetic. The coming embarkation into social change is a far greater challenge than you have faced; but you will meet it. You always have.

You deserve and should be able to expect the help of everyone, if everyone will simply look through your eyes for a moment. The issue of desegregation so far has been political and legal. Suddenly it will become human, and all of the unprecedented human problems flowing from it will be heaped upon you for solution. It isn't fair for you to bear such burdens. But history has given them to you. You do need help. I think you will have it, because the human problems you face are the problems of our children.

And I shall never forget the Speaker of the House, Rep. George Smith, rising soberly in the aftermath of the University of Georgia riot and saying to his fellow politicians: "We in politics have all taught them that lesson . . . We in Georgia politics are partly to blame for everything that happened."

Surely it is time for everyone to begin helping you shield our children from repetition of that ordeal.

June 6, 1961
New Rationality Comes to South

The plan to desegregate five Atlanta schools by admitting 10 Negro students is too little, in the view of Negro leader Jesse Hill, and too much, according to Gov. Vandiver.

But removal of the laws that compel segregation is releasing the power of rationality in the South and turning back this problem from the furnace of political conflict to the cooling chamber of the reasoning mind.

No longer coerced by law, the Negro can apply his judgment to practical steps toward progress in alliance with the white man who is faced toward the same future now, and is no less anxious to approach it in peace.

Whether 10 students and five schools are too many or too few is secondary to the setting of the year's historic precedents—repeal of the state school law that forced the Negro into segregation, and their replacement by a beginning of desegregation, in peace.

Because Mr. Hill and other Atlanta Negro leaders recognize the magnitude of the precedents being set, we believe their voluntary judgment will be to help inaugurate the new principle this year in manageable form.

As for Gov. Vandiver, his public vow to keep the peace is a powerful testimony to his responsibility. Georgians have seen what weaker or more frightened governors did to Arkansas, Louisiana and Alabama by withholding their leadership or refusing to exercise it. Gov. Vandiver said:

"Anytime the life or property of any citizen is endangered, whatever forces that are necessary to preserve the peace will be used."

That is the rock to which civilization is anchored. For one night at Athens rioters took over and shocked us all. Then the governor took command in behalf of peace. Now he has announced his principle again. And so he has strongly reassured every Georgian who respects law and order.

So begins the new rationality of the South. As man-invented force and coercion are removed, the God-given power of human beings to adjust and to determine to get along peacefully and sensibly with each other is released and begins to exert itself. Georgia honors itself by a leader on this path in the South.

July 18, 1961
Each Race Needs to Tend Vineyard

White Georgians are able now to face and reflect on school desegregation and other racial readjustments without relapse into the pains and fever of the past decade. Negro Georgians, achieving these gains, can also look around them in the diminishing combat and face the problem troubling the Lockheed plant at Marietta; the plant wants to hire Negro technicians but cannot find enough qualified ones.

The vessel of social chance is leaving the narrows. And each race must scan its widening horizon with a greater breadth of view. The white man, no longer imprisoned in a doomed defense of the past, must choose a better politics for the future. And the Negro, having cracked the walls of force that other men built around him, must consider his own course, too.

We are too close to the revolution of the last 20 years to grasp the enormity of it. Many who are reading these lines must pause to realize that, early in their own lifetimes, only two out of 10 American Negroes could read or write. Now nine out of 10 can.

Nine out of 10 American Negroes lived in the South in 1910. Only half of them live here now. Migration has moved the Negro from the Southern cotton cabin into the cities of the North and West.

The old white Southern complaint that "the North doesn't have the population problem" no longer holds water. Three-fourths of the children in Manhattan's public elementary schools are Negro or Puerto Rican, which makes Atlanta's ratio minor by contrast.

While Atlanta's population is about one-third Negro, Washington's is 54 percent; in Detroit, 29 percent.

So the Southern white can no longer claim a peculiar problem in his cities. The readjustments in schools and housing are pressing Northern urban areas just as hard or harder, and if the Southern white does not meet the problems as well, he can no longer blame it on the Negro population, but must face his own failure.

By the same token the Negro can no longer blame existence of his problems altogether on Southern white oppression, but must progressively shoulder the responsibilities he has pressed so effectively to assume. This goes deeper than an isolated riot in Chicago, or Lockheed's inability to find qualified Negro technicians. It is reflected in the climb of Negro illegitimate births from 16 percent in 1940 to 21 percent now, and in the jail populations which, in 1955, were 65 percent Negro in Chicago, 58 percent in Detroit, 80 percent in Philadelphia. The first years of any man's freedom are stormy.

The fact that only 14 percent of the jail population in Los Angeles in 1955 was Negro indicates that a city which gives the Negro equality in jobs and housing, as Los Angeles does, will find the Negro to be as responsible a citizen as the white. This needs proving in other major cities by some vineyard-tending in each race.

It is up to both of the races now to look inward more—and not simply to contest their mutual worth, as they have in the past, but to prove it.

July 27, 1961
Walter Jones Gets His Start

Back in boyhood my brother and I opened a lemonade stand on a sidewalk in Nicholls, Ga., and, except for our parents' purchases, made no sales. We drank up the inventory at nightfall and hoped for better business on the morrow. But a hurricane blowing up from Florida struck Nicholls during the night, splintered our lemonade stand and blew it halfway down the hill to the creek.

With this business background, I couldn't resist stopping the car Wednesday morning at 2160 Northside Drive where a bright-faced boy in a T-shirt was sitting all alone in the yard behind a soft drink stand, waiting for customers.

Turned out his name was Walter Jones. He's 10. He thinks he can do anything his brothers, aged 15 and 17, can do. He likes music and wanted some money to buy records. He fished bottles from Peachtree Creek for a while but the profit was low.

So he marched across the street to the Bobby Jones golf course and presented himself as a caddy. A golfer's bag is about as big as Walter is, though. He proved to be too little to caddy. A failure at 10. He brooded. Then he approached his father with a proposition.

Would Pop advance him $5.62, for which he could swing the little soda stand ($1), buy three cases of supplies from the Coca-Cola company ($1.30 a case), put down a deposit on the bottles and lay in some ice. His father went along with the transaction.

Walter got the goods, bicycled to the market for a bag of ice, and opened for business Tuesday afternoon. The first day wasn't good. "I sold five," he said. "My mother bought them all."

Anticipating a better day Wednesday, he reopened negotiations with his father Tuesday night. He wanted to buy some records with his first profit and pay back Pop later. No go. "You pay your debts first," Walter was told. He trudged up and down Northside Drive salvaging old bottles to offset his deposit expense.

Wednesday dawned bright and clear and the golfers were thick along the fairway across the street from Walter's yard. "I got the king-sized ones because golfers are thirsty," Walter said. "I knew Wednesday would be a good day because lots of them take off half a day from the office."

He was looking forward, too, to the afternoon rush hour. He knew cars would jam to a halt in the street, increasing his sales possibilities. "I'll be right here till 7 P.M.," he said.

By mid-afternoon Walter had sold nearly all of his three cases at 10 cents a bottle, or $2.40 for a case that cost him $1.30, and had made an approach to his mother for a new advance for supplies. Mrs. Sara M. Jones considered it a good investment in view of the profit he was turning. At least she wasn't having to drink his stock now. And that was the beginning in business of Walter Jones, who was too little to caddy. Men in shorts dragged their little buggies along the fairway across the street trying to be boys in the sunshine, and there in the shade behind his out-door counter sat a boy determined to be a man.

July 28, 1961
Let's Advertise South's Viewpoint

Mississippi leads in a new call for the South to take up a collection and advertise its racial point of view nationally. This is an excellent idea which can do great good.

Too many Americans in the North and West have judged Southern-ers by the activities of leaders who continue to speak, but not for the people.

What a great thing it would be for the South to junk the old jargon, which for so long has attempted to justify the impossible, and set the record straight.

Let the ad begin by announcing that many people of the South ques-tioned the Supreme Court's decision to desegregate schools and op-posed it to the limit by every honorable means; but now with honorable means exhausted, the South has determined to abide in dignity by the law without casting aspersions on the patriotism of the Supreme Court, the loyalty of the American government, or the pride of the Negro race. In return for this pledge, the South requests an end to national condem-nation and a beginning of sympathetic understanding for its difficulties as it strives to cope with the protracted pacing of a delicate change.

Let the advertisement go on to express the conclusion of the South that the Negro citizen has the same right to vote as any other American citizen and will have that right safeguarded from intimidation or unfair disqualification by the full powers vested in each of the sovereign South-ern states. In return, it requests an end to the questioning of its credi-bility.

Let the ad inform all of America that Southerners have suffered an understandable anxiety about the rearrangement of ancestral custom but are determined to move reasonably to meet its demands, either vol-untarily as they can or in compliance with law, in such fields as jobs, libraries, buses, lunch counters, transport terminals, housing. In return the South relies on mutual reason to reduce such divisive goading as extended Freedom Rides and to rule out present pressure in too-sensitive areas such as wade-ins.

The ad should state that Southern honor will no longer accept political speeches based on humiliation of the Negro as a human being, and in return for Southern determination to replace racial inflammation with a regard for the dignity of all, the South requests a fair regard for itself in place of regional prejudice.

Once these positions are meant and set forth in national publications the South can expect the patience, the understanding and the support of the nation, and an ear for its appeals to keep this whole business within reason.

But if the Madison Avenue of Mississippi happens to have some other kind of advertising in mind—and possibly it may have—we Southerners can save our money because we'll be talking to nobody but ourselves.

August 24, 1961
A Letter Asks: How Come?

Dear Editor: What is your purpose, except to fight the county unit system, in running the "Fading Counties" series? Georgia, especially rural Georgia, white and colored, since World War I has served the role of breeding ground for more populated areas of the nation, including our own metropolitan areas . . .

It is likely that most *Constitution* employees, including the editors and reporters, sprang from such roots. Also most of Atlanta's one million . . .

At a time when Georgia needs anything but a built-in atmosphere of depression, I think it rather unwarranted to use the talents of a couple of good reporters and space in your paper to needlessly expose the viscera of selected sparsely settled Georgia counties.

James A. Hayes,
Atlanta

Dear Mr. Hayes: Like most *Constitution* reporters, I am proud that my roots are in rural Georgia. And I had a talk with an Atlanta banker recently that shook me. I told him I was disturbed to see some of the rural counties so hard up, and what did he think could be done for their people.

He said do nothing: let the present political and economic trends continue and the counties and many of their people will go bankrupt, and that will be that. "That's business," he said.

But that's a pretty cruel law to apply deliberately to human beings who may be living in the belief that things are about to get better. I know enough about the horse sense and hardihood of rural Georgians to know they deserve and will achieve a better deal than bankruptcy if they are given the facts.

So that is the purpose of the series, Mr. Hayes—to go to the rural people with the facts on what was going wrong, instead of sitting silently by while self-seeking politicians mislead them any further down the road the banker marked. The needs are both political and economic.

But yes, we will fight the sort of county unit system that feeds politicians while the people hunger. These politicians are the root cause of the backward policies that are depriving so many rural children of a future.

They build the wrong kind of roads to get votes instead of the right kind to get industry; they waste money to build unfilled schoolrooms rather than seek better schools consolidated across county lines; they hold to unequal taxation that repels industry and victimizes small rural landholders, rather than risk equalizing taxes of privileged men who perpetuate them; they fritter away the substance of the state without plan in countless boondoggles for short-term political gain, while long-term planning and financing of a program of industrial growth goes begging. They strangle new ideas and block better men. And they try to cover the depression they have brought to the rural people by throwing up a dust of demands for "inviolate" continuation of the very system that has betrayed those people.

Such men should never again be entrusted with rural Georgia's future. They have failed. The people of the fading counties see their harsh handiwork in the still streets and the idle fields and the eyes of children unfairly held back. Gov. Ernest Vandiver has turned Georgia around in many respects. And the county unit politicians now attacking him will drag the state back if the rural people, lacking facts, let them.

August 25, 1961
Give These Nazis Some Castor Oil

Every man in Georgia who put on a steel hat and went to deal with Hitler's Germany, and every Georgia family that gave a son to stop the Nazi scourge, should know of a telegram we have just received from the discredited commander of the American Nazi Party.

This man, whose name is Lincoln Rockwell, sent a truck full of swastika-wearing outsiders into the South earlier this year. Montgomery threw them out. New Orleans gave them the bum's rush.

Now they are coming to Atlanta.

We don't ordinarily recommend fighting fascism with its own weapons. But we are tempted to recommend that Police Chief Jenkins use an old Mussolini remedy in this case, meet the Nazis at the Atlanta city limits, and give them all a generous dose of castor oil. Then throw them out.

"On behalf of the white Christian majority of this great American Republic and in accordance with our right under the U.S. Constitution the American Nazi Party plans to peacefully picket the schools scheduled to be integrated (in Atlanta) on the 29th and 30th of August," Rockwell's telegram said.

He sent it from Arlington, Va.

This is precisely what Atlanta does not need—outsiders trucked in here to tear down a city that a million people have labored to build. And Nazis to boot.

They wear jackboots and swastika arm bands that look something like Hitler's SS. Their intention is to engage decent Atlantans in controversy and get themselves pictured in the world press as indicators of what Atlanta is. They hope to come in here from hundreds of miles away and strut before the television cameras that otherwise would record the responsible efforts of a healthy and law-abiding city.

Montgomery wouldn't have it. New Orleans refused to put up with it. Atlanta doesn't need it.

Snug in Arlington, far from this city which he threatens to discredit, Rockwell added in his telegram: "We are not intimidated by brazen threats of illegal force and violence and will insist on the full measure of our constitutional rights."

We trust Chief Jenkins will administer the castor oil gently, not violently. He should be sure they get a full enough measure not only to protect but to improve their constitutions. And he should then scrupulously assure their rights to move freely down the road toward any state line of their choosing.

On second thought, let the Nazis come on into Atlanta with their jackboots and swastikas; let's see if they can meet the eye of the men and the mothers who remember World War II. The looks they will get from Georgians who fought that war to eliminate their sort should be enough to wilt these Hitler lilies for good.

August 30, 1961
Why Do Georgians Act Like This?

Earlier this month a farm bull reverted to some red primitive rage and fatally gored its master, Robert L. Hill, a respected farmer in south Georgia's Lanier County.

The beast was destroyed at once and butchered to be sold as beefsteak. But it was publicly announced that none of the beef would be sold in the food markets of Lakeland and Lanier County.

The community, saddened by the death of Mr. Hill, felt it only right and proper that this announcement be made.

And of course it was right and proper. This instinctive regard for intangible sensibilities typifies the respect, often raw and plain and clean as the frontier, which one neighbor shows to another in the folkways of rural Georgia.

We commend this knowledge to the visiting reporters who are here to cover the desegregation of Atlanta's schools today, and who may be searching for insights into the character which fortifies our people to meet this difficult transition with poise and grace.

They may be tempted to attribute our equanimity to one part or another of the community.

Certainly the academic aura has cast its glow of worldliness on this center of colleges, white and Negro.

The injection of national blood has made this sales and distribution center cosmopolitan.

A clergy of exceptional faith and learning has illuminated her pulpits.

A tier of business leadership unmatched in the South has contributed a powerful commitment to the cause of peace and dignity.

A political directorate, tacking and veering before the whirling winds, but too conscious of the responsibility of captaincy to swamp the state, has done its duty.

Men of wealth and men of labor have raised a common flag of reason.

The people who live in this city of a million, though troubled and divided in their apprehensions, are united in their certainty that what we do must be worthy. No ragtag remnant of little men can speak for Atlanta's people.

But three quarters of us in Atlanta come from the Georgia hinterland. Our values rest on those hills; our roots are deep in those quiet fields and forests.

And an essential part of this day's conduct springs from the ancestral spirit of a land that is combative and independent but is by instinct full of respect for neighbor and regard for the right thing, and strong enough to show it.

August 31, 1961
A School Day and a Rocket

It was a deeply moving day. It was a flash of impressions, a collision of emotions—a drama both somber and exalted, intensively alive. First, in the dewy morning, Northside High.

Reporters stood unobtrusively as requested across the street. Policemen who had come to assure order at the moment of desegregation found themselves instead perspiring at the prosaic task of untangling traffic. As parents in the scores of creeping cars delivered their young to the future's keeping, the faces of the youngsters branded the mind.

Unafraid, interested, with clear eyes lively and eager, they walked firmly up the hill and into the schoolhouse door. There was something so noble in the manner of these undoubting young people, walking confidently through a door that so many of their fathers and mothers had endured inner anguish to hold open for them, that a surge of pride and admiration brought a sting to the eye.

Then at the press center at City Hall, Superintendent Letson spoke strongly into a battery of telephones, hiding nothing from the people, directing the Atlanta school system openly and with confidence. The calm, drawling responses of the principals came through amplifiers for all to hear. ("It's more normal than usual here," said one.) These voices from the school halls suddenly brought home, with great impact, the care and courage that goes into the daily safekeeping of Atlanta's children at school.

The press center installation itself astonished, impressed, and occasionally amused the visiting reporter. Some veterans of New Orleans and Little Rock couldn't quite believe Atlanta would do this thing in the open. They kept searching for hidden motives. They found it anomalous that Atlanta could face such a tense test with free disclosure. One reporter with whom I once covered events in Europe observed, "We never saw a summit conference set up this well."

But slowly the full implication dawned on these visitors, and impressed them: What they were seeing was what they saw at Cape Canaveral when the United States launched Commander Alan Shepard into space.

There was no guarantee the rocket would lift. There was possibility of failure, and therefore great tension. But the preparation, the planning, the deep confidence in the ability of the mechanism to succeed, and above all the trust in the man to perform bravely and well, inspired the government to say to the world, "Come and watch and see. If we fail, you will know we tried. If we succeed, share our pride. This is the confidence of a free country."

The rocket fired. The heart of mankind rode high with Shepard. That bold, unhidden shot truly was heard round the world.

Atlanta had no less confidence. And now they have shown the world the worth of a great people.

September 23, 1961
A Letter to the New Mayor

Dear Mr. Winner: You ought to be very proud of being elected mayor by an electorate of such quality as Atlanta's. Now the problems as well as the honors are yours. And one of the problems is immediate: you must throw your arm around the shoulder of a town that is torn apart, and pull it together again.

Seldom has Atlanta been so wrenched and goaded as it has been in this week's runoff campaign. These aggravations are familiar enough in a state race in Mississippi, but they are new to a city election in this citadel of reason. They have dug deep into old ground and turned up long-buried bones of unease.

That has been the tragedy of this melancholy campaign. Let us pray we will never be reduced to such a time again. One man alone can calm the anger and still the fright that has been called down upon the city, and the man is you.

For suddenly you are the elected leader of all Atlantans—the ones who fought you as well as the ones who cheered you.

All of us are neighbors. You will govern us all. Reassure your opponents, then, at the same time as you thank your supporters.

Tell them you will represent them all, as you will. You obviously are a big enough man to do that or you would not have won the office in this big town.

Throw your arm around this troubled city, bring its people together again, and tell them of the respect you have for your duty to all, not some, of them.

Atlanta's people will return your faith. The bruises of this campaign will hurt for a long time. But the people of this town are good.

They have simply been subjected to tactics that were bad.

Let us devoutly hope this week's storm of passion and racial recrimination has blown itself out forever, and that a clean and unclouded sky will light the politics of Atlanta from now on.

We truly are too busy to hate, as Mayor Hartsfield has said.

Our experiment with it this week has shocked us back to realization that peace, good order, and due regard for another man's pride are hallmarks that distinguish Atlanta and draw economic growth to her.

Let us never go away from that again, or encourage any politician to do so.

Reassure Atlanta, Mr. Winner, that you will be the first to forgive and forget this week of our history, and lead us away from repetition of such a time of vengeance.

November 30, 1961
Two Letters on Patriotism

ATLANTA—I've been trying to put you in several categories, none very complimentary. You certainly always seem to be against what any good white, Southern, patriotic American stands for.

J. G. Roos

MILLEDGEVILLE—I should like to ask Mr. Patterson if there is anything American or patriotic which he or his paper support or praise. As far as I can see, his *Atlanta Constitution* attacks everything that is right of center.

Harriette A. Wilson

Dear Folks: Please. Patriotism is not confined to people who are right of center. If it were, more than half of the American people would be disloyal.

We owe it to our country not to make our differences the basis for questioning one another's loyalty.

You and I undoubtedly differ on some public policies. That is natural and good. We must use that freedom. The friction generated by our freely expressed ideas keeps America's freedom ground to a fine edge.

If some Americans didn't argue against excessive government intervention in the nation's economy and society, there might be too much intervention.

And if other Americans didn't argue for government help on demanding problems that could not or would not be handled privately, our modern nation might strangle on obsolete slogans.

But neither side can claim it is qualified to administer a loyalty oath to the other.

Neither wing of political thought has patriotism as its own property. By their very arguments, both show they care about the country and its course. I and this newspaper support and praise this freedom to differ as both American and patriotic.

If we felt otherwise—if we shrank timidly from ideas with which you might disagree for fear you might question our patriotism—we would be unworthy, un-American and unpatriotic, in my opinion. We would be selling out freedom, because freedom presupposes its holders will be bold enough to use it.

I think it also presupposes that free people will have enough faith in each other not to lose trust in each other's loyalty. If we are going to make allegations of treason an acceptable part of our domestic arguments, we will demonstrate a loss of faith in the people and the basic institutions of freedom.

So even though I judge from your letters that I support the policies of the present American government more frequently than you do, I would not presume to judge I am more patriotic than you are. That would be neither a fair nor an American conclusion on my part. We may differ politically. But we salute the same flag.

Why don't we just put this business of judging other Americans' patriotism off limits, and get on with our honest differences?

December 2, 1961
Let Us Judge Ourselves First

The tired old texts do not quite cover Donita Gaines. The defenders and attackers of segregation will engage in cruelty if they try to make their usual points out of her misery. She is not, at this moment, a social or a political symbol.

She is an exhausted, tormented child.

This Negro girl needs no excuses made for her by the NAACP and she is vulnerable to no taunts from the White Citizens Councils because of one and the same reason: Her report card at Northside High School shows all As and Bs.

She did not fail. She succeeded. Of the nine Negro students who entered white schools in this year's desegregation, hers is the finest record.

It would not be unusual for any ambitious, sensitive adolescent to suffer strain and exhaustion from making such a record under an overload of courses, as any mother or father knows.

Atlanta parents can also imagine some of the extra anxiety that these nine children must have felt this year even though most of them, like Donita, have been treated kindly.

At some schools incidents have occurred. There have been cases when some of the Negro children did not eat at midday; they sat in the library rather than go into the dining hall to eat alone. A Negro girl did not want to go to school one morning. Under questioning it was learned a white boy had been hitting her with spitballs. There have been profane notes, garbage throwing, whispers, rifles pointed on an ROTC drill field. There were bound to be incidents in this imperfect period.

Most often, though—and certainly at Donita Gaines' school—there has been a great effort by students and teachers to make the transition in good grace.

Uncertainty and overwork took their toll on Donita. While making her splendid record, she came to have a dread of the schoolhouse itself. Her parents thought it best to lighten her load by returning her to her old school. Then a storm broke, and the suffering girl was torn between fears—fear that Negroes would censure her, fear that whites would jibe. She does not know what to do.

What she and her parents decide ought to be decided on the same basis that any other parent would use in a normal situation: what is best for her as an individual, suffering human being.

That is what every feeling parent of whatever color in Atlanta wants Donita to do.

And they are not going to have much patience with any person or group that may be so insensitive as to prod for political advantage in the personal crisis of a child—especially one whose courage and ability have earned her the right to hold her head high.

December 25, 1961
We're Standing in Need of Mercy

The living room lights were out. My 7-year-old Mary sat in the crook of my arm and we looked at the gentle glow of the Christmas tree. It was one of those moments, sweet as they are rare, when a child's interest is intensely, raptly engaged.

I asked the questions and she answered for a while. Who was Jesus' mother? Mary. Where was He born? In Bethlehem. Where in Bethlehem? In a stable. Why was Mary staying there? They didn't have a room at the hotel. Was it nighttime or daytime? Night, because there was a star.

"And what did Jesus do when He grew up?"

"He praised God," she said. "And He said to love other people."

We sat quietly for a while. Her eyes were filled with wonder in the tree light.

"What else did Jesus say about God?" she asked.

"He said God was not an angry and punishing God but was a gentle and merciful Father who would forgive a sin if you were truly sorry and if you asked to be forgiven. He said God wants us to love each other always, and never to hurt each other. He said if somebody hates you, don't hate him back, but love him. Jesus said God believed in gentleness and love, and forgiveness of people who are troubled.

"Jesus said God is our eternal refuge, and that beneath us are His everlasting arms, never leaving us hopeless, but always giving us hope.

"And so here at Christmas time, nearly 2,000 years after He was born, we still celebrate Jesus' birthday. He brought a beautiful message to us. None of us can be perfect. But we know what we ought to be, because of the lessons He taught us.

"And this is what we want to be and try to be all of our lives. At those bad times when we don't do what is right, though, we know we can truly repent, and pray, and receive the peace of forgiveness in our souls, so we can go on with the hope that we can be better. He is merciful and understanding, and He never goes away and leaves us, but is with us always."

Her head was on my shoulder, her eyes intent.

"It's the birthday of the Prince of Peace, and now you know why they called Him that," I said.

Her head nodded against my shoulder. We made up a special prayer at bedtime.

When I went to work next morning, India had invaded Goa, Russia had threatened to resume nuclear blasts if we did, 200 more Negroes had demonstrated and been jailed at Albany and shooting continued in Katanga.

An NAACP picket protesting segregation passes a Klansman handing out leaflets in downtown Atlanta. By permission of the *Atlanta Journal and Constitution*.

5

1962

Acts of Honor

January   The Atlanta-based Southern Christian Leadership Conference
          (SCLC) initiates a regional Voter Education Project. Ivan Allen Jr.
          becomes major of Atlanta, succeeding William Hartsfield.
February Astronaut John Glenn becomes the first American to orbit the
          earth.
March   The U.S. Supreme Court strikes down the Georgia county-unit
          system of legislative apportionment in *Baker v. Carr.* Carl Sanders,
          a self-styled moderate, defeats arch-segregationist Governor
          Marvin Griffin in the Georgia Democratic gubernatorial primary.
April   President Kennedy authorizes the resumption of atmospheric
          nuclear testing.
June   The Students for a Democratic Society issue the Port Huron
          Statement, a call for radical change and participatory democracy.
          In *Engel v. Vitale,* the U.S. Supreme Court rules that reading
          prayers in public schools violates the First Amendment.
July–August The resumption of mass protests in Albany, Georgia, leads to the
          Reverend Martin Luther King Jr.'s arrest. Frustrated by Sheriff
          Laurie Pritchett's tactics, SCLC withdraws from the Albany pro-
          tests without achieving desegregation of the south Georgia city.
September Mob violence disrupts James Meredith's attempt to desegregate
          the University of Mississippi.
October   The Cuban missile crisis forces a Cold War showdown between
          American and Soviet officials.
November In the midterm national election, the Democrats maintain control
          of both houses of Congress. Richard Nixon suffers defeat in the
          California gubernatorial election. Carl Sanders is elected governor
          of Georgia.

January 2, 1962
Nice Guys Do Finish First

A handshake now becomes the only link between Atlanta's political future and its bright past. But the handshake of Bill Hartsfield and Ivan Allen Jr. is a strong bond.

Hartsfield goes out of the mayor's office possessing Allen's affectionate regard. Allen takes up the seals of office with Hartsfield's best wishes.

And Atlanta is promised a continuity of excellence for which the gods be thanked.

They make quite a pair.

Hartsfield came out of a little depression law office, unmoneyed and unknown, and clawed his way up from obscurity to become the best-known mayor—and quite possibly the best one—in America.

Allen teethed on a silver spoon and had to claw his way out of the velvet cage of privilege to become a shirtsleeves slugger who could take it and dish it out in the ring of politics.

The father of one is an aristocrat. The father of the other was unschooled. But their instincts are the same. Both believe in honesty, rationality, and a sensibly progressive administration of the people's business, and they combine it with a passionate drive for something more than mediocrity.

They typify democracy. Foreign visitors—particularly those from countries that know communism—find it hard to understand why money czars do not take over and dictate in America, since Americans seem to revere money and the men who make it. Marx built a quack political science on the supposition that capitalism would thus strangle on its own greed.

Yet again and again they find moneyed intellectuals like Roosevelt and Kennedy placing service ahead of comfort and joining themselves (traitors to their class?) with the plain, the poor, the concerned and the voiceless whose vote dwarfs that of the mere moneymaker.

Or they find a scrapper like Harry Truman fighting his way up from nowhere to win the confidence of the people and the respect and support of the intellectuals.

No matter which side of the bank window he begins on, the successful American politician must pursue an ideal, not greed, or the people won't have him. The system works. It turns up worthy men. It sustains freedom and disproves Marx.

The nation had Truman and Kennedy.

Atlanta has Hartsfield and Allen.

They started a long way apart. But they were warmed by the same fires. They stand side by side at the same place now, and their handshake is an expression of democracy's main strength—a set of ideals.

February 3, 1962
Anybody Want to Wrestle an Ape?

"Oh, I got a girl named Minnie, she is 10 yards around; she weighs a ton in her stocking feet and she covers an acre of ground." I remember the hired man singing that as he ambled along behind a team and a steel beam turning plow.

He wasn't a tenant farmer; he was just a hired man who finished school in depression Ohio and got stranded in south Georgia trying to hitch-hike to Florida.

So he turned off the highway and came out the dirt road until we fed him some sweet potatoes and gave him a place to sleep at our house after he split us some stove wood.

He kept on working and we kept giving him food and shelter and a little pocket change for Saturday nights in Adel until finally he went on off down the road singing one more verse about his monstrous big Minnie:

"I put my Minnie in the sideshow, and sat her on a stool; and I charged the rubes a dime apiece to pay my way through school."

The hired man and his Minnie came back to mind when this carnival advertisement appeared recently in the *Valley Times* at West Point, Ga.:

"WANTED: ATHLETIC MEN. We pay you $5.00 to try to hold 85-pound Ape shoulders on the floor . . . No experience necessary. Apply at the Gorilla Show, every night of the Fair."

There is unemployment in the Valley. And in the jobless days of the '30s, that hired man would have rassled Gargantua for five bucks and thrown in big Minnie's contract to boot. But it is reported they had trouble finding ape wrestlers in West Point; unemployed fathers don't have to get down in the sawdust for their children's supper any more. The hired man is gone, praise be, and the tenant who so far excelled him in worldly goods is going too.

The Federal Reserve Bank of Atlanta says three out of five Southern farmers were tenants in the mid-1930s. Now only one out of four is a tenant. Tenants are racing from the land fastest in north Georgia— probably going into the big factories; they're staying on the land longest in Louisiana's cane belt.

The tenant who remains on the land is changed. He no longer sells his labor and relies solely on the landlord for the land, the capital and the management.

Without hired men, he manages complex machines, conserves the soil, carries a note at the bank and builds up property of his own. He has lived to see his patch of land become part of a world where foreigners buy half his cotton and a quarter of his tobacco and beckon him toward a common market. But he is also seeing the fields where he once made nickel cotton going into crops of pine trees that brought farmers $14 million cash money last year in Georgia. He has seen his sons go to town and his fields go to trees and he has had to work very hard himself because the pines and machines have replaced all but the best tenants.

And he hardly ever wonders any more what happened to that hired man of so long ago who always sang the last verse as if he truly missed his one-ton Minnie from the sideshow; it sounded very soulful in a summer dusk: *"And now I'm up in Heaven, a badly battered wreck; for when I proposed to Minnie, she fell about my neck."*

March 19, 1962
Harry Truman Likes Atlanta

Harry Truman surveyed Atlanta from the top of the Bank of Georgia building yesterday, shook his head in wonder at the city's growth and said, "Wouldn't old Sherman like to get at it now!"

"I like this town. I always have," said the former President.

Square-rigged and chesty, Mr. Truman welcomed the chance to zip downtown and have a quick look around between planes. He liked what he saw, a great city bathed in sunlight. We told him he had been cussed a good deal in these parts but that Georgians deep down admired him.

"I don't care what they call me, as long as they can prove it," he grinned. He pointed to Kennesaw Mountain on the horizon.

"If you'd had Stonewall Jackson running things instead of Joe Johnston, Sherman wouldn't have got here," he said.

"If Andrew Jackson had been president instead of that do-nothing Buchanan, there wouldn't have been a Civil War anyway.

"When South Carolina tried to nullify the tariff act, you know, old Jackson offered to go down and hang 'em all.

"All my kinfolks are Southerners," he added, "and I like the South. But if the South had won that war on the issues at stake, this country never would have been the leader of the world."

Somebody suggested one snort of bourbon. "Well, well," said Mr. Truman.

Then it was a rush back to the airport. "Ralph McGill is a fighter and a great newspaperman," he said, upon being told our publisher had sent his regards. "He's one of the real ones. Can you imagine me saying anything nice about a newspaperman? When old Gov. Cox got the *Constitution* he got more than a good newspaper; he got McGill."

Riding out the south expressway, he mused about politics.

"I'll tell you this," he said. "I could have won it again in 1952. Eisenhower probably wouldn't have gotten in it if I'd been going to run again."

The blessing-out Mr. Truman once gave a music critic for criticizing his daughter's singing came up. "Whew, did the madame and Margaret get on me about writing that letter," he said. "They said I had ruined myself. But I knew better. Every man in the country who had a daughter was for me."

We suggested this habit of reacting in natural and human ways made him a better politician than a careful and cautious responder like Richard M. Nixon. "Nixon was a loss," Mr. Truman said. "What a terrible thing it would be if he were running the country."

He barely made his plane—and only with the forbearance of a Hapeville policeman who, after flagging down the hurrying car, was told this was President Truman, and believed it.

"You've got a great city here," said the snowy-haired gentleman. He was told he ought to come back for a two-bourbon tour next time.

"I want to do that," laughed the former president, and was gone.

March 23, 1962
Emory Acts with Honor

The stewards of Emory University performed an act of honor Thursday. Their lawsuit seeks clearance to admit Douglas Aaron Rucker, a Negro, to the Emory School of Dentistry. But the suit was brought less on behalf of Rucker's rights than on behalf of Emory's rights.

Emory is claiming the right to choose its course—to decide for itself what is full and what is hollow in academic values.

The Emory campus is a very beautiful one, with its buildings of pearl gray marble set in green hills and pines. Its faculty is distinguished, its colleges renowned among private universities, it is a jewel of Southern education; it aspires to be the Harvard of the South.

But all of its assets are hollow if small thinking shapes its course. Emory has a mind of its own—and has now made it up.

Honorably, the trustees have announced they wish to accept Rucker's application because he is qualified.

But a section of the state constitution threatens to tax the endowment of any Georgia private college which, if "established" for white students, admits a Negro.

Under its charter Emory was not "established" for white students.

Therefore its trustees are asking the courts to declare that Emory may admit any student it chooses without threat of a punitive tax.

And if the courts do not remove the threat in Rucker's case, then Emory asks that the tortured section itself be struck from the constitution.

This is lawyer talk, of course. It is the ordered drill by which a society of laws moves its magnificent weight forward on little, vital wheels of petty words.

The plain facts are less complicated. The state already has desegregated two state-operated colleges—the University of Georgia by federal court order, Georgia Tech voluntarily.

How can the state demand of private colleges what it does not and cannot practice in state colleges?

The constitutional threat against private colleges should have died when the public school segregation laws expired. Emory, biggest of Georgia's private colleges, has an obligation to remove the threat, and is meeting it.

It has gone to court less for one Negro than the right of all private colleges in Georgia to be free of academic discrimination.

And even behind that, in the complex layers of Southern change, is this growing truth: an educational institution that wishes to be truly great, and not simply a provincial center of certain merits, must pattern its goals of learning on convictions larger than racial discrimination.

Emory has had increasing difficulty in keeping some superior professors who could not equate their search for academic truth with a policy of white-only merit.

The trustees themselves have wondered how much longer Emory could get $2.5 million a year in federal research grants while violating federal policy against racial discrimination.

Most important were the feelings of a new generation of Southern students—some of whom were willing to accept the past in its entirety, but many of whom were not. And those who saw the increasing need for change and understanding could not, with comfort, be part of forced segregation much longer and be untroubled in their minds.

Without honesty, there is no learning of much value.

So Emory acted. The trustees need the understanding that all of the South needs in this difficult time. What they have decided to seek is greatness.

April 7, 1962
Birmingham Uses Biscuits

Atlanta is fully occupied with racial problems in its own back yard. So Atlantans do not make a habit of passing hasty judgment on the racial problems of other cities. What has just happened in Birmingham, however, is noteworthy here, if for no other reason than to induce thankfulness that Atlanta's people have been spared such a shockingly primitive act as the Birmingham city commission perpetrated in the name of that city's people.

It is a lesson for Atlanta in how not to meet its problems, a reminder of the kind of politicians not to elect, ever, in this city.

Negroes were reported boycotting downtown stores, pressing them to end some segregation practices. Atlanta has been through this, and knows it is not pleasant for anybody concerned. But the Birmingham mayor and his commissioners reacted in a manner so unpleasant as to put that city on page one of the *New York Times* and other papers throughout the land with the kind of promotion money couldn't buy— or undo.

"To nip this boycott in the bud," Mayor Arthur J. Hanes said, the city was withdrawing its support from the surplus food program which feeds the needy.

This plan—to starve the helpless for acts of the ambitious—was stated explicitly. "If they come in and tell the mayor that it (a boycott) is not so, then I'm willing to reinstate the money," said Commissioner Bull Connor.

And so the people of Birmingham see these politicians, acting in their name, use the helpless and the hungry as hostages to counter acts beyond their knowledge or control.

They see the elected officials unashamedly using public power to punish the people least able to protect themselves.

They see a great city's name identified with a morality that would take the soup from the pots of the poor, hold a biscuit away from an unfed child, as a tactic in a social, political and financial contest.

Exactly where bottom is, we do not know, but we suspect these Birmingham politicians have just about hit it.

Karl Marx started communism on the theory that capitalism leaves no other connection "between man and man than naked self-interest, than callous cash payment . . . naked, shameless, direct, brutal exploitation." Marx was wrong, and America has been proving him wrong from the time when Pilgrims shared their harvests to the present maintenance of soup lines for the luckless in a time of general plenty.

But the officials who were entrusted with the power to represent the people of Birmingham did not help much this week, except by making Atlanta voters resolve anew not to let that kind of leadership happen here.

April 9, 1962
From Protest to Performance

History is hard to recognize up close as it happens. But a discernible turning has come in the hard path the Southern Negro has walked from the slave cabin to the modern lunch counter.

The explosively climactic years of march and demonstration were, by their nature, limited. They quickly widened the openings which the courts broke in the old walls of forced segregation. They were instruments of shock action, never to be used lightly.

And the sit-ins and similar shows of physical mass have about run out of missions in cities like Atlanta, where schools, planes, libraries, trains, lunch counters, buses, terminals, golf courses, colleges and auditoriums have been or are being desegregated, and where theaters, hotels and the public hospital are moving in good faith to wind up the last big arguments.

Where, then, are the Negro energies to turn? Freed of causes to protest, they can turn to performance.

Two examples occurred last week.

First, Henry Grady High School held its annual banquet, honoring students who rank in the top 10 percent of their classes. Both of the

Negro students who entered Grady in this first year of desegregation were members of the honors group.

The long hours of study are known only to them. But their superior performance makes the way surer for others of their race who will follow them.

The second sign of future performance came when Dr. Martin Luther King's organization and others like it allied themselves with the Southern Regional Council and launched a two-year effort to get Negroes registered to vote in the South.

The vote is the basic civil right. From it, all other opportunities flow. It isn't as flashy as a freedom ride. But its potentiality for lasting good is incomparably larger.

Persuading voters to register may seem prosaic at first to people recently preoccupied with picket lines.

But as the Negro is able to bring his fight out of the streets and into the main channel of orderly, democratic political action at the polls, tension will drop and opportunity will rise, not fitfully, but in steady and continuing measure. And respect for the rights of the Negro, sought for so long in isolated skirmishing, will come to its permanent and peaceful place in the framework of an ordered society.

May 11, 1962
Their Alphabet Spelled a Lament

In 18th-century Tennessee, a German trader won the love of the sister of a Cherokee chief and their son was named Sequoyah. This child was destined, in the words of Georgia's J. Roy McGinty, to exemplify "how a single individual could have a profound influence on history."

Sequoyah was illiterate. His tribe could speak but had no [written] language. Intrigued by the white man's alphabet, Sequoyah listened to the sounds of his people's syllables and made a symbol for each. Within months his syllabary taught the Cherokee people to read and write.

But the statue of Sequoyah stands in Oklahoma City, not in the region of northeast Georgia which was part of the Cherokee nation. The proud and industrious Cherokees had honored Georgia by building their national capital, New Echota, near the present Georgia town of Calhoun. They founded the place only 35 years before the Civil War.

But two years later frontiersman Andrew Jackson, an Indian-hater, was elected president, and this immediately emboldened the white man's state of Georgia to smash and grab the Cherokee nation.

The proud new capital of New Echota, where the Indians were practicing a republican form of government and modeling a civilization on the white man's, fell.

The Georgia legislature stripped all legal rights from anyone of Indian blood, voided all Cherokee laws and property rights, seized the Indians' land, divided it into 160-acre plots and handed it out to white men who drew lucky lottery cards.

Cherokee heads of family were allowed a reservation of 160 acres in their dismembered country at first. But they received no deed and no protection of property rights from state or federal government. The U.S. Supreme Court tried to curb the white man's avarice. But President Jackson refused to execute the court's decision.

In 1838 the Cherokees who remained were forcibly expelled from Georgia and sent on the trail of tears to new territory in Oklahoma, only to lose even that in later years and be penned on reservations.

This ignoble episode cost Georgia the contribution that might have been made by a vigorous people whose system of schools, roads and self-government was achieving swift advances within the framework of a truly native American culture. But Sequoyah's alphabet, which had enabled the Cherokees to have a national newspaper by 1828, was finally fated to write only the lament of a misused people.

That is why Georgians owe it to themselves as well as to the Cherokee Indians to perform an act scheduled for tomorrow near Calhoun. The ghost capital of New Echota, restored by the state, will be opened as a shrine of history. It will be a good place for us to go and reflect on our ideals.

May 31, 1962
Facts Denied Are Still Facts

George C. Wallace and Vieslaw Gornicki have never met. One of them won a fight this week and the other lost one. The only connection between them is that both addressed themselves to the same issue—the race problem in the American South.

Mr. Wallace won the Democratic nomination for the governorship of Alabama, defeating a candidate of somewhat more moderate racial views. Mr. Wallace proposed to defy the nation's courts if necessary to hold the Negro in a segregated status.

Gov. Orval Faubus of Arkansas and Gov. Jimmie Davis of Louisiana tried defiance, of course, and found it could not and did not preserve segregation. It only brought down crushing damage on their states, followed by desegregation.

Despite those lessons Mr. Wallace still proposes defiance of the court as a way to hold the Negro where he is, by force of state law, regardless of the Negro's aspirations and the overriding authority of federal law. The fact that federal law is not going to allow this did not deter him from proposing it.

Vieslaw Gornicki, unlike Mr. Wallace, is a Communist. Communism holds that no lower classes of people can shake off the forcible hold of classes above them, and rise to a life of greater dignity, if they rely on the democratic process of gradual reform. Communism says that a lower class can rise only by revolting against the classes that are holding it down and smashing them with blood and iron.

Gornicki believed this theory of revolution applied to the South's Negro problem when he arrived in Georgia last winter on a visit. But he spent three weeks observing the peaceful progress the Negro is making in Georgia's reasonable political climate.

And when he went back to Poland Gornicki had the courage to write in his Communist magazine that perhaps gradual reforms under democracy will, after all, permit the Southern Negro to rise without revolution.

This was a body blow to communism. It made news worldwide. It struck at the cornerstone of Marxism, which holds that evolutionary reforms are phony and meaningless, and that revolutionary force is the only instrument by which lower classes can raise themselves. But some things are more important than the facts to people who do not like the facts.

Gornicki lost. Poland's Communist Premier Gomulka has slapped him down hard for "pro-western ideas" and has barred certain other Polish editors from making planned visits to the United States and the South.

Communism must go on believing that the Southern white will hold down the Southern Negro by defiance and force, and that gradual reforms are impossible.

Gornicki reports the contrary was true here, and that was fact, of course.

He lost.

Wallace proposed to do in Alabama that which Arkansas and Louisiana have shown is impossible.

He won.

July 13, 1962
The Verdict Rests with the South

The people of Atlanta recently witnessed the refusal of an Atlanta hotel to admit the Nobel prize–winning American undersecretary at the United Nations because he was not white, and until Atlantans can end such humiliations in this city they are not qualified to pass easy judgments on Albany.

So this comment on the jailing of Martin Luther King and other Negroes at Albany is a general one that any of us can apply to ourselves.

Some Southerners sincerely believe that King got a jail sentence he deserved because he broke the parade-permit ordinances of Albany.

Some Negroes just as devoutly believe they can get no hearing of their grievances through polite requests and therefore must either parade or else give up hope of redress.

It seems to us the question here is not whether one of these positions or the other is accurate and in accord with the facts. They both are, as the evidence plainly shows. King broke the law. Negroes have been unable to get their grievances heard. To argue over which statement is true is aimless. Both are.

Both sides obviously have weaknesses also. The whites have little defense for denying the Negroes a hearing. The Negroes have made emotional demonstrations without making clear what grievances they want heard.

With that out of the way, then, the larger question may as well be faced. And Dr. King himself stated it as gently as the South will ever hear it put, after he was sentenced to jail:

"I am sure the judge rendered a decision which he considered just," King said, "and which I consider unjust."

That is the entire question, phrased with understanding and without condemnation.

The verdict, therefore, has not been reached. It rests with the people of the South sitting as a jury of the whole, and weighing the deep conflicts within their own troubled hearts.

Where lies the greater justice—that of citizens who ask a hearing of their grievances, or that of those who use their laws to deny it?

History indicates that if the czar had heard the people's grievances at Petrograd instead of setting the Cossacks upon them, the Russian revolution might have been stayed. It indicates that if Britain had heard its colonists and granted redress, the American Revolution might have been avoided.

The people of this generation will write the history of the South.

So there is no intelligent point to be made here by arguing the empty question as to which of the two positions is being accurately stated. Both are, and Dr. King himself had the understanding to realize that the Southern people are painfully divided between them, and that nothing can be gained therefore by angrily arguing over the obvious.

It is time then to get on to the larger question which is going to have to be answered in the Southern heart: Which position is the more just?

Dr. King left that one up to you.

July 23, 1962
The Quiet Hour Begins at Albany

Federal Judge J. Robert Elliott has ordered Negroes to stop demonstrating in Albany. That order must be obeyed. If it is found unjust an appeals court will strike it down. If it is found just, an appeals court will sustain it. But only an appeals court has the power to make that judgment. In a society of law the people have one duty while a court order stands: Obey it.

Dr. Martin Luther King's initial comment—"I cannot say whether we will obey, or disobey the injunction"—was a mistake. The Negro demonstration which came after the order was issued cannot be justified. If the Negro leadership persists in the folly of violating law itself, instead of demanding white compliance with law, it will be trading away its surest shield. It ought to get back onto sound legal ground forthwith, no matter what it thinks of the temporary restraining order.

In the interim there can be a quiet hour during which the white and Negro citizens of Albany can reflect on what it is they are trying to do.

And what are they trying to do?

Are the responsible white men of Albany dedicated to a sport no cleaner than proving they can push people around and hold them helpless, disregarding their petitions, denying them a hearing, and calling that justice? No. The Albany white majority is honorable.

Are the responsible Negroes in the movement dedicated to agitating strife for its own sake, with more desire to disrupt relations through theatrics than to improve them through orderly means? No, that isn't true of the Negro majority either.

Then what are they trying to do?

Dr. W. G. Anderson, president of the Negro Albany Movement, recently said that if the Negroes had been able to see any other way to get a hearing than by demonstrating, "we would have chosen it."

During this lull, then, when pressure has been removed, the white majority of Albany has its opportunity to open a way for its citizens to seek redress and find it reasonably within the democratic process.

And the Negro movement has its chance to specify rather than broadside the whites with diffuse grievances, and to take out of the streets issues which should be in the courts.

The South has endured long enough a national accusation that its white majority snickers at justice for the Negro and, standing with one clodhopper on his neck, kicks him in the face with the other foot when he dares to make a plea of supplication. That was the South of the white trash. Albany now has its chance to show that the white South holds a more honorable attitude than that.

And that would place an obligation on the Negroes to respond cooperatively.

Let no man delude himself through emotionalism or partisanship: If one side fails Albany on this, be it Negro or be it white, that will be the hand that bears the stain.

In the quiet hour now beginning, some men will be measured.

July 28, 1962
There Is a Way out of Blindness

It was a week heavy with symbols and irony bearing on the racial conflict in Georgia. It ended with a thief, identified by witnesses as a Negro, entering our editorial offices and stealing Ralph McGill's typewriter.

Nothing could have been a more forceful reminder to Negro leaders that they must devote themselves to raising standards among their people, in addition to seeking rights for them.

But if Mr. McGill were here he also would be the first person to remind the white man that he cannot escape guilt for the high Negro crime rate so long as he holds the Negro in slums, short-changes him on education and blocks him from jobs.

At Albany, the week brought a rain of rocks and bottles directed by a Negro mob against white men—a senseless blow against all that the Negro nonviolent movement stood for and a stinging defeat of the Negro at the hands of nonviolent white men who did not strike back. Violence, the nettle that has betrayed the white Southerner for so long, was inexplicably grasped by the Negro and he learned it betrays him too.

But the white Georgians who are so exasperated by the Negro excesses at Albany cannot escape the guilt they also bear there: when the white government flatly refuses over a period of months to give a hearing to its citizens, how are they to get a hearing? What are they expected to do? Any fair white man will have to give himself an answer to that before he finds a verdict of innocence in his own heart.

The week affected politics. In this election year, when the state had progressed to the point of discrediting racial demagogues, and the voters had a chance to hear a campaign pitched on issues instead of on the traditional inflammation of emotions, the Negroes chose in a master stroke of ill timing to press, goad and demonstrate at the very hour of history when a Georgia election might have been emancipated from the hot chains of heedlessness.

But who are the voters? More than 8,000 Negroes live in Terrell County and only 51 are registered to vote. So a group of Negroes met in a church at Sasser Wednesday night to hear how to register. And into the church walked some white men, some wearing badges. "We're a little fed up with this registration business," the sheriff said. A deputy told the Negroes it would not be "to your interest" to continue the meeting. Outside the church, white men called out the license numbers of cars there. The Negroes wanted to vote, but the sheriff said he wanted them to live "like they have for the last hundred years."

Exactly how does the white man expect the Negro to seek his rights by democratic processes if he is intimidated when he tries to exercise the basic democratic process—the peaceful, nonviolent, non-demonstrative vote?

The week was heavy and deep with the symbols and the irony that dramatize the simple truth.

The truthful symbol, which offers the only salvation there is going to be for Negroes and whites alike in this suffering South, was seen Wednesday afternoon by those Atlantans who happened to be standing at the corner of Broad and Walton streets. They saw two men, both blind, help each other across the street.

One was Negro. One was white.

September 4, 1962
Lester Maddox Is in the Lead

This will shock Atlantans and it is meant to. A greater shock is going to come in the morning after next Wednesday's election if Fulton County voters fail to wake up to what is happening in the lieutenant governor's race.

Lester Maddox, whose chief accomplishments are frying chicken and abusing Negroes, holds a clear lead—according to a poll which I believe to be reliable—and is on his way to winning Fulton County's vote if our non-Maddox citizens will simply continue to do what they are doing.

What they are doing is splitting the vote that ought to be going to Peyton Hawes, a responsible candidate who has a chance to win—but who cannot win unless the responsible voters rally round him and quit scattering their votes as if this were a game of Pattycake.

The poll figures on my desk show Maddox is leading in Fulton County with 30 percent of the vote.

Hawes is second with 24 percent. He is second to Maddox because Ed Wilson has split away 15 percent of the vote and Hawes needs it if he is going to top Maddox in Fulton County.

We like Ed Wilson. He is a fine candidate. But we do not think he is as strong as the other fine candidate, Peyton Hawes, and the poll supports that. We think he is just strong enough to take away the votes Hawes needs to handle Maddox. The poll supports that too.

And if the 15 percent now backing Wilson continues to do so, instead of getting behind Hawes, then they can be pretty sure Maddox is going to take this county and that's all there is to it.

It is not pleasant for this newspaper to have to say that. We oppose Mr. Maddox's radical politics, deplore his blacking of Atlanta's eye, and detest the foulness and fanaticism of his race-baiting.

But this uncomprehending man, who got beat 2 to 1 when he ran for mayor last year, is suddenly about to become Fulton County's choice for the second highest office in the state through benefit of his bloc vote if the other voters of Atlanta continue their leisurely scattering of their support and refuse to unite behind Hawes.

And any man who goes out of Fulton County with a solid lead is going to be a serious contender for election. Peter Z. Geer who was thought to be out-Maddoxing Maddox, got only 19 percent in the poll.

With these figures in, therefore, and with only a week to go until election day, we think it is time for every voter who opposes Maddox's disastrous politics to take a frank look at the facts.

It is our considered judgment that the responsible vote must unite behind the single strongest responsible candidate, Peyton Hawes, or else an irresponsible candidate is going to carry Fulton County and, conceivably, the state.

September 7, 1962
Shall the Guns Speak for Georgia?

So now the guns are speaking in Georgia. The night knocks are coming from masked men at the door. Bullets rip the planks of sleeping houses. Free people are terrorized because they want to vote. The curtain of civilization is torn away and the bleeding and the dying have begun.

What kind of state do we want?

Georgians are going to vote next Wednesday.

Everyone who casts a ballot will have deep feelings on the racial issue. This historic ordeal in the South cannot pass without stirring deep emotions, testing us with conflict, challenging us in restraint, responsibility, reason.

Is such an issue safe in the hands of an unrestrained, or irresponsible, or unreasonable candidate? He will say always that he is against violence. But when violence follows the tension he creates, what has he really said?

What kind of state do we want?

The guns are now speaking in this campaign.

A week ago night riders pumped bullets through the walls of four houses in Lee County, Georgia, where Negro citizens had expressed a wish to vote.

Early on Wednesday of this week, blasts of gunfire pierced the walls of a house at Sasser in Terrell County, Georgia, where Negroes wanted to vote. Buckshot wounded a man inside.

On Wednesday night armed white men wearing stocking masks drove into the yard of a house occupied by Negro women and children in Paulding County, Georgia. One of the callers opened a political discussion by putting a pistol through the door and in a terrifying exchange of volleys in the darkness a man fell, shot fatally through the heart.

No candidate has advocated violence.

Violence is loose.

Is this the kind of state we want—a state where people cower behind chained doors and watch for approaching headlights; where mothers put their children to bed in back bedrooms lest bullets come from the road; where men can be so unhinged by emotion that they would put on masks and turn to bloodletting?

This will be the kind of state the people want it to be.

They can place it, with self-respect, in the hands of strong, firm, responsible men who know great challenges require great responses—and above all, responsibility. Or they can give it to men who play with fire and insist they are innocent when the cross burns.

That is the political question that Georgians will answer at the polls next week. It is not a question of whether we will have a challenge; the challenge is present. It is a question of how we are going to meet it.

The guns of Lee and Terrell and Paulding are speaking to us all.

September 11, 1962
Attention Georgia:

There has been some talk that money is going to be raised in the North to rebuild the Mt. Mary and Mt. Olive Baptist churches which were burned Sunday at Sasser, Ga.

But many Georgians will feel the honor of the South is involved in this matter. Honestly differing views on segregation exist in our state. But church-burning is not approved anywhere in Georgia as an acceptable method of expressing them. Instead of letting other sections of the country rebuild the churches that were burned in our section, some Georgians will want to demonstrate that we can handle these matters on our own.

An Atlanta architect has offered to design replacements for the two burned churches as his contribution. Any Georgian who wishes to contribute any amount, no matter how small, to the rebuilding of the two Baptist churches may mail a check, payable to "Church Fund," to the *Atlanta Constitution*, Atlanta, Ga., and it will be conveyed to the two congregations. Dr. Roy McClain, pastor of the First Baptist Church of Atlanta, will act as treasurer of the fund.

September 13, 1962
Georgians Are This Kind of People

"We are sorry it can't be more," wrote an elderly Atlanta couple, "but being retired for a number of years, we feel this is the best we can do." Attached was their check for $10. It was made payable to "Church Fund" and mailed to this newspaper. A lot of people who do not have much money are sending what they can. This kind of gift comes right out of the grocery money, and from the heart.

Anyone who wants to measure the fineness of this state and its people ought to see these letters.

Scores of them came in the first mail after we offered to receive contributions to rebuild the two Negro Baptist churches which were burned at Sasser, Ga., last Sunday.

Several hundred dollars already has come in. We are putting it into a special bank account. Dr. Roy McClain of Atlanta's First Baptist Church will be the treasurer who will write the checks on it to help the two congregations rebuild the modest houses of worship which they raised originally from their own humble purses—only to lose them to night-riders in one fiery night.

The letters that are coming may be more important than the checks.

"I hope the two churches can be rebuilt from help entirely from Georgia citizens," wrote one Atlanta woman who sent $5.

From Savannah a woman sent $1, saying, "The burning of these churches is a very dark blot on Georgia history."

An Atlanta businessman sent $200 without comment. Two dollars came from a woman who said, "I am sure that the Christians of all churches deplore the burning, and we in the South want to restore them ourselves.

From College Park came $1 and the note: "I wish this could be a whole lot more. I feel so deeply about this shameful thing."

From Dahlonega, $10 and this: "In a profound sense it is our responsibility, for we must share the guilt in such actions. The guilt of many of us may be negative—the guilt of doing nothing."

A Decatur businessman sent $50, "grateful for an opportunity for the people of Georgia to help in a small way to redress this terrible wrong."

A Carrollton woman sent $10 to express "shame and vicarious guilt for these unspeakable crimes."

"I do believe the best answer to this . . . for the image of Georgia before the rest of the country, is for the people of the state to contribute the funds for the rebuilding of these two churches," an Atlantan said, attaching $50.

One woman sent $10 with the simple note, "I thank you for the privilege." A Decatur man gave $10 saying, "I was born and reared in this state. It breaks my heart to think that people live amongst us who will do such things."

"I feel this is a definite obligation of fellow Georgians who feel humiliated," said an Atlanta businessman, giving $50.

A woman in East Point, who was able to give $5, summed up a good deal about the sense of honor that endures in this state's people. "This letter is partly an answer," she writes, "to future questions by my children as to where I stood when terror reigned in Georgia."

These churches are going to be rebuilt. The kind of people who live in Georgia will see to it.

September 18, 1962
A Letter to the President

Dear President Kennedy: You were understandably emphatic last week when you denounced the burning of Negro churches in Georgia. By now you will have received word that another one was burned in Terrell County Monday.

But we are in position now to report the rest of the story to you in the hope that you will tell it to the world.

The state of Georgia and its people also are appalled, and what is more important, they are bearing witness.

They are setting out to rebuild their own ruins.

They have recoiled from church-burning as swiftly as other Americans, and they agree with the words of their own governor who describes these fires as the work of "demented minds."

How do we know what Georgians think?

We have nearly 300 letters here already from individual Georgians who attached money to help the Negroes rebuild their burned churches.

The amount is not as important as the show of sentiment, but the amount itself is climbing toward $5,000.

That is a lot of money when it comes in small sums from the old, the poor, and the humble as well as from the comfortable.

Men of wealth have sent personal checks for up to $200. Struggling widows have sent as little as 25 cents taped to a sheet of tablet paper. Dozens of letters have contained $1 bills clipped to notes that express a faith beyond price.

These letters have come from the cities and the farms, from the south and the north of the state. They are postmarked Pearson, Adel, Hogansville and Social Circle as well as Atlanta, Savannah and Columbus.

Nobody has pressed these Georgians to give. Their names are not being announced. Their almsgiving is a personal act of conscience. Their collective desire to right a wrong that has occurred amongst themselves is, we believe, a measure of the goodness and the decency and the rightness that endure in our state.

These coins and bills and checks, made payable to "Church Fund" and mailed to this newspaper, are being put into a bank account which can be drawn upon by the fund's treasurer, Dr. Roy McClain, pastor of Atlanta's First Baptist Church. He will administer the conveyance of the money to the building committees of the burned churches for the construction of new ones.

We felt you ought to know of this determination Georgians have shown to undo the sacrilege that has occurred here, and we hope you will let the world know how an honorable people responded to a wrong in the Deep South.

September 25, 1962
The Story of a Moderate Minister

Dr. Henry J. Stokes is 52 years old. He is now at the point in a preacher's time when he should be secure and safe in the love of his congregation. But Dr. Stokes is a Southerner and heir to our region's burdens. His great-grandparents are buried in Twiggs County. His was the pulpit of Macon's First Baptist Church. It no longer is.

On Sunday morning he resigned his pastorate when he concluded that many in his congregation wanted him out of the pulpit.

He harbors no rancor.

"The funny thing is, I'm one of the most moderate preachers in Georgia," he mused. "I've never ever been a member of any interracial group.

"I just came to my conclusions as a minister."

How many other Georgia ministers are suffering, at this moment, a sense of divided direction from their God and their congregation on racial issues? Dr. Stokes said:

"I am American enough to believe that the Supreme Court until altered by subsequent opinions still speaks with legal authority for the nation in disputed affairs; I am Southern enough to have bone-chilling feelings and emotional upheavals as some accustomed patterns dissolve before my eyes, and I am Christian enough, I hope, that my trust in God will guide me to be charitable to those who differ and that He will temper my tongue and acts under all provocations."

With that he ended his occupancy of a pulpit where he had become uncomfortable. He honestly admitted being torn himself by the emotional upheavals which many in his congregation felt. But secular logic required him to face the truth of legal authority.

And finally, turning to the religion he professed, he tried to find guidance and moderation for his preaching of the truth.

But he could not and would not dodge this most painful issue confronting Southern Christians. He did not believe his congregation wanted him to "Say unto us smooth things." And a large number of them did not; they tried to hold up his hand.

At last, though, he did not feel welcome. So many Southern ministers could keep their pulpits tenable if they would avoid the difficult. Some can and do, believing they can serve by preaching what the Bible said long ago, without needing to apply it to problems of the life we live.

Others like Dr. Stokes cannot in Christian conscience divorce the spiritual guidance they draw from the Bible from the spiritual problems that confront their living flocks. These prophetic preachers see their faith as a strength and a guide to the living and they cannot go on if they must withhold their honest convictions for fear of offending the congregations that hired them. They cannot feel honest and do that.

These ministers are bearers of the Southern burden. Georgians like Dr. Stokes fully understand the emotions of their congregations. They ask understanding in return as they try honestly to show the way as they see it. But the understanding often is not returned and the lonely man in the pulpit is left to choose between his honesty and his daily bread.

At 52, Dr. Henry J. Stokes does not have a job and does not know what he is going to do.

September 29, 1962
The Patriots of Mississippi

Nobody can force Mississippi to desegregate its schools. That state can simply close its schools. But if Mississippi keeps its schools open, it cannot admit some American citizens and bar others because they are colored differently.

The United States Constitution says so. It says a man like James Meredith, who was good enough to offer his life for the American nation in its Air Force, cannot be treated like that when he returns home to live in his American state.

The Supreme Court so interpreted the Constitution. The Congress declined to change the interpretation. It is, therefore, a part of the American law, supported by the legislative and judicial branches of the

United States government and handed over to the executive branch for enforcement. It must be enforced or there will be no United States.

The tragedy of Mississippi is that its politicians have told the American citizens who live there that they do not have to obey the American law.

This is what the politicians of the South told the people a century ago—that a Southern state had the right to hold Negroes as slaves regardless of the national policy, seceding if necessary. In a fair and honorable test of arms, the American government challenged and the Southern states defended that position.

The issue was settled in favor of the Union after the most brutal bloodbath in the history of civil conflict on this earth. Since then Americans have tried to follow Robert E. Lee's advice to accept that verdict in manly pride and make a nation at peace. The Cause had been fought to its settlement in the ultimate forum—the battlefield. Yet, as if Lee had left no testament, the politicians of Mississippi are again saying a state has a right to treat the Negro as it chooses regardless of the national law.

But this time, instead of standing for a Cause, they are cornered in a deception.

Instead of raising a living issue that is in honorable doubt, they are rustling mice-like in the dead leaves of history.

Instead of Davis and Stephens, they have Ross Barnett.

In place of the magnificent Gray army, they have tin hats on a highway patrol.

Instead of Lee and Jackson, they have Edwin A. Walker.

Instead of rallying the people of the South to their side, they are convening the crackpots.

Instead of meeting the truth like men, they are asking for punishment like children.

They are shaming Mississippi, dishonoring the South, humiliating the nation and soiling its flag.

A gracious Providence spared Georgia such leaders as these.

October 8, 1962
A Georgian Goes to Mississippi

I wish the students at the University of Mississippi knew Herbert W. Biles of Atlanta. He is 45. He is a correctional officer at the Atlanta Federal Penitentiary. I first knew him when he was 28. He came to my platoon of the 10th Armored Division as a replacement during combat in Germany.

One snowy night I saw him ride with a small armored column, 10 miles behind the enemy lines in a longshot effort to seize the Echelsbach bridge over the Ammer River. It was a long concrete span connecting cliff tops above a breathtaking chasm. The waters raged in rapids below. The towering bridge was presumed to be wired for demolition, ready to be blown by Germans at the far end if attacked.

Biles was one volunteer in a four-man patrol [that included Patterson] that crept forward to run across the bridge on foot and try to take it, by surprise, intact. Each man held an open knife in his hand. The four knelt briefly in the blizzard and one said a prayer: "God help us." Then Biles and the other three ran straight across the bridge into the unknown, expecting it to be dynamited under them at each instant. They made it. They took the bridge intact, and surprised and captured between 30 and 40 Germans who were napping in the woods. I saw this happen. The division drove south across the bridge into Bavaria. Biles was awarded the Silver Star, the Army's third-highest award for heroism. He finished the war without being hit though he repeatedly offered his life under gunfire.

On Sunday night a week ago this same brave Southerner stood shoulder to shoulder on the Ole Miss campus with his brother Robert, also an Atlantan and also a penal correctional officer. Both had been ordered deputized as U.S. marshals and they did their duty to the flag they serve. Their country had commanded them to guard the life of James Meredith. But federal troops had not come, Mississippi police had withdrawn, and the thin line of marshals faced a terrible mob of rioters with tear gas running out.

Bricks and bottles struck them but they stood. A shotgun blasted in the darkness and wounded Herbert Biles in the arm. The man who had fought a gallant war abroad without being hit was shot in Mississippi. A .22 caliber rifle began cracking near the marshals. But still Herbert stood with his brother and with his flag.

They had pistols which they never drew. They were surrounded and could not have retreated if they had tried. But these quiet, slow-talking Biles brothers do not run. They stood and held until the paratroopers came—"the prettiest sight in the world," Herbert recalls. By then he was one of 166 marshals who had been hurt. But they held.

Robert Biles was one of five marshals who went to Washington and received personal citations for bravery from the president. "If you had failed and they had taken Mr. Meredith," the president said, "it would have been a blow from which the United States and Mississippi would not have recovered for many years."

Herbert Biles, back in Atlanta, was philosophical. "It was worse than anything we saw in the war," he said, without bitterness. "During the war you could shoot back. That was the last thing we wanted to do out there, and the students could do anything. Their screaming and hollering was what got me. I've never been cursed like that in my life.

"Being born and bred a Georgian, I might have felt out of place there if I had thought of it as something I was doing only for Meredith.

"But the way I looked at it, I felt I was doing more for those Mississippi students than I was for Meredith. I felt like, by standing there, that I was saving them from themselves."

I wish the people of Mississippi could know the kind of man they shot, and then do for themselves what this gallant American from Georgia risked his life to do for them.

November 22, 1962
"No Cause for That Kind of Doing"

Thanksgiving Day is a good time to give the final financial report on of the most selfless and inspirational acts of giving that Georgians have undertaken in recent times.

Nearly three months ago two Negro Baptist churches were burned on the same night at Sasser, Ga.

1962: Acts of Honor | 117

We placed a quiet note on this page saying that anyone who felt the honor of the South was involved here, and who felt it was a matter of conscience to help rebuild the two houses of God, could send any amount of money, no matter how small, to "Church Fund," in care of the *Constitution,* and we would turn it over to Dr. Roy McClain of Atlanta's First Baptist Church as treasurer to help the little country congregations restore their places of worship.

The response was immediate and overwhelming. No huge amount of money was raised; there isn't enough in the fund to build back the churches alone. But the truly important thing was the number of people who responded—more than 800 of them sat down separately in individual communion with their own consciences and decided, without expecting any recognition, to give.

And notes expressing their sentiments came along with the coins and the dollar bills of the humble, the $200 and $400 checks of the wealthy, the $500 check from a single congregation. The letters crossed all class, regional and religious lines. Most of them expressed a true depth of religious feeling. But none was more eloquent than the message from a 16-year-old Georgia boy penciled on tablet paper to which he had taped 25 cents as a token of his feeling about church burning.

"I don't see no cause," he wrote, "for that kind of doing."

In sum, these hundreds of envelopes have built a fund of $10,030.

We have therefore informed the Rev. William Boyd of Mt. Mary Baptist Church and the Rev. F. S. Swaggott of Mt. Olive Baptist Church that $5,015 is on deposit at the Trust Company of Georgia to assist each of their congregations in rebuilding the two churches.

This, we have told them, is a pledge of the people of Georgia.

Because we felt the givers would want the fund used for the most basic replacement of the holy structures which the fires consumed, we have specifically pledged on behalf of the people that the contractor's bills for the first $5,015 worth of lumber, nails, masonry and mortar in each church will be paid by checks which Dr. McClain will draw on the Church Fund.

Other groups have raised other monies to finish filling the rebuilding needs of these and other burned churches. Joseph Amisano, the Atlanta architect, is designing modest churches free for the congregations. We hope he will remember to work a little stained glass into the design so that one of the most moving offers can be accepted; the Trappist monks in the monastery of Conyers, who live in silence without any worldly goods, have asked if they may make some stained glass with their own hands as their contribution to the rebuilding.

Thanksgiving seemed to be the right kind of day for giving this report.

December 10, 1962
Ed Danforth Didn't Doubt

To come back from vacation and find Ed Danforth gone leaves me feeling like a cub alone in the press box of a stadium that has emptied. He always was at my elbow, steadying my hand. As a boy on a farm, I wrote him letters about ball games and he would print them in his column with breezy replies. And I was hooked by the printed word.

As I kid I saw him in person at a Marietta Street lunch counter. He was having a bowl of soup. I didn't have the nerve to say anything to the greatest sports writer in the world but I stood on the sidewalk and watched him through the window until he left.

When he wrote, the words hopped and sang. He felt them. Reporters can still learn color writing from such passages as this, written 23 years ago when Danforth went out to cover a Baptist World Alliance meeting in Ponce de Leon Park:

"Over the stands was a pleasant hum like the noise one hears through the windows of a church while the faithful are gathering, magnified. Then from outside the park came the rhythmic thrumming of heat-tightened drums and the staccato spat of motorcycles. The parade was approaching. The grass arena devoted to the pursuit of an athletic contest became a vast church. It brought back memories of a little brick church in a maple grove, a wooden arbor covered with brush by a purling stream . . . Through a gate in left field came the band . . . Colored silk umbrellas loomed in the infield. The brightly colored cotton print dresses of the women looked like flower beds in bloom. The soft popping of bottle caps did not disturb the serenity of the occasion. The gathering rose, and 30,000 voices, led by a man in a white suit on the platform, burst tremendously into the hymn, 'All Hail the Power of Jesus' Name.'"

Danforth was a hard-bitten professional, accurate and contained. But the emotion he flaunted least counted most in explaining his power as a writer. He had a secret handhold which he tried to share with me the day I became editor. He walked in, put his hat on the desk and asked, "You scared, kid?"

He got an honest answer. "Well," he said gruffly, "here's how I did it.

"If you start to wondering how you can have anything worthwhile to say in print, every day for the rest of your life, it'll scare you out of the game. What you have to do on the tough days, when you're dry, is come in and sit down in front of that typewriter and say to yourself: 'I didn't ask to be put here. I didn't ask to come into this world. But Somebody brought me into this world, and moved me here in front of this type-writer, and so I don't think He's going to let me run dry now if I'll just unlock the mind the Lord gave me, and use it the best I can, and trust in an idea to come, instead of doubting whether one will.'

"After I got to thinking about it that way, I never worried about being able to write a daily column again," Ed Danforth said. "You see what I mean, kid?"

The whole world saw what he meant.

The Reverend Martin Luther King Jr. delivers his famous "I Have a Dream" speech in Washington, D.C. By permission of the Associated Press.

6

1963

One Small Shoe

April–May   Civil rights marches in Birmingham, Alabama lead to mass arrests
            and mounting criticism of Public Safety Commissioner Bull
            Connor's repressive tactics. In South Vietnam, a Buddhist revolt
            challenges the Diem regime.

June   President Kennedy addresses the nation on the moral imperatives
            of desegregation and racial equality and proposes a comprehensive
            civil rights bill. NAACP leader Medgar Evers is assassinated in
            Jackson, Mississippi. Alabama governor George Wallace "stands in
            the schoolhouse door" at the University of Alabama, in Tuscaloosa,
            to protest school desegregation. Following the federalization of the
            Alabama National Guard, the university is desegregated. President
            Kennedy visits West Berlin.

August   The March on Washington, highlighted by the Reverend Martin
            Luther King Jr.'s "I Have a Dream" speech, attracts more than two
            hundred thousand civil rights advocates.

September   The bombing of the 16th Street Baptist Church in Birmingham kills
            four black children. The U.S. Senate ratifies a nuclear test ban
            treaty.

November   South Vietnam President Ngo Dinh Diem is assassinated during a
            successful military coup. President Kennedy is assassinated in Dal-
            las, Texas. Lyndon Johnson becomes president.

January 15, 1963
Why the South Will Rise Again

It will be a valuable enlightenment if both the South and the rest of the country will pause for a minute and think about the deeper meaning behind Sen. LeRoy Johnson's presence on the floor of the Georgia Senate.

Sen. Johnson is a Negro, fairly elected to membership in the legislative body, and he has been received and accepted with courtesy and understanding by his colleagues. Yet if he had even shown up in the spectators' gallery one year ago just to watch the activities, they would have ordered him thrown out of the place. Quite a change has occurred.

This abrupt turnabout from rejection to acceptance will astound only those people who do not know the white Southerner very well. And since few of us even know ourselves, it is interesting to look for the meaning behind the switch.

It is completely in character. The white Southerner is a man of manners. Sometimes they are very bad manners, and sometimes they are quite good, but they are manners—a way of going.

He carries passion in him like a fever. In bad causes it is a destroyer. But in good causes it makes conviction. It does not congeal into the cold suet of cunning.

His crudely expressed prejudice has been the shame and despair of the South—but also an evidence of a hypocrisy level that is below the national average.

The white Southerner believes fiercely. When he is wrongheaded he is granite. But when he takes up a right idea, he is also granite. This stony quality is strength, not a weakness. His weakness comes only when he commits his strength to wrong ideas.

But when he rights a wrong idea, he backs it up with all of the manners, the passion, the conviction and the granite that he previously placed in the wrong cause. And this is why Sen. Johnson is a symbol of something important.

A year ago he wouldn't even have been allowed to sit with whites in the Senate gallery. Today he sits as a respected member. There is nothing particularly odd about this violent shift to the white Southerner. Having seen what was fairly required of him, he reacted with open face, and all the way.

This may bewilder those who do not understand the cyclonic but basically simple code and temper of the South. But it helps to explain the recent comment by the Rev. Dow Kirkpatrick, an Oxonian liberal who, after moving from Atlanta to a pulpit in Evanston, Ill., decided the white South is going to solve its racial conflicts in better style than the white North is.

Mayor Ed Wilson of Macon, a perceptive scholar and politician, likewise believes that the chief racial frictions of future years are going to occur outside the South because the white Southerner, as he understands and accepts, tends to act in good faith.

He is passionate and he can be brutal when he is wrong. But he is not very devious. He puts openness ahead of cunning. And when he is right, he is a strong man.

Sen. LeRoy Johnson is a symbol of the honorable accords that are beginning to come in the South's long racial ordeal. The strength and pride of the South, once liberated from small aims and mean leadership, are its key to greatness.

February 16, 1963
A Scene That Nobody Noticed

Today's worldly young don't know, and their fathers may have forgotten, those recent days when terror seized the heart of the farm-bred person when he visited the clangorous city.

He stood in a flush of indecision as street cars clanged past him with the wrong street signs posted. In the greasy spoon café he anxiously searched the unfamiliar menu which might have been written in French. As he walked he looked behind himself for landmarks; he darted awed glances at the city people, assuming they knew every store and every person in the whole great city just as he knew everyone back home. He was a stranger, uncertain of his adequacy. And no place confused him more than the busy, noisy bus station.

Our Harold Martin, who moved to Atlanta from Commerce, Ga., not too many years ago, remembers how it was, and he happened to be in the bus station Thursday.

He was there because a down-and-out gentleman, suffering a touch of insobriety, had come to his office and asked for bus fare to a small town and a better life. The last time Martin gave him bus fare the gentleman got in jail on his way to the bus station. So this time Harold frogwalked him to the bus station, bought him a ticket and sealed him in the bus with instructions to the driver not to let him off short of his destination. First, however, Martin administered a bowl of soup to his reluctant friend in the bus station cafeteria. While there, he began to watch a humble fellow diner.

The embarrassed Negro was sitting at a table wearing a clean old blue overcoat. He had stacked his packages on a chair beside him. Patiently, looking neither left nor right, he waited for someone to take his order. He did not know it was a self-service cafeteria. He may never have been in a cafeteria. Of course, nobody came to take his order. His discomfort undoubtedly was heightened because of his color and his uncertainty as to whether he was in the wrong place.

Finally he rose slowly and began gathering up his packages to leave, unfed. Martin gestured until he caught the man's eye across the room. He made roundabout motions of guidance until the puzzled traveler, carrying his packages, circled tentatively into the cafeteria line. Martin motioned as if picking up a tray. The man took one, then looked along the steam tables and began to comprehend. As those behind pressed him along the servers asked him if he would like this kind of meat, that dish of vegetables, and to each he made the same reply: "Yes'm, that'll be all right."

He reached the cash register with a great load of food, paid for his meal and with growing confidence returned to his table.

Before he began to eat he went over to Harold Martin, bent and whispered, "Thank you, sir."

That was all that was said between the two men from small towns.

March 10, 1963
"Car Butter"

A Superhighway Trip with Strange Results

"Where does butter come from?" asked the 8-year-old, and her play-mate from the city echoed it with her eyes. So we made some "car but-ter."

It had been a good day on the farm, tramping the woods of one's boyhood with the two children to ask questions.

The winter woods were clean and open and you could see the hawk on top of the dead tree. The doves still could whistle to cover in the South Georgia evergreen of pine and gallberry. But the hardwoods were bare as bones and the hot, rich underbrush of summer was missing.

Field larks made their low glides and landings to pick the fallow fields. A covey of quail shot up underfoot in the edge of the cypress pond. Cows lowered their heads and watched the children. The city dog made treble threats to an unmoved sow, then scrambled for distance when the old hog gave a companionable grunt.

The Recipe

Where does butter come from? Why you skim the cream off the clabber and put it in a half-gallon Mason jar and you shake it for half an hour, letting the cold jar bottom slap your hand. Or you put the cream in an old crockery churn and pump the broom handle up and down. Or you take the Dazey churn out of Grandmother's cupboard and put it in the car with the wooden butter mold, as we did.

We put a quart of cream in the clear glass churn and screwed on the top so that the paddles dipped down into the cream. Then we showed the wide-eyed little girls in the back seat how to turn the geared crank so the paddles went round and round and spun the cream.

For 30 miles they alternated by turning the little crank as the car sped back toward Atlanta. They tired, so we leaned back to the back seat and spun it for them awhile.

Passengers in other cars on the interstate highway stared curiously as we passed. So there was nothing to do but lift up the Dazey churn and point to it, all clouded with white spun cream. Not one seemed to know what it was. But oh, how they stared.

Fifty miles and 5,000 crank turns up the superhighway and the whipped cream began to produce yellow specks. The thinning liquid washed the churn sides clean and bit by bit the butter formed into a yellow ball. The mesh top of the peephole had to come off each 25 turns, of course, so the forming golden content could be examined and assayed.

And then it was done. A cupful of the fresh buttermilk disappointed all, as it will; too bland.

But a stop at a store for salt and wax paper made the next adventure possible at the roadside park. With plentiful water we washed and kneaded the butter clean, then worked in the salt and halved the lump.

People who had come to picnic stared, but the children stared back with glowing eyes. Each had half, and each saw it packed into the round mold, pressed and expelled with a daisy on the top. Each little girl arrived home carrying a fine golden half pound of butter and because they knew where it came from, they ate it up.

March 29, 1963
Small Hotels in a Big Town

While buckshot is being fired into homes of Negroes who want to vote in Leflore County, Mississippi, and dog-handling Greenwood police arrest Negroes who protest it, President Kennedy is clinging stubbornly—at his own political risk—to a belief that moderating influences within the South itself will stop these outrages without the duress of sharp new civil rights laws.

Is his faith in us well-placed?

A group of Republican senators including Scott, Keating, Case, Kuchel and Saltonstall think not. They have put together and introduced a sweeping package of strong civil rights bills that go far beyond the limited reach of the president's restrained program.

"If the president will not assume the leadership," they said, "we in Congress must."

It is not the president's leadership that has failed: it is the South that has failed the president and itself when Negroes get shot at for wanting to vote, or when a few Atlanta hotel owners airily jeopardize a reputation that other businessmen labored to build for this city.

The Republican senators will, of course, derive some profit politically from their bills, combined with Southern failures. But Southern successes, demonstrating the successes of the Kennedy program of low force levels coupled with high persuasion, are becoming too numerous to be lost under our flashy failures.

We think Mr. Kennedy bet right when he placed the South more on its honor than on the defensive. We only hope it doesn't require him to say in 1964 that he'd rather have been right than president.

His present civil rights program, which the Republican senators attacked as insufficient, places the emphasis where it most obviously belongs—on the enforcement of Negro voting rights.

He withheld proposals for more federal force in wider areas and left it to the South to show what it can do. Atlanta and Georgia have done all right, and we're moving toward Southern supremacy in the field of reasonable racial solutions, which is why the current readiness of some hotel men to black the eye of Atlanta is all the more hurtful.

The segregated hotels are their private property, of course, as they are in other Southern cities where they have been desegregated. But the lunch counters were the private property of Atlanta store owners, and the theaters were the private property of the motion picture men, and they didn't let the fact that they could do as they pleased deter them from doing what was right.

That is how Atlanta got its reputation as a place where people try to do what is right. And Atlanta is one of the places that encouraged President Kennedy to place more faith than force in the South.

The GOP's Sen. Scott and company, who are excellent politicians, think Mr. Kennedy is politically vulnerable because of it. If he is, it's not his fault for believing in the quality of the South. It's ours for defaulting on the trust, not just in Greenwood, Miss., but right here in this big hotel town.

April 26, 1963
The Negro Who Proved Himself

Dean Bill Tate literally fought Hamilton Holmes' way into the University of Georgia; he spent the night of the riot raging through the thick of it, collaring white rock throwers. Now, three years later, the dean has written Holmes a letter informing him that he, the first Negro boy admitted to a white Georgia school, has been selected to Phi Beta Kappa.

This is, of course, the most distinguished symbol of scholarship in American academic life.

Taking a pre-medical course heavy on chemistry and zoology, the cool, athletic young Negro knocked down 24 A's (many of them A plusses), four B plusses and one B during his three years of performance under pressure. One of the B's was in German.

He already had four B's on his record at Negro Morehouse College when he transferred in his sophomore year to the university under the state's first desegregation court order. "The transfer was good for me. It gave me some purpose," Holmes says.

He promptly shunned invitations to speak as a civil rights pioneer on the banquet circuit, forgot about football (he was a potential star as a pass receiver, with good hands and movements), and, except for regular basketball workouts at the Negro Y in Athens, he went to the books.

Holmes was in Atlanta Wednesday to qualify again for the summertime job he has held for the last four years—life guard at the Washington Park pool—before entering Emory University Medical School this fall.

He is a confident fellow, full of the quiet self-sufficiency that often comes to the eldest of many children. He handles himself neither humbly nor arrogantly, but matter of factly. He assumes the answers are in him. He depends on himself. Was he ever afraid he couldn't do the work at Georgia? "No." Is he apprehensive about his ability to do well as the first Negro in Emory medical school? "No."

Well, there must have been times when his scientific courses got a bit deep; what then? "The only thing to do then," he said, "is just bear down with it."

James Meredith has had academic troubles at Ole Miss. Four of the six Negroes at Georgia Tech are struggling to stave off failure. The few Southerners who might be unfeeling enough to try to use this to prove a point for school segregation are simply missing the point of desegregation.

This is a land of the lone man, the individual. Americans aren't weighed in bulk. They are measured singly. Their rights include the right to fail. But when desegregation gives one single American the right to succeed, whereas segregation of his whole race would have hobbled him, the point of individual rights, and the worth of the U.S. Constitution, is proved.

This week a segregationist struck a priest in the face in Louisiana. A Mississippi legislative committee blamed U.S. marshals for their own shame at Ole Miss. Alabama murderers killed a former mental patient. They had been falsely told their individual rights included the right to push other individuals around.

Georgia showed what individual rights mean. It gave Hamilton Holmes the right to be what he could be.

April 27, 1963
Now It's up to Alabama's People

Robert F. Kennedy's hawk nose is very hard and he is widely regarded in the South as a civil rights firebrand. Southerners usually see the attorney general only when he goes into public action, fighting fire with fire from Anniston to Oxford.

His visit to Alabama Thursday finally showed him in the role that only a few know he has played consistently. The fact is that ever since Kennedy entered the Cabinet he has been an enormous moderating influence on racial strife in the South.

Not many people know this because he cannot talk about his method of operation. He operates on confidence. His trip to Montgomery, a futile one, was one of his few public displays of the technique. Usually the public never knows what he does and he will not break the confidences necessary to defend himself against the firebrand charges.

It is a matter of fact, however, that the Justice Department under Kennedy has never brought a single civil rights suit to court without first having tried patiently behind the scenes to gain cooperation without coercion.

Impending crises have been solved without ever being heard of. Demands for civil rights actions have been mysteriously stalled for months on his desk while he maneuvered to achieve justice without force. He has asked for the counsel of Southern senators and congressmen, and has offered both time and political understanding to local officials. He has held off action to desegregate the University of Alabama until now.

The president and the board of that university are now said to be determined not to let it be ruined by violence and defiance. Birmingham's voters recently rejected the racial extremism of Bull Connor and important parts of that city's business community hope to temper the stridency of Alabama segregationists so that Tuscaloosa will not become another Oxford. Many students on campuses of the state are expressing similar hope.

But all of it depends on one man—Gov. George Wallace. Only he has the troops to keep the peace. If he will not, Robert Kennedy must.

So Kennedy went to Montgomery. He did not go as a firebrand, but as a moderator; not to threaten intervention of federal troops in Alabama, but to prevent it.

The reward for his effort was zero.

In the face of all the lessons of Oxford and Little Rock, Wallace seems determined to force yet another intervention of federal marshals or troops when the University of Alabama is desegregated, with all the damage that implies for the university, the state, the South and the nation.

The attorney general has done all he can. Only the people of Alabama can put a hand on Wallace now. If they fail, and another heedless governor permits the flames of violence to rise once again around a Southern university, Wallace will, of course, raise the old awful squall— that Kennedy is a firebrand. The time to judge that charge is right now.

May 28, 1963
The Businessman in Race Relations

In the massive realignment of race relations in Atlanta there is cause for reassurance. Genuine fears that the sky would fall down have faded one by one—with astonishing rapidity—as change has come, been noted, then been accepted and no longer noticed.

Atlanta's Negro citizens now attend movies, ride buses, play golf, read at libraries, travel on planes and trains, hold jobs, go to school (some flunking, some gaining top honors) alongside white citizens, and there is no novelty about it.

The old fears that Negroes just couldn't be treated like other citizens evaporated, once the thing was tried, and in place of trouble there was, more than anything else, a great relief. We simply rediscovered the oldest truth—that human beings are individuals, not masses, and any man deserves to be treated as an individual.

While there is cause to feel reassurance, then, there also remains a need to reassure.

In particular, some restaurant owners in Atlanta are in the lonely position of being under pressure for service from Negroes without a corresponding encouragement from whites to go ahead. Some fear competition disadvantage if they do go ahead and meet the inevitable, as many of their colleagues already have done without incident. They need reassurance, and Atlanta owes it to them.

In the smaller North Carolina cities of Raleigh and Charlotte, the merchants' bureaus or chambers of commerce have seen it as their duty to take a stand in support of their restaurant owners.

The business leadership of both those cities has come out publicly for public service, including restaurant service, for all citizens without discrimination. Instead of leaving their restaurant men to face a decision they fear alone, the business leaders have formed a solid front to help them and have even set up negotiating committees to assist them if needed in working out desegregation.

This emergence of business leadership in a progressive role in race relations is a vastly important new factor in the development of the South. At Birmingham it was an emergency proposition—the town was on fire, the elected leaders had lain down, and somebody had to lead so the businessmen did.

But in Raleigh, Charlotte and elsewhere the power structures have acted to prevent fires instead of waiting to fight them.

Atlanta's business leadership, which has a history of leading and not simply following lesser cities of the South, cannot have failed to note the initiatives taken in places like Raleigh and Charlotte to meet problems precisely like the restaurant difficulties here.

Many Atlanta eating places have long been serving all citizens alike, in some instances right next door to restaurants that do not. Atlanta can ill afford such anomalies. Only yesterday, two bewildered visitors from the Ivory Coast who came here to observe American freedom were ordered out of a Forsyth Street cafeteria. As many Atlanta lunch counters and restaurants have already proved, fear of change is groundless. But the city can be sorely damaged if fear, and not progress, rules.

This is a time when a little reassurance as to what Atlanta stands for can go a long way toward helping the restaurant men take the steps that other Atlanta businesses have taken for the enduring good of the city and its citizens.

June 6, 1963
We're Weary of Civil Rights Bills

Whether President Kennedy proposes new civil rights bills next week is not now the central issue. The law has served its valuable purpose as the starter on the engine of racial progress. But the engine must run on the sustained power of voluntary decision in the hearts of people. Slowly but with gathering sureness that power is taking hold.

If the president thinks it is not yet enough to meet the emergency of this revolutionary day, he will ask Congress to pass a law barring discrimination in places like restaurants, theaters and hotels.

Maybe it would help more than hurt. It might indeed help and be silently welcomed by white managements in places like Mississippi where, the managers explain, they can't move unless they are forced. But . . .

The engine of individual opinion still must run ultimately of its own accord. That is where the real progress is coming. By comparison, civil rights bills of the future, laws present, and those past, are small parts.

The true status of progress is being found far higher up the ladder than these low rungs of force. The central decisions are being made up there by men like Atlanta's Bishop Randolph Claiborne when he states the Episcopal stand: "Segregation on the sole basis of race is inconsistent with the Christian religion."

He has told it gently to the troubled trustees of the church-related Lovett School as they search for answers to give Negro applicants.

For the trustees, and the parents they represent, are having to face something more basic than force; legal force cannot reach into their private school. Their decision, with their church as their guide, ultimately will answer a simpler question: Can a school built on racial discrimination be a good school, or will it have poor sills? Is this really why we are sending our children here—to buy segregation? Or is it because we want them to go to a great school and be trained for larger lives? Then, can any great school, or any large life, be born of so small an aim as racial rejection? Can segregation be part of a curriculum that is worth much?

This is the point where the enduring decisions are being made, as they have been made at private schools like Emory, Agnes Scott, Mercer and Oglethorpe. Often they come in fear, or anger, or torment of spirit, but they are the ones that will endure. A civil rights law is a small thing beside them.

Atlanta needs no new laws because it is thinking beyond force already. Downtown theater owners have made their decision, and desegregated. Surely hotel owners are going to do the same. As for the remaining segregated restaurants, we cannot believe they will evade the voluntary decision other businessmen here have made. Voluntarily the Chamber of Commerce board has publicly come out for service to all Americans by all businesses without regard to their color. A weariness with holding back the Negro has come; a willingness to help him rise is growing.

The relief of this decision, voluntarily made, cleanses a community and the citizens in it and leaves us all a little astonished that only yesterday we believed such a just change was unthinkable.

June 16, 1963
Right against Right

Choice Is Narrowed to a Swift Ending

A nation sorely perplexed by racial rough-housing might turn for light to Hegel's dictum: "The real tragedy of human existence is the conflict not between right and wrong—but between right and right."

It is right for a private property owner to be free to run his business as he wishes.

It is right for a Negro to protest being thrown out of a place of business that is open to serve the public.

It is right to condemn lawless protest demonstrations and to demand just and orderly settlements in courts of law instead.

It is right for the president to propose the necessary new laws if just settlements in court cannot be had without them.

So, the choice reduces itself, as Hegel warned, to a painful choice between the greater right and the lesser right.

Certainly the greater right, in the decisions now facing Americans, will be for private business owners to make just settlements voluntarily.

An End

Then there would be no new laws, nor more demonstrations, and an end to degrading treatment of Negro Americans.

Some may still deny at this point that segregated treatment is degrading. But the Negro is the one who is segregated, and he has found it degrading. Any reasonably fair white man can see why, if he will consider what it is to be a Negro.

He would not be content to go on trying to find excuses for saying no when his child asked if he could to see a picture show that had been advertised for all to read about. He would grow very weary of making up lies to spare his child's pride.

He would not be happily content to take his family on trips along a road without knowing where he would be able to find a restaurant to feed them, or a hotel to house them, and worse—not knowing where his inquiry for food and shelter might cause him to be abused and ejected in front of his children.

No, no white man of any pride would be content to leave that kind of world to his children.

And no white man of complete honesty can say it is right for him—despite the torment he may feel over torn traditions—to go on forcing a Negro father to humble his children to such a life when he knows he would not put up with such a life for his own.

The white private businessman now has a full legal right to go on degrading the Negro. When he exercises it, though he knows it is wrong, the Negro has no legal right to correct the wrong. But he no longer will accept it, any more than the white man would. So he has started a revolution outside the law in the streets of America.

Out of Streets

To bring the hot danger of this rebellion out of the streets and back into the coolness of the courtroom, President Kennedy proposes laws to take away the private businessman's legal right to inflict the degrading wrong.

But even the president knows such laws alone would mean little except as a damper on the fires of street riots; only the changing heart of the white can end the Negro's degradation.

That change is coming. The white American owes it to himself to hasten it; the Negro American owes it to the nation to exercise a prudent patience. The choices between right and right narrow down the urgent need for voluntary, peaceful, unforced—and swift—end to a wrong. Atlanta is moving courageously in that direction.

What is the alternative? Every page of history records the folly and the fall of men and societies that tried to lock up just protests in jails, and lost their power, or who exercised what they considered to be their right to do wrong, and lost the right. That history stretches back from Colonial America, and forward from Homer's Greece, to Christ.

July 16, 1963
The Bass Ate the Bream, but . . .

Jack Wingate warned me to watch the thunderheads building up in the southwest. Wingate is an amiable rock of a man and the finest of fishermen. When he talks, men listen. So I set out alone from his fishing lodge last week with an eye on the sky. The outboard drove the boat smoothly south across still water, flat as black glass, toward the place where the big bass might be in Southwest Georgia's Lake Seminole.

The thunderheads grew. The southern sky blackened totally. Swiftly rising wind blew up waves and tore off whitecaps. Roughening water thumped and spanked the boat about in plumes of spray. Valor to the winds, I made for the lee of a low green island near the center of the big lake, snubbed the bow line to a cypress snag and drove the anchor down astern, and waded ashore.

I squatted on wiregrass under scrub brush and watched the squall roll in. The gale rose rapidly from a howl to a shriek. It buffeted the tied boat like a paper cup offshore. It flattened the low trees and grasses of the island and churned the lake channel into heavy sea. The rain broke. Suddenly I was alone, wrapped in hard gray rain and a wild wind, while lightning bolts struck about the island like white hammers in great rips of sound.

One wet man, huddled on an island in a storm, is a lonely specimen.

The heavens were at work; there was nothing much a mere two-legged son could do but take refuge under a bush and concede their power. About a mile away another fisherman failed to make for land in time. It was a punishing moment of supremacy for the elements; the man's body was taken from the water the next day.

At the height of the storm, in the angry waters in front of my bush, as the wind shrilled and the rain drove down, a bass rose to the surface in a great boiling splash and ate a little fish.

So that's how it really is, I began to think. Perhaps the merciless power of nature, with its unbending laws, demands its sacrifices. The big bass eats the little fish, and that's how it has to be.

Maybe there isn't time in the savage storm for gentle ideals. Maybe this was it—all there is. Dog eat dog, bass eat bream, and what are a man's aspirations for anyway in the face of nature's power.

Back at Jack Wingate's lodge at Johnson's Landing, I told him it had been quite a blow. "One of my little girls used to be afraid of these storms," said the big man. "Then one day in the middle of one I took her by the hand and led her out in it. We stood there and she looked at the lightning, and maybe it was because her daddy was there, but she wasn't scared any more and she hasn't been since."

And that is the real point of it. A man, like the other creatures of nature, must be able to meet and master the roughest storms in a life where predators feed on the weak, like the bass on the bream. But Jack Wingate showed the other side—the side that raises a really strong man above the lower creatures. He used his strength to help someone less strong.

July 17, 1963
Gov. Barnett and the Rock Thrower

The NAACP is serving Georgia well by trying to stop the Savannah-type mob scenes. When Negro demonstrations degenerate into violence they are indefensible. The NAACP, long the steadiest of the Negro organizations, had the strength to say so.

"We don't condone the kind of thing that is happening in Savannah," said Leon Cox, Georgia field secretary for the NAACP, last Friday.

What had happened in Savannah the night before was plain, dangerous folly. To a vacationing traveler like myself, driving through Savannah along West Broad Street with his family in the car, the sudden scene was appalling. Flaming kerosene bombs were being thrown. Three fire trucks clanged past and blocked the street to fight a blaze. A house and two cars were set afire that night.

With a child in the car, a detour through the seething back streets to get around the flames became an unacceptable situation. Before that night was over, cars had been stoned, tires slashed and shop windows shattered. Police came in with tear gas and a mist of it hung over West Broad Street at dawn.

This was no peaceable assembly. It was not a nonviolent demonstration. It was what the NAACP official called it—a mob on the loose. Pillagers out of pool halls had been handed the onetime banner of nonviolence and they were soiling it.

"The kind of mob action taking place hurts the cause," Mr. Cox said. It was good to see the responsible Negro leadership in the NAACP and elsewhere asserting itself to lay a hand on the vandals.

President Kennedy gave American Negroes the right guideline in a section of his civil rights message, which opposing politicians have left widely unmentioned. "These demonstrations have increasingly endangered lives and property, enflamed emotions and unnecessarily divided communities," the president said.

"They are not the way in which this country should rid itself of racial discrimination. Violence is never justified. I want to caution against demonstrations which can lead to violence."

While his civil rights bills are before Congress, Mr. Kennedy urged "all community leaders, Negro and white, to do their utmost to lessen tensions and to exercise self-restraint."

After Savannah, it is time for the Negro American to read again what the president said.

Just as it is time, after a century, for the white American to listen fairly also to something else the president said.

"I ask you to look into your hearts," he said, "for the one plain, proud and priceless quality that unites all of us as Americans: A sense of justice."

The Negro American deserves fair treatment. He has been denied it by force and often violence in the past, a thing his white judges should remember. That fair treatment is going to come, as the president said, "because it is right." It is not going to be forcibly withheld by Mississippi's itinerant governor, nor is it going to be violently attained by the Negro rock thrower in Savannah, because they are wrong.

August 3, 1963
Needed: A Season of Understanding

This has been a harsh summer, heavy with heat and anger. Calm talk comes hard. Friends separate in petty spats. Mayor Ivan Allen attributed much racial progress in Atlanta to a Negro leadership that goes after "results instead of rhetoric." Yet some of that leadership, heroic only yesterday, is now called Uncle Tom because it questions the wisdom of blocking traffic with street lie-downs.

And too many angry whites are reacting, in this harsh summer, by denouncing the street lie-downs to the point of forgetting there are calmer Negro leaders like Sen. LeRoy R. Johnson who, in Newark, N.J., recently was saying:

"The people's revolution which is being advanced in these uneasy times must undergird its cry for freedom with a strong sense of social responsibility."

The calm talk is hard to hear.

Heat and anger weigh like a weight on the land. Negro and white, Americans are making easy judgments of each other instead of directing calm judgment toward the goal of racial fairness.

"The Negro may be gaining rights but he is losing acceptance," said an experienced Atlanta politician, disturbed by the more extreme demonstrations.

"Who are you to advise the Negro what he should do," snapped a militant Negro, forgetful of that politician's pioneering in the recent, harder days.

The Negro does not need to lie down in a street, or let violence creep into his demonstrations, to make his point. Those tactics obscure his point.

And the point, which the Southern white man cannot and must not evade with legalism or angry half-answers, is a simple and human one. Martin Luther King Jr. stated it so simply that any man who wants to be fair can understand it:

"I guess it is easy for those who have never felt the stinging facts of segregation to say, 'Wait.' But when you see the vast majority of your 20 million Negro brothers smothering in an airtight cage of poverty in the midst of an affluent society; when you suddenly find your tongue twisted and your speech stammering as you seek to explain to your 6-year-old daughter why she can't go to the public amusement park that has just been advertised on television . . . and see the depressing clouds of inferiority begin to form in her little mental sky; when you have to concoct an answer for a 5–year-old son asking, 'Daddy, why do white people treat colored people so mean?'; when you take a cross-country drive and find it necessary to sleep night after night in the uncomfortable corners of your automobile because no motel will accept you; when you are humiliated day in and day out by nagging signs reading 'white' and 'colored'; when your first name becomes 'nigger' and your middle name becomes 'boy' and your last name becomes 'John,' and when your wife and mother are never given the respected title 'Mrs.'; when you are . . . living constantly at tiptoe stance never quite knowing what to expect next, and plagued with inner fears and outer resentments . . . then you will understand why we find it difficult to wait."

A cool season of understanding is needed now in America.

August 13, 1963
The Great Kudzu Flood

Take kudzu (assuming it doesn't take us first). A few years ago everybody was planting it. The tough vine would stop rain from eroding ditch banks along the roads men had cut through nature's wilderness. It stopped the erosion, all right. The question now is how to stop the kudzu.

The mountain roads through North Georgia's Chattahoochee National Forest are leafy green tunnels of kudzu.

Up the telephone poles it goes and comes back down to the shrubs.

Once graceful trees are cocooned and dying in shrouds of kudzu.

It creeps ever farther into the forest and may even yet—who knows—approach the towns—a rolling, velvety tide threatening to engulf us all in a Great Green Kudzu Flood. Hang onto your hoe. At least Pompeii got it all at once.

The national forest rangers have long since quit planting kudzu. They've gone to lespedeza. But to stop what they started will take chemicals—and who knows where that will lead?

Consider how rancher Ray Cerna of Toppenish, Wash., must have felt last Saturday when he looked around and saw his cows dropping dead. A white cloud hung over the landscape. It was insecticide that crop dusters had sprayed. Thirty-eight people went to hospitals from breathing the stuff.

Secretary of the Interior Udall is asking Congress for more money to study the effect of pesticides. His tests show the wild ducks are passing along residues of DDT and other poisons to their progeny "in a yet unexplained manner."

Also, the Interior Department adds, "marine fishes from different oceans of the world have been found to contain DDT."

The U.S. Public Health Service had another uncheerful note for us all. Due to Soviet and American nuclear tests during 1962, there was almost twice as much strontium 90 in the nation's milk this year as there was a year ago.

And so it goes. If the roads hadn't been cut through the wilderness, the kudzu wouldn't have been planted in the first place. But leaving nature just the way it was won't work either.

Men keep working themselves into corners like these because they're expected to explore nature's laws and enlarge their lives within those laws. As long as they don't break the laws they're all right.

But everything from kudzu to fallout reminds us that it's a good idea to know what we're doing before we do it.

Men are adventurous jokers, though. They aren't likely to quit making messes yet. Take the Tennessee copper industry around Ducktown and Copperhill. Fumes from the smelters have killed the trees and shrubs and even the grasses. Ragged red hills stretch like a desert for many square miles. Rains are slicing the hills like cleavers, and the gullies are turning into canyons. But they can't quit making copper. So do you know what they've planted on the hills?

Kudzu.

August 30, 1963
"I Have A Dream"

WASHINGTON—The march was ended. The marble Lincoln brooded over meadows snowy white with litter and placards. In the sudden silence left by 200,000 departed people, the meaning of what had happened here slowly settled into shape. It may have been historic.

It may be that this will be marked down as the date when the Civil Rights movement grew up.

Two upheavals occurred here.

1. Breaking a rising national fever of shrillness and disorder, Negro demonstrators embraced a constructive discipline.

2. Rejecting a further rise of bitterness and anger, Martin Luther King defined a new purpose, expressed in bright hope through love of a country.

What this Negro maturing will mean to a nation that is much in need of both pacification and racial progress will depend on the response of the country, of course. The country saw it happen, and has been handed the challenge.

The reaction of the marching Negro multitude and its leaders was unmistakable. They were proud, awestruck and more than a little bewildered by the implications of the new vein they had struck here. It all seemed slightly accidental.

For the first time the various Negro leaders had concerted their efforts. Those efforts had been getting at ragged cross purposes.

Here, for the first time, the leaders sat down in council. They decided to show the country discipline and order, instead of making a bitter and trouble-fraught march on the Capitol to goad and anger Congress. The crowd obeyed. The council of leaders got together on the March day itself and pressured SNCC's John Lewis to temper a bitter and negative speech he had planned to make. More than preaching, they wanted progress.

But it still would have been just a large turnout of people who came and heard predictable things if Martin Luther King had not gotten carried away to spontaneity by the roars of an electrified crowd. In a few impassioned and triumphant moments below the great seated statue of Abraham Lincoln, King swept the marchers to a new vision of the Negro's destiny in America by praising and celebrating America, and lifting their eyes from the "valley of despair" to purple mountain majesties.

"I have a dream," he boomed, again and again, and each dream showed him liberty and pursuit of happiness for all races of Americans soon, from the cliffs of the Rockies to the slopes of the Alleghenies, from Stone Mountain in Georgia to the broad Mississippi. "I have a dream," he roared, weeping, and his dream stretched from sea to shining sea, and all the way from the speaker's stand at the Lincoln Memorial to the far end of a crowd that stretched to the Washington Monument.

The rapt crowd was on its feet, seeing the Negro's dream really wrapped in the red, white and blue, and the answering ovations seemed to seal a very important bond.

King has preached hope, and not despair; faith in the white man, not bitterness; identification with America, not doubt of its capacity for social justice. In this tremendously positive and upbeat moment, he found 200,000 Negro Americans had that dream too, and responded.

How the country will respond is up to its individuals. (On my way home the airliner stewardess said, "I haven't been for this civil rights stuff and I've never liked King. But I watched him on TV, and after it was over I was proud of the Negro and proud of America. I'd thought they were just going to criticize us white people. He made my country seem so beautiful I felt like I wanted to shake his hand.")

September 4, 1963
Newest Minority Is White

America's newest minority is the Southern poor white, hunting work in the impersonal stone valleys of Detroit, Cleveland and Chicago. Machines are driving him from the mine and the farm. But he does not know how to work or live away from the land, and the cruelty he once brought to bear on the Negro is being visited upon him ruthlessly.

He is called, in the cities, a "hillbilly," and it has come to be a term of opprobrium resented by him as hotly as the Negro resents "nigger." So the derisive city dwellers use it on him all the more.

He is taunted for his Southern accent, ridiculed for his illiteracy, rejected as a worker because he has no skill, bilked by loan sharks and salesmen, overcharged by slumlords and driven, by his frustration, into outbursts of wife-beating and knifing in the ghettos where he is segregated.

Donald Janson of the *New York Times*, reporting on the 30,000 of these poor people who are massed in Chicago, says three murders have occurred in one of their apartment houses in the last six months.

Thirty shells of abandoned cars must be removed from Chicago's streets each week. The rattletraps that brought the white migrants are stripped and left by the curb when they break down.

Their children go barefoot in the harsh Chicago winter, shivering in their thin Southern shirting. While mothers and fathers hunt work, children run loose. Too often they are hungry and sick.

But they simply go on being hungry and sick. Astonished Chicago authorities find these self-reliant people will not accept help. Welfare agencies open, then close because nobody comes. These self-reliant people want only to work. But there is no work that they know how to do. Stoically, then, they suffer.

The store-front church does not reach them, because this is not home. Health authorities cannot treat sick children, nor can welfare agencies feed them though they have gone hungry for days; their parents reject charity. In a terrible twilight between the rural life they know and the hard city where they live, they suffer in helplessness and degradation. "The only hope is in the kids," says Robert J. O'Rourke, the alderman for their Chicago ward.

But the parents who cannot read and write even reject education for their young. Mass truancy bewilders Chicago school officials. Only when these children can be gotten into school will there be hope of a generation that can make a living.

Until then, the city agencies can only go on trying to find job opportunities for a few of the white migrants and fend off, as best they can, the human hyenas who creep everywhere to mock and snap and feast their sick souls on the misery of any minority that cannot help itself.

It is to the everlasting honor of the South that most Southern whites are ceasing to treat the Negro like that.

September 15, 1963
Deep Fears

Racial Segregation No Answer at All

David Lawrence writes accurately that rationalizations "do not erase the deep feelings of fear and the emotional hostility" that many parents of both races feel about the possibility of intermarriage of their children.

Mr. Lawrence correctly defines the problem. But he offers no guidance as to how the two races might solve it or at least live with it.

Nearly everybody knows this fear is the main emotional base of segregation.

What they seek now is some indication of an answer for the future, now that the answer of the past has failed. Americans have learned what they cannot do. The job now is to learn what can be done.

Segregation failed as a rational system for meeting the fear, no matter what point of view one assumes.

From the point of view of those who oppose mixing of the races, segregation failed because under it the races have been mixed on a monumental scale. It is a generally accepted estimate that nearly three out of four American Negroes now have white blood. Put the other way, three out of four are whites with Negro blood. That happened under a system that was ostensibly designed to prevent it.

In the fact of what has happened, it is self-delusion to defend segregation still as a means of preventing race-mixing. Some sociologists think segregation in fact has contributed to the mixing, by holding down the Negro's pride and security and by investing the issue with the dark novelty of things clandestine.

Another View

Additionally, from the point of view of those who wish to treat the Negro citizen in a civilized manner, segregation failed because his separate life was not made an equal life. It became simply a vehicle by which the white majority expresses its own fear by oppressing somebody else. The fear is real and unquestionable, as Mr. Lawrence said. But to express a fear by taking it out of another's hide is no longer a method that sits easily on the American conscience. Americans have learned what they cannot do.

Since segregation failed as a way to prevent mixing of the races, and since it failed as a worthy way of treating American citizens, there is no point in holding to the delusion that it is an answer.

Yet the fear, as Mr. Lawrence said, remains. It is deep, real and basic in many parents of both races.

What guidelines are there, then, as Americans turn away from the failure of forced segregation and search for a successful future way for the races to live side by side, with equal rights, in peace? There are some.

Northern public schools and colleges have educated children of both races in the same classrooms for generations. There has been no appreciable growth of any tendency toward intermarriage. Surely this is a guideline the apprehensive Southern white can note as he faces the unfamiliar.

Not a Trend

And what does the Southern Negro feel, as he rises toward equality of rights? "We need not get excited about occasional so-called interracial marriages," says the Rev. M. L. Tobin, of the School of Religion at Atlanta's Morehouse College. "This is not a trend nor is it a harbinger of the future. There is a healthy and growing sense of race pride among Negroes that deters such a trend."

Dr. Tobin defends the right of any individuals to marry—"races do not marry"—but adds:

"Sensible Negroes do not consider it a badge of honor or distinction to marry a white person. 'If he did, he would be calling true what he knows is false, namely that the white person is innately superior' (Wentzel).

"Dr. W.E.B. DuBois expressed it admirably in his best book, *The Souls of Black Folk.*

"'(The Negro) would not Africanize America, for America has too much to teach the world and Africa. He would not bleach his soul in a flood of white Americanism, for he knows that Negro blood has a message for the world. He simply wishes to make it possible for a man to be both a Negro and an American, without being cursed and spit upon by his fellows, without having the doors of opportunity closed roughly in his face.'"

The fear is not erased, as Mr. Lawrence says. But if it is looked at rationally, the new answers that will develop as the future unfolds may prove more reassuring than the old answer of forced segregation, for that turned out to be no answer at all.

September 16, 1963
A Flower for the Graves

A Negro mother wept in the street Sunday morning in front of a Baptist Church in Birmingham. In her hand she held a shoe, one shoe, from the foot of her dead child. We hold that shoe with her.

Every one of us in the white South holds that small shoe in his hand.

It is too late to blame the sick criminals who handled the dynamite. The FBI and the police can deal with that kind. The charge against them is simple. They killed four children.

Only we can trace the truth, Southerner—you and I. We broke those children's bodies.

We watched the stage set without staying it. We listened to the prologue unbestirred. We saw the curtain opening with disinterest. We have heard the play.

We—who go on electing politicians who heat the kettles of hate.

We—who raise no hand to silence the mean and little men who have their nigger jokes.

We—who stand aside in imagined rectitude and let the mad dogs that run in every society slide their leashes from our hand, and spring.

We—the heirs of a proud South, who protest its worth and demand its recognition—we are the ones who have ducked the difficult, skirted the uncomfortable, caviled at the challenge, resented the necessary, rationalized the unacceptable, and created the day surely when these children would die.

This is no time to load our anguish onto the murderous scapegoat who set the cap in dynamite of our own manufacture.

He didn't know any better.

Somewhere in the dim and fevered recess of an evil mind he feels right now that he has been a hero. He is only guilty of murder. He thinks he has pleased us.

We of the white South who know better are the ones who must take a harsher judgment.

We, who know better, created a climate for child-killing by those who don't.

We hold that shoe in our hand, Southerner. Let us see it straight, and look at the blood on it. Let us compare it with the unworthy speeches of Southern public men who have traduced the Negro; match it with the spectacle of shrilling children whose parents and teachers turned them free to spit epithets at small huddles of Negro school children for a week before this Sunday in Birmingham; hold up the shoe and look beyond it to the state house in Montgomery where the official attitudes of Alabama have been spoken in heat and anger.

Let us not lay the blame on some brutal fool who didn't know any better.

We know better. We created the day. We bear the judgment. May God have mercy on the poor South that has so been led. May what has happened hasten the day when the good South, which does live and has great being, will rise to this challenge of racial understanding and common humanity, and in the full power of its unasserted courage, assert itself.

The Sunday school play at Birmingham is ended. With a weeping Negro mother, we stand in the bitter smoke and hold a shoe. If our South is ever to be what we wish it to be, we will plant a flower of nobler resolve for the South now upon these four small graves that we dug.

October 5, 1963
Savannah? Or Americus?

This newspaper has expressed opposition to the public accommodations bill. We have done so because we believe a property-owning American will act justly without being compelled to.

We don't believe that many white men would consider it to be just if they and their families had to live their lives in this country without knowing where they could find a place that would let them eat or sleep when they took a trip, or without knowing which theaters would embarrass and reject their children if the kids wanted to go to a movie.

Our faith that white men will voluntarily stop treating people like that has been shaken somewhat by the continuation of such discriminatory treatment by some restaurant owners in Atlanta. Certainly their refusal to act voluntarily is strengthening the argument of those who say it will take a public accommodations law to make them act.

But faith endures.

And in Savannah, it has been furthered this week by hotel and theater owners. Instead of standing obstinately and inviting passage of the public accommodations law, they voluntarily stopped discrimination and strengthened our argument that such voluntary action will obviate the need for the law.

But what can be said to Congress, when the public accommodations bill comes up for debate, about situations like the one now existing at Americus, where public accommodations owners not only decline to stop discrimination voluntarily, but where four persons who protested are being held in jail without bail from August until November when a grand jury meets, and who may be held in prison for months after that awaiting trial if the grand jury indicts them? Is imprisonment the South's alternative to a federal force law?

That does not give us much of an argument against the need for a public accommodations law.

The South is asked to meet a difficult change, and needs time. But it must be recognized that a national impatience with obstinacy is growing and sooner or later, unless Southerners act voluntarily, it is going to be reflected in Congress.

Who in the South is strengthening the case for the public accommodations law?

October 7, 1963
The Mind of the South

Beyond the grave, the words of W. J. Cash hang like smoke on the Southern air: "The Old South was a society beset by the specters of defeat, of shame, of guilt—a society driven by the need to bolster its morale, to nerve its arm against waxing odds, to justify itself in its own eyes and in those of the world. Hence a large part of its history . . . is the history of efforts to achieve that end, and characteristically by means of romantic fictions."

To justify slavery, the Old South stultified itself.

To justify its present treatment of the Negro, the South goes on with fictions that it does not believe. That is the funny thing about it—the non-belief. The Negro and the Southern white (not the trash) rather like and trust each other.

How, if ever, can the mind of Cash's South be freed of the myths it never has believed in its heart—a heart that beats and lives individually like a lion's, yet pursues destruction in herd like a sheep's?

I don't know.

I do know this:

The Southerner is a stronger, gentler man than his fictions paint him.

He knows things in his heart that his tongue denies.

He is, in lonely test, a fair, brave and compassionate man.

The Southerner is in nearly every way a better man than he presents himself to be. In a world crowded with posing men, he will be a refreshment to the discoverer when he does reveal himself—just as he finds an astonishing sense of relief within himself each time he finds it was possible, after all, to let the Negro take a new step upward.

The Southerner does not fit the mold in which other men are cast. He is "driven by the need to justify." Yet the Southern man would have so little to justify—if he could only rid himself of the remaining folds of his raiment of fiction—that he might stand unique in the height of his revealed worth.

How can he do that?

I don't know. It's a personal matter with every man. His leaders could help by quitting their cheap fictions and confessing their own worth. But a man has to make up his own heart.

I only know what the Southerner is, behind his fictions. He is a better man than his condemnors think, a better man than he himself knows.

I've fished, fought, plowed, prayed and marched with him all my life. He is hard of will, soft of heart, and honest beyond any meanness when he decides to be—but first, he tries to get his pride disentangled by justifying and that's where he's stumped.

He's more proud than angry—so he acts angry; more unsure than ignorant, so he acts unknowing. That's the funny thing about him; he covers up the best of himself—the very part that other men over-advertise in themselves.

When the brusque outlander tries to penetrate these subtle Southern tissues with the blunt blade of a different judgment, I say to him again and again, be careful, because one of these days when the cocoon of fiction breaks, you may find here men who can judge you.

Then they ask the question that one of these days we'll have to answer: "When?"

December 6, 1963
Joseph Parham Told the Truth

Joseph Parham has left Woodland, Ga., now. The PTA asked him to apologize and of course he couldn't do that. He resigned as principal of the Woodland school without denouncing anybody and left town quietly because he thought his continued presence would create animosities. He doesn't have a job. But he preferred to leave the one he had rather than harm the school by causing further controversy.

What this brave, mild-mannered man had done, of course, was to teach the children and the PTA of Woodland the most important lesson they will ever learn.

He taught them that no matter the cost, no matter the peril, an American—and especially a teacher—ought to have the courage to stand up against wrong and speak plainly for what is right.

Mr. Parham had never written a letter to a newspaper in his life.

But when children in his school cheered, upon being told of President Kennedy's assassination, Mr. Parham sat down and wrote an open letter to the people, saying this was wrong, and he sent it to this newspaper to be printed. He did not bite his tongue in his own self-interest and choke back the most important lesson growing out of the president's death. He grasped its importance and he taught it. The American people need to be taught it. The nation is weaker because they have not been taught it.

Mr. Parham did not indict his sixth- and seventh-graders who reacted to their president's murder with cheers. He indicted their parents for letting such disrespect be bred into the children. "There can be no justification, no excuse," the principal wrote unflinchingly.

"A parent who by flaunting the law, tolerating hatred and scorning justice brings a child to hate has eternally condemned himself. He has forfeited his birthright as an American, renounced his Christian heritage and forsaken his child."

The parents of Woodland did not appreciate the lesson Mr. Parham taught, of course. It was their children who had cheered. It was their guilt. That lesson hurt. So they asked for an apology. They should have raised his pay.

Now this brave teacher, under the angry pressures that truth has a tendency to generate when it is spoken by a humble man, has taken the guilt of Woodland on himself without complaint and been driven like a scapegoat from the town.

He doesn't have a job now. He has only his honor as a courageous American. The Woodland PTA may not yet have grasped the importance of that. But their children will. He taught them.

If there is no place for such a teacher as this, God help our children and their country.

Gene's editorials raised money from white Georgians to help rebuild this black Baptist church, one of two burned down by white terrorists in Sasser, Georgia, in September 1962. By permission of the *Atlanta Journal and Constitution.*

7

1964

How Do You Reach Them?

January	The surgeon general declares that cigarette smoking causes lung cancer, and the Federal Trade Commission authorizes warning labels on cigarette packages. President Johnson calls for an "unconditional war on poverty" and creates the Office of Economic Opportunity.
February	Ratification of the Twenty-Fourth Amendment eliminates the poll tax in federal elections. Cassius Clay defeats Sonny Liston and becomes world heavyweight boxing champion.
March	In *New York Times v. Sullivan,* the U.S. Supreme Court restricts libel actions by public officials.
June	Congress passes a comprehensive civil rights bill. Three civil rights workers involved in the Freedom Summer project are murdered in Philadelphia, Mississippi.
July	Arizona Senator Barry Goldwater wins the Republican Party's nomination for president. Goldwater selects New York congressman William Miller as his running mate.
August	Congress passes the Gulf of Tonkin Resolution, giving the president broad powers to respond to military aggression, and approves the Equal Opportunity Act. President Johnson wins the Democratic Party's presidential nomination and selects Senator Hubert Humphrey of Minnesota as his running mate. At the Democratic National Convention in Atlantic City, New Jersey, the black-led Mississippi Freedom Democratic Party challenges the legitimacy of the state's white delegation. A major race riot erupts in the Harlem section of New York City.

September   The Warren Commission declares that the assassination of President Kennedy was the work of a lone assassin, Lee Harvey Oswald. The Free Speech Movement at the University of California, Berkeley, leads to sit-ins and student strikes.
October   The Reverend Martin Luther King Jr. wins the Nobel Peace Prize.
November   Lyndon Johnson wins a landslide victory over Barry Goldwater, and the Democrats solidify their control over both houses of Congress.

January 7, 1964
Atlanta and the Negro

For a very long time the white community of Atlanta condemned the Negroes for demonstrating and demanded that they take a quieter and more reasonable approach to racial problems. So they did.

The Negro community united under leadership of A. T. Walden and Clarence Coleman, and proposed to supplant conflict and crisis with calm negotiations around the conference table.

In the months since this widely applauded move was made, the leadership of the white community has declared itself as favoring an end to many of the discriminatory practices the Negroes find humiliating—particularly discrimination in the basic human necessities of food and shelter.

But restaurant and hotel owners held the power of decision. There is not yet a public accommodations law to require them to desegregate. There is not yet a storm of direct action by the Negroes seeking to compel them to desegregate.

There is only the quiet voice of the Chamber of Commerce, the mayor, the Retail Merchants Association, the Fulton County Commission, 200 clergymen, the Board of Aldermen and many other bodies, public and private, assuring the owners that the leadership of this city supports them in ending discrimination and coaxing them, for the good of the city, to go ahead.

Many of the owners haven't bothered.

The bulk of Atlanta's leadership, while trying to shield them from Negro pressures, has done everything it can to encourage and assist them in the change.

Now the hour is fast approaching when the leadership must turn and try to shield the city.

Atlanta doesn't want demonstrations. But the positions of Mr. Walden and Mr. Coleman are deteriorating rapidly because they have been unable to do at the conference table what the demonstrators want to do in the streets.

The ground is being cut out from under opponents of the federal public accommodations bill because these owners will not do voluntarily what civil rights advocates want to do in Congress.

The Negroes of Atlanta extended the hand of good faith, and the white leadership of Atlanta tried to respond. But the key decisions—those affecting public accommodations—have been withheld.

Everything has been done that can be done to help these owners. Now if they are ever going to shoulder their responsibility to help the city in return, it had better be immediate; time has run out for the moderate Negro leaders who didn't think Atlanta would let them down.

January 20, 1964
Reflections on a Quiet Sunday

This was a quiet Sunday in Atlanta. Legislators were back home consulting the folks. There was a rummaging around to find the meaning of things. What really is important? The psalmists told us a man's mere days are consumed as smoke; his days are but a shadow that passeth away.

What will you leave of yourself on earth? asked the pastor, preaching in the soft light of the sun through stained glass. The answer seemed clearest when a father stepped to the baptismal font holding an infant, who took a lively interest in her sprinkling and grumbled only when Pop blocked her vision of the congregation, upon which she wished to bestow an intent, wobbly-headed inspection.

After church, a fellow at a neighboring cafeteria table turned out to be Zack Cravey. Never have our political views squared and never has either of us minced words about it. But things that will endure beyond our days and differences don't change. "How is your family at Adel?" he asked. And we talked about his grandchildren.

At home in the quiet afternoon, the telephone rang. Our daughter's gifted, sweet-tempered piano teacher, Mrs. Prentice Hightower, had slipped into death in her sleep. As smoke, her days were consumed. What thing of importance remained? The tears of a child who loved her. And the magic of music, forming for a lifetime, in the stubby little fingers she taught. Where does a song, released into many children, and through them into their multiplying generations, ever end?

Children endure. Whatever is worth having must be put in their keeping. If battles must be fought for them, so be it. If burdens must be borne for them, let them be taken up, as Archbishop Hallinan and Atlanta's Roman Catholic community are shouldering them today.

They seek to build a village for dependent children of the church on a tract they own on Fairburn Road. Some real estate men object to use of the land and seek to block the building; they have a dim vision of the uses to which they should put their days. The churchmen are asking the Board of Aldermen to stand with the children. When the vote comes tonight, how can the aldermen stand otherwise? What do they wish to leave as a marker of their days?

And as the legislators return to begin voting on the governor's program for education, the question is the same. The bills are imperfect, the taxes unpopular, and the details require handling with care. But the program is to help children. It is a good day for Georgia that we have come down to this truth: That education must be made sufficient unto their day, not ours—or ours will pass, poorly spent, traced in smoke.

January 24, 1964
Young Men Please Note

It has been said, cruelly, that conservatives are admirers of dead rebels. A conservative organization, Associated Industries of Georgia, has disproved the saying. For the last three years the AIG has awarded its medal for Distinguished Public Service not to men who conformed to the status quo, but to living rebels.

The first winner, John Sibley, had all the comforts and honors that most men dream of when he presented himself at the fiery doors of the racial furnace in Georgia. He saw that public schools would close unless strong men stepped forward and held them open in the name of reason and justice. He rebelled against drift and placed his strength on the side of change. He prevailed, and was honored.

Bishop Arthur Moore received the second annual award—not for leading the Methodist Church toward confirmation of its comforts, but for recognizing that Jesus spoke for people who could not speak for themselves. The Methodists under his leadership moved up to a new dimension of courage and understanding. This did not surprise those who knew Bishop Moore as one of the early pioneers in recognizing the responsibility the white people of the South had to join with the Negro in a common elevation. As long ago as 1938 he was one of the signers of the charter for the Southern Regional Council. At the time, they called him a rebel.

Now Rep. Carl Vinson has received the AIG's third annual award. And what a rebel he is! A rural Southerner, he supported John F. Kennedy, as he now supports Lyndon Johnson, while others hid or jibed.

An armorer who helped build the American military establishment, he says, "Every shot that is not fired . . . is a victory in the war for peace."

A conservative who suspects government interference, he expresses faith that what the federal government will try to do is only that "which the people cannot do for themselves."

A Georgian bred, he warns us plainly that "there is no longer room in America for any form of parochialism or sectionalism."

An 80-year-old, with every right to defend things as they are, Rep. Vinson instead instructs us: "We either move forward or we fall backward. There is no such thing as maintaining the status quo."

As the small men sift through the sieve of history until the big men remain, standing alone, a truth recurs. The men who grow big usually have stood alone all along, presenting themselves at the breach in time of trouble—not hanging back to conform with the approving crowd. It is not surprising that such rebels turn out to be the honored men. It is just. They are Georgia's true leaders, for they used their power not to gain momentary approval for themselves, but to serve men who were less fortunate.

January 25, 1964
To Atlanta's U.N. Visitors

To the United Nations Subcommission on the Prevention of Discrimination and Protection of Minorities: Welcome to Atlanta. You will find no better American city to observe. Race relations here aren't as good as they ought to be but they may be better than some citizens of your homelands have thought.

This Deep South city is not trying to justify injustices that remain, but to rectify them. It is not boastful about the progress it has made, but is genuinely proud of it.

You are worldly and knowledgeable enough about the difficulty of social change to recognize what is real and what is not, coming as you do from Great Britain, the Soviet Union, France, the Philippines, Italy, the Sudan, India, the United Arab Republic, Chile, Finland, Mexico.

As a city representing the United States of America, Atlanta welcomes your appraisal.

You will find that during the past lone decade Atlanta has abandoned centuries of discriminatory custom and desegregated its swimming pools, libraries and parks; its train, plane and bus facilities, including its local city buses; its large department and variety store lunch counters and some of its best restaurants; its theaters, most of its good hotels and all of its city auditorium facilities; its public schools and colleges and some of its private ones; many of its churches and some of its hospital facilities.

You will find Negroes serving on the Fulton-DeKalb Hospital Authority, the Atlanta School Board and in the State Senate of Georgia, and you will learn that the first Negro boy ever admitted to the University of Georgia was graduated with high honors and is now studying medicine as the first Negro ever admitted to Emory University, a Methodist private institution. (The Baptists' Mercer University is also desegregated.) You will note that the Georgia Senate voted unanimously this week for a constitutional amendment to abolish the poll tax—a device that was still serving in some Southern states to retard Negro voting, though Georgia scrapped it in 1945.

You will learn that Negroes vote with complete freedom in Atlanta and have, in fact, become one of the great forces in electing responsible leaders such as Mayor Ivan Allen—and not by breaking away from the white moderates and the city's business leadership, but by allying themselves with that white leadership to form a progressive majority. Elected officials are in turn responsive to the rights and needs of all.

Problems remain. You may see demonstrators protesting those restaurants that still are segregated. The U.S. national government is committed to ending that, if local owners will not do so voluntarily. Job opportunities and housing needs are getting increased attention. Much remains to be done. In Atlanta, justice will be done. We would like the world to know it, for liberty and justice to all is a living American ideal.

January 31, 1964
Who's Out of Step in Atlanta?

In blunt terms this newspaper has denounced the lawlessness evident in SNCC demonstrations here. If it occurs again, it will be denounced again. If it has now abated, Atlantans can turn calm attention back to the problem of the city's segregated restaurants. Owners of these places have not abated their outburst of excuses.

They announce, "We still have the freedom of choice to operate our businesses as we see fit." But having that freedom, they have exercised it in ways that other Atlanta businesses have found to be unfit.

Why? Why is the private property argument right for restaurant owners if owners of other private properties in Atlanta found it wrong to discriminate?

Downtown theater owners had the freedom of choice to operate their businesses as they saw fit. They saw discrimination as unfit.

Most of the major hotel owners had the freedom to operate as they saw fit. They found it fit to end discrimination.

Owners of department store and variety store lunch counters had the right to do wrong on their own property. They didn't find it worthy to exercise such a right.

The Chamber of Commerce, speaking for Atlanta private business in general, has repeatedly urged the restaurant owners to cease discrimination.

All of these people are owners of private property, with the same rights and freedoms of the segregated restaurant owners. Yet the restaurant owners alone, in voluble isolation, claim it is fit to discriminate. For the damage they are doing to this city, and for the destruction of private property rights which they are making inevitable, they deserve no civic awards.

But it is important to note that this shortsighted view is held by only one segment of Atlanta's restaurant owners—a segment which has tried to cow the others by bullying, demagoguery and economic alarm. These people are the ones who deserve the lash of public opinion for what they have done to Atlanta.

But two other groups of restaurant men deserve credit, encouragement and public understanding. One is the brave band of leaders who desegregated last year and who stand as models now so the others can see it can be done if an owner is only determined to do it.

The other is the large middle group of restaurant owners who have come to see the folly of discrimination, but who have been whipsawed into inaction thus far by care-nothing competitors and their own doubts. Many of these men want to move, and with public understanding and support, will move as they increasingly discover the emptiness of the shortsighted segment's mouthing, and draw determination from their own judgments. May this be soon. The bullying segment has had charge of the others' reputations—and Atlanta's—long enough.

February 11, 1964
Visualize, Then Multiply by 391

You may not fully understand this piece until you have stood at dawn in a hot room lit to surgical brightness, heard a babbling man forced down into a chair, seen him buckled and strapped tight while he asked, "Will it hurt?" and watched spitting white arcs of electricity kill him in a kettle spout of steam. After you watch this obscenity once—as few have, besides us reporters—you are ready to review some figures.

Georgia has executed more persons in its human abattoir over the last 38 years than any other state in America.

Since 1926 Georgia has executed 391 persons, 314 of them colored.

Of these 45 were teenagers, 43 of them colored. Three were 16 years old.

One woman has been electrocuted. She was colored.

The number of people we have killed has declined steadily over the last four decades; in the years 1943–52, for instance, the lives taken numbered 128, and in the years 1953–62 the toll fell to 64.

Last year, after a 15-year-old colored boy was sentenced to death, the Legislature passed a law exempting any boy or girl under 17 from electrocution.

But Georgia remains the long-term leader in this dubious business of handing out the death sentence. Meanwhile such other states as Michigan, Minnesota, Wisconsin, Maine, Alaska and Hawaii are getting along with no death penalty at all. So are most European countries. New York, Oregon and North Dakota have restricted the death penalty. At least 19 state legislatures considered bills to eliminate their capital punishment laws in 1963, the AP says.

Perhaps it is time, then, considering Georgia's record, to ponder Rep. Wilson Brooks' bill to restrict capital punishment.

Rep. Brooks' original bill went too far, in my opinion. It would have abolished the death penalty outright. But without a death penalty to apply to nothing-to-lose life-term prisoners, how could you keep them from killing prison guards at will? The bill also would have made life imprisonment mandatory in place of capital punishment. But prison experts promptly noted that murderers, instead of being repeaters, are among the best risks on parole.

Rep. Brooks has now amended his bill to apply the death penalty for the killing of any guard or law officer, and would permit parole in life sentences in certain instances. He has served the state well by putting this matter on our consciences. Certainly a study commission should be set up, at the least, to come to grips seriously with the problem and to recommend a program that will drastically alter such wholesale execution procedures as Georgia has practiced.

If you have not seen a man led into a room and deliberately killed, visualize it. Multiply that by 391. Then compare it with the rest of the country.

March 27, 1964
A President, a Preacher

When President Lyndon Johnson stepped into the White House rose garden Wednesday and told a Baptist gathering that "no group of Christians has a greater responsibility in civil rights than Southern Baptists," he added an expression that was personal.

The civil rights cause demands prophets who are "unafraid of the consequences of fulfilling their faith," he said.

And to the consternation of the Secret Service, the president is understood to have expressed a desire to fulfill his own faith by flying to Birmingham, Ala., Sunday and standing with evangelist Billy Graham at a mass Easter worship that will be bi-racial.

Those responsible for the president's security were not as unafraid as he.

A Birmingham white citizens group has been petitioning the city government to bar the integrated Graham rally in 54,000-seat Legion Field, saying otherwise it will not be responsible for bloodshed. Dr. Graham, a Southern Baptist, refuses to preach if the service is segregated. The Southern president's remarks on Wednesday showed he agrees with Graham, and his privately expressed wish to go to Birmingham with the evangelist handed his security people a Good Friday jolt. Security requirements will ultimately determine what he does.

Meanwhile Billy Graham, who feels Mr. Johnson's Wednesday statement was one of the finest things any president has said yet, is going straight ahead with plans for his Easter rally, confident that "the Lord is going to handle it all."

He isn't going to Birmingham "waving a big red flag" or "aiming to ruffle feelings with my preaching on the subject." Just by being there at

Easter, and inviting any child of God to worship with him, Dr. Graham feels he will have served. His 2,000-voice choir will be about half Negro. Many Birmingham ministers have stuck their necks out to help arrange the meeting.

The service, as the evangelist sees it, will be "a testimony and a witness to the whole South, and to the whole world." He believes Birmingham, whose name has been blackened by some, can be an Easter symbol of redemption for all if its believing masses pray together.

"There are preachers and there are teachers of injustice and dissension and distrust at work in America this very hour," President Johnson told the Baptists Wednesday.

They seek, he said, "to turn back the rising tide of human hope by sowing half-truths and untruths wherever they find root. Help us to answer them with truth and with action. Help us . . . build a house of freedom where all men can dwell."

Meditating in North Carolina before leaving for Alabama for Easter, Billy Graham asked simply: "If the church can't help solve this, who can?"

May 3, 1964
Mr. President

The Ship's Lantern Is Still Lighted

WARM SPRINGS Nineteen Aprils have lit their glow to the laurel and azaleas on Pine Mountain since the president of the United States died here.

But at dusk each day a ship's lantern is lighted over the portal of the plain little house, and it burns through the night just as it did in Franklin Roosevelt's life to signify his presence within.

That great presence still is very much here. There is the table where he signed state papers, the room where he brought rural electrification into being for the vast American land.

He loved the Georgia fields and pastures where his cattle grazed, the woods of pine and hickory sloping down to a deep valley beyond the French doors of his living room.

Among Them

He loved the people he came upon in Georgia—the mule traders, the crippled children, the slow-spoken farmers who scratched for a living in the red earth. With hand clutch and brakes, the crippled president drove among them in his little open Ford, which is still here in his garage, encased in glass.

He found these farmers were paying four times as much for electricity as he paid at Hyde Park, in New York—yet nine out of 10 U.S. farmers couldn't even get electricity. So Roosevelt created and signed here, at Warm Springs, the REA act; today nine out of 10 rural homes in the United States have electricity.

The half-burned logs remain in his fireplace just as they were on April 12, 1945. Whose mind does not go back to that day, and to the place where he heard the sorrowful news? It came to me on a foggy morning in Germany, crackling over the radio of a medium tank. Men took off their helmets and stood silent. The news was hard to believe. It seemed Roosevelt had always been president.

A Portrait

Here is the brown leather chair where he was sitting for his portrait. Across the little plank-paneled room—the house has only six rooms—stands the portrait, unfinished. Beyond it is the president's small bedroom, and the single bed where they placed him gently. Death came two hours later. Outside it was April, with the dogwoods in bloom—a beautiful sight for a tired man.

His old Panama hat still lies on a shelf. Up an avenue of flags and stones from the 50 states, in the new museum, a 12-minute motion picture is run over and over for the visitors, and especially for the little children who never saw this remarkable man in life. There he is in the old hat—the quick smile, the intelligent glance, the huge vitality.

The children who never knew him react to his presence even in the dim old films. They walk with awe through his little house, catching reverence from their elders, perhaps—or maybe it's something more they catch. A sense of his great presence, continuing still.

Nineteen Aprils have come to the mountain. The ship's lantern glows through all the nights.

May 8, 1964
The President Must Have Help

Lyndon Johnson comes to Georgia possessed of the deepest presidential understanding of the South since Franklin D. Roosevelt, who lived much and died here.

FDR called the South "this truly American section." It contained, he noted, "a population still holding the great heritages of King's Mountain and Shiloh."

The region happened to be busted when Roosevelt said that. But he honored its worth as he set about restoring its means.

Now another president comes to a generally prospering Georgia, intent still on restoring its remaining places of poverty, and possessed still of respect for the South's inherent worth.

Georgia in turn has taken steps to merit that respect. As State Rep. James Mackay said Wednesday, "We are beginning to function like a state, and not like a province. It is giving us all a sense of belonging to our nation, which is a heartening and inspiring thing."

President Johnson comes as the spokesman for all Americans, not just Southerners. But he is in great measure dependent on the help of his fellow Southerners if he is to succeed in speaking for all Americans.

If Southerners quaver, cavil and quit on the first of their number to hold the presidency since the 1860s, he cannot succeed in convincing the country that Southern leadership is worthy of national trust.

In his guaranty of racial justice, he especially needs the South's help, not its hindrance. For he, too, is a Southerner. He is trying to show a still-doubtful nation that a Southern president can and will do the right thing. If his words are negated by Southern acts, he can be unhorsed by his own legion.

So it is that in a particular way President Johnson needs the hand and the help of the South. The South—both of its races—needs presidential understanding; they have that. He in turn needs Southern deeds to sustain his words. He is getting some from Georgia, which is determined to be a state and not a province.

There is a Baptist preacher in Richmond, Va., who has played a leading part in persuading that city to end racial discrimination (60 of Richmond's restaurants have stopped discrimination voluntarily compared to about 20 in Atlanta). Yet the preacher is from Ohio. Why did Richmond accept a Yankee's leadership? An old preacher told him when he went South, he says, to approach Southerners in only one way: "First, earn their love. Then speak softly to them." He took that course.

President Johnson was born with the affection of the South, and once in power he has spoken softly to us. As in Richmond, the response now is ours to make. I think the Southern president can count on this Southern state not to fail him.

May 27, 1964
The Changing Land

ADEL—Hot sun has dried the rains of the planting season. Yellowing tobacco has sent some farmers hurrying for the irrigation man. He puts a suction pipe in the farmer's water hole. The power takeoff of his tractor sucks the water to the field.

A gun-nozzle swirls white spray across the field and draws down the water hole almost to the bream beds. But the springs will fill up the little pond again. And the tobacco is greening up under the wetting. The South's richest resource is water; at last it's being used.

The small corn stands thicker in the drill than some old farmers like to see it. They used to thin the corn this time of year by pulling up every other stalk or so to leave growing room.

But nitrogen dressings and hybrid seed, together with irrigation if needed, can end the day when Georgia grew 35 bushels per acre compared to 75 in Iowa. Still, some farmers don't change lightly.

Many still are spacing the hills at about 8,000 an acre when the rich land can support a stand of 14,000 if plants are spaced a foot or less apart with a yard between rows. There's moisture and fertilizer enough for the thicker stand; the wind will shake more pollen from the tassels onto massed silks, and yields of 60 to 100 bushels beckon.

Cotton has come up and peaches are ripening. Pines are straightening from the twisting and breaking of the winter's freeze. Hogs root and grumble in fat indolence in the pens and cattle crop the grazing lands in growing herds.

Under the barn shed, rust cakes the fittings of old single-trees. Only the ghosts of patient mules who pulled them linger in the cobwebbed stable. For all their devotion, the land yielded less when they drew the plows. The time of water guns, nitrogen and clattering engines is better.

In town, with its light industrial jobs, there's another kind of abundance. The consolidated high school is graduating 103 youngsters—three more than Dr. James Bryant Conant specified as the ideal minimum. A 900-pupil consolidated elementary school assures continuing good flow to the high school. The children are better read and instructed than their fathers were. (The scattered elementary schools where their fathers studied only seven months out of the year are storage sheds now, or meeting houses, and some are simply gone.) These children study Spanish in the third grade.

It is very easy to believe, here among the neighborly people born of this kind land, that life is getting better with our passing years.

May 28, 1964
The Young Are Not Buying

CARROLLTON—Robert Kennedy ordered his driver to stop in the hot street when he saw a swarm of school children waving to him. He walked among them. They crowded close to touch his hand, jumping and pressing and shouting to him. Across the street, two old men under a grocery store awning didn't get up out of their chairs to look at him.

The attorney general drove on to the West Georgia College campus. A warm cheer went up as he mounted the bunting-hung platform under the shade of oaks. The audience was small but honest. Students predominated. He spoke quietly of his dead brother's beliefs, of faith and tolerance, and of the "consensus of good sense" that has guided America.

But it was later in the college auditorium when Robert Kennedy sharply struck new fire to an old fact: The Kennedy ideal speaks to youth. The new generation of Americans that identified itself with his brother finds itself in him also.

The students' questions were blunt and penetrating, weighted with the civil rights reservations they had heard as a staple of Southern oratory.

Kennedy's answers were direct and rough-edged, never tangential or slippery. And the students responded to what he said with profound, rolling applause that visibly startled him and then strengthened him.

It might be tempting for older Southerners who were not present to scorn this overwhelming student reaction as proving only the gullibility of the young and naive who do not yet understand things like property rights. If they do, they will simply be gulling and deluding themselves. These students had heard and pondered the George Wallace doctrine all their lives. Their questions reflected that. Kennedy's answers did not seem so much to create as to confirm their doubt about the soundness and rightness of the Wallace doctrine.

Kennedy was asked, what about the rights of states to handle their own racial matters? It would be "much better" if the states and not the federal government did it, he replied. But there continue to be some states "that won't deal with it." He excepted Georgia, and mentioned Alabama and Mississippi. "They have made it quite clear they're not going to do it."

Thus, he said, even though he considers it "unfortunate" that the federal government should have to act, "I don't see any alternative to it."

Neither, obviously, did an applauding majority of students.

What he had pointed out, of course, was the central weakness of the old Southern segregationist position, which sought to justify wrong instead of trying to rectify it. It was pretty clear here that the young generation is not buying that tortured old position. It did respond to a man who talked straight. This is a major Southern political fact.

June 9, 1964
What'll Rights Bill Do in Georgia?

If the Senate invokes cloture this week, and goes on to pass the civil rights bill, how will the new laws affect Georgia? The section on voting rights may not be noticeable, and for a laudable reason: In most of Georgia, Negroes already can register and vote freely.

The new law is designed to expedite court decisions on voting cases. It also establishes a presumption of literacy for a citizen with six years of schooling.

Principal effect will be felt in about 100 Southern counties—most of them in Mississippi, Alabama and Louisiana—where some 89 percent of voting age whites are registered, but only 8 percent of voting age are Negroes. Most Georgia communities have long since gotten out of this business of disfranchising Negroes.

The bill would authorize the attorney general to initiate desegregation cases involving school and public facilities for individuals who can show they are unable to do so themselves. Georgians have long since grown accustomed to such cases, brought from the Eisenhower years.

The bill would forbid discrimination in programs receiving federal grants and loans. This general precedent is already pretty well established in Georgia.

Employers and unions covering 100 or more employees, and whose activities affect interstate commerce, would be prohibited from discriminating in hiring against women, Negroes, or others solely on grounds of race, religion, national origin or sex.

The 100-or-more coverage would drop gradually until after four years it would cover employers or unions representing 25 or more employees. Employers would continue to set their own job qualifications; where sex or race is irrelevant they would simply be forbidden to use it as a sole cause for disqualification. Setting of any racial hiring quotas is specifically forbidden. Georgia, with Lockheed and other major companies, already has become a pioneer in opening up jobs for qualified Negroes.

The one title of the bill that will be most noticeable in Georgia probably will be the public accommodations section.

It forbids racial discrimination in hotels, motels, restaurants, theaters, gas stations and sports arenas. It exempts owner-occupied lodging houses that rent no more than five rooms. Neither does it cover sale or rental of private homes. Neither does it affect doctors, dentists, lawyers or others offering professional services.

Georgia cities have voluntarily made such a broad beginning that they already are pretty well accustomed to desegregated hotels, theaters, restaurants and public facilities.

On balance, the great progress this state has made for itself has prepared it to meet the new laws without severe dislocation. If other states had done as well, some of these new laws might not now be on the verge of passage.

June 29, 1964
It's a New Need for Bold Courage

WASHINGTON—Traveling the South and the nation on the eve of the Fourth of July, an American is heartened by the steadiness and quiet reason he encounters, though many people are troubled. Adjustment to the new civil rights law is about to test again the durability of the republic.

But the old national commodity of courage is still there—a widely held courage to face the unfamiliar honestly.

Here in the capital the agencies of government are casting the tools to enforce what Congress has overwhelmingly voted to make into civil rights law. Yet the primary aim still is not to punish but to persuade.

Businessmen like Julius Manger, who desegregated his hotels at Savannah and Charlotte, are shuttling across the country because the government has asked them to. They are offering advice to colleagues in the business world who might also comply voluntarily ahead of the new law if quietly assisted.

Great power to compel will shortly lie in the hands of the chief executive. "For once a law is passed, no man can defy it and no leader can refuse to enforce it," President Johnson, a Southerner, said Saturday. "If our laws are flouted, our society will fail."

Nevertheless the president at the same moment was recruiting another Southerner, Florida's LeRoy Collins, to be the government's official seeker of voluntary compliance in place of compulsion.

Southerner Brooks Hays, former head of the Southern Baptist Convention, was telling a religious gathering here that churchmen now have "a great opportunity," by encouraging voluntary action ahead of the law, "to live out our religious belief in the brotherhood of man."

All of the elaborate soft-speaking here in place of emphasis on the big stick reflects a Southern president's preference for implying power, instead of applying it. His success will depend on the South's willingness to reciprocate his courtesy with its courage. That courage is not likely to be supplied by politicians like George Wallace and Ross Barnett. Who, then, will lead and tell them at last to be quiet?

"Courage is required of the businessman in this crisis," says Walter F. Carey, president of the United States Chamber of Commerce. "He must face up to hostility and perhaps economic reprisals, but such demands are nothing new for him. Historically he is the risk-taker who lays the foundation for social and economic progress."

Historically also the South has a steady people, ultimately responsive to men who have the courage to be honest with them. The only real risk is to believe otherwise.

July 7, 1964
A Test Now of Christianity

". . . How, in God's name, do you reach them?" Reg Murphy of this newspaper asked that question in anguish. He had just returned from Atlanta's Lakewood Park on Saturday. There to cover the George Wallace–Ross Barnett speechmaking, he had been an eyewitness to the savage beating of two Negroes.

Whites had cornered the Negroes against a fence. They did not strike simply with their fists. They swung metal folding chairs, again and again, with crushing force against the bodies and heads of their human quarry. Murphy saw blood splash and spurt. "Kill 'em," people were screaming.

"I thought I was watching two men being killed," Murphy said. "I was almost physically sick,"

Policemen who braved blows themselves got to the bleeding Negroes in time, took them away from their butchers and sent them to the hospital. Murphy came to the newspaper office and tried to write quietly of the brutality he had seen, and the screams he had heard.

The frustrated, violent men, "have lost their way in their search for their kind of government," he wrote.

"Any sort of analysis would have to point out to them that they undercut their own cause—any other conservative cause—by such conduct."

At this point, quiet, analytical words failed Reg Murphy and he concluded his commentary with one shattering question. "But how, in God's name, do you reach them?"

That is a question for the men themselves, for their families, for their ministers—yes, and for the heedless, imported political opportunists who came from out of state to please them cheaply after Georgia's own responsible leadership had been honest with them. There is no alternative but compliance with the law, Sen. Herman Talmadge had said.

But how do you reach the people who smashed metal chairs against bleeding bodies, or people who cried, "Kill 'em" at the sickening sight? There are a few mean men in any society, of course, who can be reached only by the police, and convinced only by the chain gang. Recent outcroppings of violence at places where Georgians are trying to obey the law are a challenge to the professional honor of law enforcement officers, as well as to the honor of the state.

But what of those who are not basically brutal, yet who are swept along, when herd leaders inflame them, until lesser men's passions sway their own humane code?

Murphy asked, in God's name, how they can be reached. Perhaps the answer can only be in God's name, and through the counsel of those who preach in it, like Atlanta's Pastor Robert E. Lee. He told his flock Sunday that Christ has never been, and cannot be, served with "pistols and ax handles."

July 8, 1964
A Segregationist Speaks

When I read what Louis Dersey, 50, of Columbus had done at Lakewood Park in Atlanta, I telephoned him long distance. "You probably don't agree with my views on race relations and my opposition to Gov. George Wallace," I began.

"I certainly don't, Mr. Patterson," replied Mr. Dersey, who is a segregationist, a believer in Wallace and a member of the Columbus Citizens Council.

"I know you don't," I said. "But I wanted to say to you, man to man, that I admired the courage you showed here last Saturday."

When other white men began beating Negroes with metal chairs, Mr. Dersey shielded a 19-year-old white girl from the attack and took many blows while doing it. He later expressed disgust for the violence of a few, which "has given us a black eye nationwide."

"Mr. Dersey," I said on the telephone, "I think most people agree with you and me that this violence in our state is wrong. You and I disagree on Wallace and other things. But I believe the people who agree with you on those things would listen to your thinking about violence, when they might not listen to mine."

So I asked him to give his views and told him I would print them. They follow:

"I don't think it's constitutional for people to be told what to do with their own property. I think the civil rights law is unconstitutional. I'm against it. I believe we've got to legislate it out. Repeal it.

"The people who went up from Columbus to Atlanta with me felt the same way, I think. They're peace-loving people who feel they're being forced into things they ought not to be made to do.

"But they don't want violence. Lots of them had their families with them. Most thinking people don't want violence. It just hurts your cause. Of course you're always going to have some hotheads. I figure if you got 10,000 preachers together you'd have some fistfights.

"But I don't believe anybody had the right to beat up on those people. That girl didn't have much of an idea of why she was even there. You could say she had a right to be there. You could also say she and those others had no business going in there. It was a little like me going to a Black Muslim meeting in Harlem and expecting not to get beat up.

"But I don't think the white people down here ought to lower themselves to that kind of thing. I don't believe anybody had the right to beat up those people."

Mr. Dersey, a Citizens Council segregationist and Wallace backer, got a blow in the head from a metal chair, and several nasty phone calls, because he stood up for his belief and shielded a girl from physical injury at Lakewood. What he really stood up for, I think, was the honor of Southerners who are still segregationists but who don't believe in beating and hurting people.

July 28, 1964
Big Day in South Georgia

The South Georgia tobacco market opens tomorrow, and time turns back . . . My grandfather, a devout man, did not think the use of tobacco was a Godly pursuit. He said he never would plant the stuff on his land and he didn't. While it became South Georgia's cash crop supplanting cotton, he stuck stubbornly to his corn and peanuts, melons and peavine hay.

The abundance of field and garden loaded his family table with plenty. And nobody was making much cash off of any crop in the 1930s anyway.

But across the post road on our family farm, as on most farms in the flatwoods, tobacco was planted, watered, poisoned and suckered, cropped, strung, cooked and packed. And at this time of year the mule-drawn wagons, laden with the golden-cured leaf in burlap sheets, lined up through the nights outside the warehouse doors.

The creaking wagons moved their loads in the damp night air so the tobacco would be in good order. It was a magic time—sitting there at midnight with a sleepy mule team, waiting to weigh in a year's work and see it placed on the warehouse floor for auction. The neighboring sheets of tobacco from other farms looked alien and unfamiliar (and of course never quite as fine quality as one's own). It was the highest form of competition. In those days of graded tobacco, a farmer personally handled nearly every leaf of his harvest.

He developed an intense pride in the fruit of his work. He waited with unsteady breath while the passing lines of buyers inspected it, assessed it and made their bids. If he missed the final price in the auctioneer's singsong (as most of us youngsters did), he would hurry to each of his sheets and read the price tag, impersonally affixed but deeply personal in meaning to him.

To the buyers, who simply were purchasing a certain number of carloads, it was a routine moment. It was not a routine moment to the farmer who had nursed that tobacco, from the seedbeds (torn from new ground) at Christmastime, to this summer sale. Each leaf was nurtured by his skill and watered by his sweat.

The big check he drew at the warehouse window usually had to go to the bank first for cashing and settling up. Then came the division with the landowner if the crop had been raised on shares. And finally, in his pocket, was the free cash from his crop. It bought new shoes, new dresses, sometimes a car and rides at the carnival. The thrifty put some in the bank or invested in new equipment, ranging from a plowpoint to a better mule. It was the busiest time of the year for the merchants.

In many South Georgia cities it still is. Great machines have replaced the mule-drawn tobacco sleds in the fields; and thermostats control the curing heat that sleepless farmers once handled with wood-fired furnaces; modern truck engines have drowned out the comfortable clink and creak of an old mule's harness at midnight. But some of the magic remains on opening day.

August 21, 1964
Sanders States the New Issue

Gov. Carl Sanders said it. Attorney General Robert Kennedy echoed it. And the Democratic platform committee is indicating awareness of an abrupt shifting of issues in America: Civil rights per se is rapidly yielding priority to the issues of economics.

Americans have made their decision against racial discrimination. The next step, which President Johnson's anti-poverty bill anticipated, is to deal with the causes and the results of it, now that discrimination itself has been acted upon.

This is a major change. It will affect the political vocabulary for years to come. New words, fresh ideas and different efforts will supplant the worn terms of old debates.

Gov. Sanders put it this way: "I don't think there's any need to harangue about civil rights any more. The question now is how are we going to solve the problem this (civil rights) bill seeks to cure."

That means, in turn, how are we going to create an economy that will provide enough jobs for men, and how are men going to equip themselves to fill the jobs, and how are opportunities going to be opened up to put the qualified men and the job vacancies together. With rights guaranteed, a chance to make a living is the next step.

As Attorney General Kennedy said, the need now is not for more civil rights laws. The new challenge is "continued, unflagging effort toward economic opportunity."

Mr. Kennedy properly added a sentence that ought to be in the Democratic platform, where Gov. Sanders is trying to put something similar. Specifically speaking of race riots in the North as well as violence in the South, he condemned "lawless disregard of the rights of others . . . when it is used to deny civil rights and when it is used to obtain civil rights."

"What we need in our platform," Mr. Kennedy said, "is not so much a promise to seek new civil rights laws as it is a promise to generate the spirit in which our country can and will solve its racial problems.

The new civil rights act is being obeyed in the South with a readiness that most of us are not yet conscious of. Exceptions are in the headlines. But the history of this year will show it as a time of massive respect for law by the great Southern majority. All problems of discrimination won't cease at once, or perhaps in a lifetime. But the issue has been decided; the American people—and, most honorably, the Southern American majority—have shunned the path of lawlessness.

A great turning has come toward a new No. 1 domestic issue, which will be far simpler and less explosive than the old one because it will deal not with emotion, but with economics. The worst is over. Americans understand, and cope extremely well, with economics. They owe no man a living. When they cease to deny him one, the rest will be up to the man.

August 23, 1964
Old System Dies a Painful Death

ATLANTIC CITY, N.J.—"This IS the convention," said a White House staffer in the wings as the Credentials Committee met Saturday. What followed was drama played with the absolute clarity of sharp pain. For a Southerner it was not pleasant to watch.

The Mississippi men sitting there with their pale heads and sunburnt faces were the substantial, tough-gentle men all Southerners know and generally respect.

Yet here in an echoing cavern of the Atlantic City Convention Hall they were being stung with a terrible brand. They had stood aside, and let beatings, burnings, bombings and murder be committed while they denied guilt.

What made it painful was that they deserved it. It was doubly painful because they hadn't really looked at it that way before. Their closed society had insulated them from the accusing gaze of the race their political bullying had injured. Now the nation was staring at them. They couldn't have helped but look within.

There facing them stood Rita Schwerner. Her husband had been lynched in Mississippi and buried with two other men in a farm pond dam. "They have not even given me a death certificate," she said quietly.

Edwin King, a white Mississippian, told of the beatings and the attempted murder he had lived through because he dared differ.

Fannie Lou Hamer's breaking voice sang with power as she told of one man sitting on her feet and another on her head while a third beat her polio-wracked body in a Mississippi jail.

These stories and the others simply could not be denied. Nor could the society responsible for them be defended. This was no longer the atmosphere of a smoke-filled room, but of an execution chamber. Dispirited and shaken, the spokesmen for white Mississippi could say little in their own behalf, and they fumbled that. It didn't seem to matter what they said. Conviction was not in them.

It was clear that these white delegates legally deserved to be seated. Right or wrong, they still represented the Mississippi majority.

The real point of the Negro challenge was not so much to unseat them as to confront the members of Mississippi's white majority and expose them to themselves. This they did. It was a purging experience. Surely, after this, the shock of self-recognition in Mississippi cannot be fully assuaged by the ease-oil of slick demagogues. And the nation, which has been understandably shocked and angered by the Negro riots in the North, received due reminder of the other side of the thing.

As usual the drama of the moment tends to obscure what will be historically significant. Significant here is the fact that the Southern states no longer stood in confederacy to defend their most backward forces. Alabama and Mississippi stood alone. And this Democratic convention, placing heavy pressure on them to advance with the nation, may mark the last stand of their old element.

For the sturdy old men with pale heads and sunburnt faces are good men, not evil; they have simply been caught up in a system that will produce evil until their revulsion against its excesses, which were evident here, gives them the courage to change it. As their spokesman noted here, Mississippi has produced proportionately more Medal of Honor winners than any other state. They know how to die. Their challenge is to learn how to live.

December 15, 1964
Merry Christmas

SAIGON—This is one quiet word about the Christmas we are about to spend in Georgia. Value it, and thank the Lord for it. Especially for the life our children have, in warm houses, with clean clothes, and security from gunfire.

These people from Southeast Asia love their children too. You see the mother standing at the door of her rice straw house holding a baby to her breast as a supplication to the tramping troops—don't shoot this house.

You walk the streets of Saigon and find father and mother sleeping on the sidewalk at midday, with the little ones cupped between them. Many of the little ones don't have pants, much less diapers. The older children steal whatever they can pick from passing pockets, and smile.

Small sisters wash baby brothers in the muddy streams that pass their huts, bringing their drinking water and carrying their sewage.

In an isolated base at the foot of the mountains in the North, a U.S. colonel who drinks a great deal sits in his small room alone at night after a day of killing and plays Christmas carols on a tape recorder.

In the southern delta, a helicopter pilot, Capt. Tim Bisch, of Baraboo, Wis., opens a big bundle of letters that a courier plane has dropped in his barbed wire compound. His sister's child has taken a letter of his to Saint Anthony's sixth grade in Dubuque, Iowa, and Sister Gertrude Mary has sent back letters from the whole grade, written to soldiers of Capt. Bisch's company, with the hope that "sixth grade enthusiasm (a special gift from God)" will help the soldiers to "enjoy the coming days of Christmas—not in splendor but with more of the true spirit of the feast—the poor and the peacemaker's spirit of Christ."

The letters serve the purpose. Half a dozen tough pilots sit drinking beer and swapping the children's letters and they read every one, hungrily, and sometimes with a little fog in the eye.

"What the hell are you guys reading?" asked Capt. Al Iller, exec of the helicopter company, as he walked in on the preoccupied pilots.

A captain looked up at him distractedly from a sixth grader's letter. "Did you know," he asked, "that the Great Lakes are shrinking?"

In a quiet convent at the edge of their air strip at Vinh Long, five Irish sisters wash the filth of the streets from child prostitutes and feed them and pray with them as the birth date of the Redeemer approaches.

But here, and in most of the earth, babies die on the sidewalks and in the huts, and those who live to old age chew betel nut until their lips are red and their minds are drugged so that they do not have to look at the filth and hopelessness and death at their muddy doorsteps. Men with guns pass their dirt-floored houses at Christmas time. They would not take for granted what our children in Georgia are blessed with.

Civil rights demonstrators at the Old Post Office building in downtown Atlanta. By permission of the *Atlanta Journal and Constitution.*

1965

Thumping the Melon

January	President Lyndon Johnson is inaugurated. In his State of the Union address, he proposes an ambitious "Great Society" legislative program.
February	U.S. bombing raids in North Vietnam signal an escalation of armed conflict in Vietnam. Former Black Muslim leader Malcolm X is assassinated in New York City. Congress passes the Elementary and Secondary Education Act, requiring the withholding of federal funds from *de jure* segregated schools.
March	Alabama state troopers attack civil rights protesters preparing for a voting rights march from Selma to Montgomery. Following federal intervention, the march goes on as planned.
April	NASA launches *Early Bird,* the nation's first commercial satellite. President Johnson dispatches U.S. Marines to the Dominican Republic, which is in the throes of civil war.
July	President Johnson signs the Medicare Act. Adlai Stevenson, the U.S. ambassador to the United Nations, dies at age sixty-five.
August	President Johnson signs the Voting Rights Act. A major race riot in the Watts section of Los Angeles leaves thirty-four dead.
September	The Department of Housing and Urban Development is created, with Robert C. Weaver, the nation's first black cabinet member, as its secretary. Employees of several New York newspapers go on strike.
October	President Johnson signs a major immigration act that abolishes the discriminatory immigration quota system established in 1924. Congress passes the first federal anti-pollution bill regulating automobile emissions.

February 21, 1965
Despotism in the South

The Evil of Slavery Lasts Till This Day

Cassius M. Clay of Kentucky noted in 1856 that free labor among Germans in Texas was out-producing slave labor in cotton. This proved, he said, "that whatever is right is expedient."

Thomas Jefferson feared the economic penalty of slavery less than the judgment of a wrathful God.

"Indeed, I tremble for my country when I reflect that God is just," Jefferson said in his notes on Virginia. "The Almighty has no attribute which can take side with us in such a contest."

History shows both men read the heavens right. Slavery and its 20th-century remnant, racial exploitation, were depressants on the South while other regions were elevated.

Only now is the South emerging into the clear light of its full promise after nearly two centuries under the dark cloud which the British slave traders laid over it.

In the beginning the Southern states actually started ahead of the other regions. Theirs was the economic and political leadership in revolutionary days. They were better than even in the natural resources of soil, climate, rivers, harbors, minerals and forests. Theirs could have been the great ports and centers of manufacture, as well as of agriculture. What happened?

Commerce Shifted

The slaves came, and the South dealt with them. Slave ownership soon locked the landed owners to cotton and the land.

Commerce grew elsewhere.

Free labor also created an agriculture elsewhere that rivaled or exceeded the slave South's in most particulars by the time of the Civil War.

Undiversified and inert, the South inevitably fell victim to exploitation by the regions to whom it had ceded economic strength. High tariffs protected Northern manufactures at the expense of Southern agricultural exports. This whipsawing of the South, to which the economic invalidism of slavery laid it open, extended into this generation, when bald freight rate differentials still were strangling Southern manufactures.

The original sin of slavery compounded itself. Slave labor drove out much good free white labor to hunt a living in the West.

It discouraged immigration of the industrious European labor that enriched other regions.

It encouraged inefficiency because the slave and his hapless post-bellum successors, the poor white and Negro sharecroppers, lacked the spurring enterprise of ownership and self-interest.

Exploitation

The small oligarchy of slaveholders and their economic descendants controlled Southern politics educating few and using the passions of the poor whites against the black man to blind them to their own poverty and exploitation.

But what was wrong was not expedient. It was bad business, fated economics.

Worse, as Jefferson foresaw, a master-slave society could only loose "the most boisterous passions—the most unremitting despotism on the one part, and degrading submissions on the other."

"Our children see this," Jefferson said, "and learn to imitate it . . . The parent storms, the child looks on, catches the lineaments of wrath, puts on the same airs, gives a loose rein to the worst of passions; and thus nursed, educated and daily exercised in tyranny, cannot but be stamped by its odious peculiarities . . . with the morals of the people, their industry also is destroyed."

As the wrath born of slavery and its bitter aftermath flickers out only now across the South, the lights of industry and progress undreamed of are coming on.

February 26, 1965
Malcolm X Didn't Laugh

My memories of Malcolm X are personal. I saw him once. He was standing on the mezzanine of the Statler Hilton in Washington. He was the center of a sea of at least 200 Negroes.

It was the eve of the Washington March. Negroes from every area of America had come to stand before the Lincoln Memorial and testify, by their presence, to a belief in this country and its institutions.

Malcolm X stood on the mezzanine the night before, trying to convert all of them who would listen. I went up the stairs to hear him because his Black Muslim newsboys were hawking scurrilous hate-white papers on the street corners outside the Statler.

When I finally edged up face-to-face with him, he had been talking so long he was hoarse. But an inner spring of passion flowed on, untired. His eyes were amber, wise and shrewd. He was altogether an amber-looking man, even his hair. He said he hated every drop of blood he had inherited from the white rapist who had been one of his ancestors.

His genius sprang from the fact that he didn't look angry or outraged—just reasonable. He spoke with impassioned conviction that reached for effect, if not sincerity, and achieved it. To a Southerner who had seen his white counterparts, he was recognizable. To others he was impressive.

The Negro audience was intensely unfriendly. These people wanted to be part of America. That's why they had come for the Washington March. He wanted to separate, isolate, segregate them. They railed at him, accused him, denounced him, and he replied always with an unsmiling and disconcertingly intelligent equanimity. But always, he attacked.

"You talk about America," he said. "Why? You Negroes went to Korea. You threw yourselves up against those Chinese hordes. For what? I wouldn't fight for a country that had done to me what it has done to you."

Grumbles and jibes answered him. "Look at him," Malcolm X said, pointing to me. "Do you think that white man is your friend? He's a rattlesnake. He's ready to kill you." Beyond the finger pointing in my face were the malevolent amber eyes.

"Malcolm," said a stumpy Negro next to me, "you ought to come to Chicago and go into politics. You really ought to do that because you can dodge more questions than any Chicago politician I ever saw." Everybody laughed except Malcolm.

He was a man who may have forgotten how to laugh. The Muslims ran him out for cheering, in effect, when President Kennedy was assassinated. Now he is assassinated, and squalid wars ferment in the little corner of black America he tried to cultivate.

But the great, gentle and gifted Negro community he tried to alienate from America did not follow him, though it listened, judged and understood him just as whites understand and reject their own demagogues.

March 6, 1965
Georgia Has a Way with Words

When Bill Emerson of Atlanta was named editor of the *Saturday Evening Post* this week, it kept the honor in the Georgia family. The editor of that renowned national magazine who preceded Emerson was Clay Blair, a native of Valdosta.

And before Blair the editor was Bob Sherrod, who came from Thomasville.

The contributions of Georgia and the South to national public offices are elaborately noted—the World Bank's Eugene Black, from Atlanta; Secretary of State Dean Rusk, from Cherokee County; Adm. David L. McDonald, chief of Naval Operations, from Maysville; and so forth.

We like to connect our path of earth and sky with its native sons who bestride the wider scene.

But one fact often overlooked, in the Southern orientation toward public affairs, is the unusual extent to which Southern writing men move into seats of editorial power, as at the *Post*.

The *New York Times* is an example. Its executive editor, Turner Catledge, is a Mississippian. Its managing editor, Clifton Daniel, and its Washington bureau chief, Tom Wicker, are North Carolinians. Its national affairs editor, Claude Sitton, and its United Nations bureau chief, Tom Hamilton, are Georgians.

A fact that impressed me equally, however, has been the national fame that Georgia writing men have achieved by operating from their own home base. Two examples will suffice—two men whose talents brought the world to their own doorsteps in Atlanta.

One is Harold Martin, whose essays appear on these pages. As most *Constitution* readers know, Martin is perhaps the finest magazine writer operating in the country—a veteran staffer of the *Saturday Evening Post* whose travels have taken him from Commerce to Kuwait and pole to pole. He writes, as Red Smith said track star Mal Whitfield ran, like honey on hot biscuits. Instead of letting the world come and take him, he settled in Atlanta, went out and took the world as his beat.

The other example, of course, is Ralph McGill, who is quite possibly the best known newspaperman—the one best known personally to the most people—in the entire United States. Atlanta is his home. He let the world come find him. Living around him every day, as we do here at the paper, we forget to salute. But McGill, punching a typewriter in Atlanta, Ga., has won the world's respect and some of its highest honors, including the treasured National Medal of Freedom, the Pulitzer Prize, and an astounding list of doctoral degrees from Harvard, Columbia, Brown, Notre Dame, Colby, Oberlin, Brandeis, Mercer, Emory, Miami, Morehouse, Wayne State and St. Bernard.

It must be something in the water.

March 29, 1965
The Teachers Will Teach Us All

Memo to the GEA: As the son of a Georgia schoolteacher, I have indulged a lifelong prejudice: A deepgoing belief that schoolteachers are among the most dependable guardians of the civilizing virtues, and that if we only would follow half the guidance they offer us, this would be twice as decent a world.

So now that you've returned home from your convention in Atlanta, I'd like to bring to your attention a matter that has just come to mine, and leave it with you for your determination.

It relates to a problem that many of you will some day face in your communities—racial desegregation of your schools, not in terms of politics any more, but in terms of children.

The following is written by others, and left to you without my comment, because the important thing is what you think.

"The white high school in Douglasville was integrated by one Negro in January," the *Austell Enterprise* commented recently. It continued:

"The boy's parents are being paid to keep him there, but the 'pore' boy isn't happy and is failing all subjects . . . This is just one example of what Martin Luther is doing to his race."

Mrs. Nobbie H. Morgan of Winston, Ga., wrote a letter in reply to the editor of the *Austell Enterprise*. She asked him:

"Would you have this written about you or your child?"

She went on to question certain of the editor's facts. "Thomas Zachery's parents are deceased. This disqualifies your statement that the boy's parents are being paid to keep him there."

Mrs. Morgan continues: "My source was very conflicting with your (information) that Thomas was failing all of his subjects. If this is the case, and I understand it is not the case, let us glance at the other side: Can we place all the blame on Thomas?

"Can we say that you are completely without blame?

". . . We, not only Negroes, but those that are aware of God as a superior being, regardless of race, creed or religion, must continue to pray for the ignorant . . . 'What ye do unto my least ones, ye do it also unto me.'

"The Negro race is also one of God's creations," Mrs. Morgan concluded. "Thomas Zachery is a human being."

As the good teachers of Douglas County High School know, the challenge of desegregation falls very heavily upon them as well as upon the unprepared boy. Some critics who are not daily in the classroom may not fully grasp it, but isn't a child—any child—a human being to a schoolteacher? I expect I know your answer.

April 4, 1965
'Enjoy the Days,' Jack Wingate says

In the middle of a hard week, when Vietnam was on fire and Alabama was in a slow burn and steady rain was flooding out the paving of the parking lots at Atlanta Stadium, a good letter came. It quieted the spirit and turned the mind back to important things long neglected.

The letter was from my friend Jack Wingate, down at Lake Seminole in southwest Georgia, where he runs a really good fish camp and rears his children with the whole outdoors—sun, woods and water—for their back yard.

"Just a line to say hello and to tell you that the bass are on the prod," Jack wrote.

The cares of the day evaporated. Back came the musky smell of the dark water, the melodious plunk of a topwater plug at dusk, the staccato wake of ducks taking wing—peace.

"I intend to wade some this afternoon," Jack went on.

He took me bellyfishing one morning, in the silver light before dawn. We got out of the boat and waded chest-deep toward a drowned treetop. "Throw right up against it," he said.

Plunk. Pow! The bass had my popping bug and he zigged and he zagged and he bent the rod hard but he came on up and we looked at each other.

What Now

"What do I do with him?" I called to Jack. The water was up to my neck and the wiggling fish was staring me down.

"Hang him on your belt and catch another'n," he laughed.

Oh, it was really good to get that letter in the middle of a hard week. Listen:

"I intend to wade some this afternoon about sundown," Jack wrote, "when the old Master upstairs mixes up his sundown colors to paint the clouds.

"I don't care too much about the good fishing, just so I'm out on the lake."

It's really fine out on the lake. In the sundown hush the water smooths. It's quiet as a cathedral font, dark as wine. The boat carves soft patterns in still water. The sounds of wild things, settling in for the night, float out from the banks, and the western sky wears a sash of crimson, with ribbons of gold tied through purple clouds.

Smoke House

"I'm tickled to death with my new place," Jack wrote.

He built the new dining room himself—dug out the foundations, poured the cement, laid the bricks, right by the bait house. He built an especially fine chimney. It only smoked once, he claimed. That was, of course, when I was there. That didn't spoil my appetite a bit for the mountain of fried catfish with golden hushpuppies.

"I don't ever expect to make any money out of this thing," Jack wrote—the same way he says he doesn't ever expect to catch any fish, but he does—"just a living and to be able to fish, hunt and enjoy the days."

Enjoy the days. I leaned back in my chair for a minute and thought about the lake, the sundowns, the swift boiling strike of a bass on topwater, and the calm ease of spirit it puts in Jack Wingate. Enjoy the days. So many of us don't. And they go very fast.

Old Jack knows what's important, more than most of us. "Next time you're down we'll go to the pot holes wading," he concluded. Man, I sure want to.

July 5, 1965
A. T. Walden: A Great Southerner

In the hot August sunshine of 1963 a frail old man climbed slowly up the grassy slope to the Lincoln Memorial in Washington and turned, leaning on his cane, to look out upon one of the most profoundly meaningful sights in American history.

Tears stood in his dim old eyes as he observed the ultimate glory of his lifetime, the Washington March. His people, his race of Americans, had come up from the slave cabins to their national destiny and there they stood, a quarter of a million of them, proud at last and moving on.

The old man was A. T. Walden. He was not even asked to speak that day. He understood that. The younger men up there at the microphones had to take over sometime.

Mr. Walden was perhaps the Southern Negro's greatest single soldier manning the gap of history between Booker T. Washington and Martin Luther King. Yet he understood his day was over, his battles won, his sword passed on. He was content to stand there, leaning on his cane, and weep quietly at the great glory of what he saw.

Now the old man, my friend, is dead. There will be no other like him because the days of his battles are dead. But his valor, his commitment, his loyalty and his labors will not die. Mr. Walden was a brave man, a gentleman, and one of the great shapers and servers of the modern South.

He was the son of slaves. His father was poor, black and proud. The father found the industrious boy shining shoes one day on a street in Fort Valley, Ga., and took him home. He told the boy not ever to shine any man's shoes, not ever to get on his knees again except to pray.

The father also told the boy to work hard for the man whose wages he took because if he did not work hard, and still took the wages, that was stealing. The father's pride and strength got into the boy; white men sensed that and gave him respect, not trouble. He was bright and wanted to study law. Nobody encouraged him. "I asked my unlettered parents about it," he recalled.

"Austin," his mother answered, "if you think you can do it, then you do it."

He took his law degree up North, served as an officer in World War I, then came home to Georgia, which lacked Negro lawyers, because, as he said simply, "I was needed."

His client swiftly became the Negro race. In the 1940s it was A. T. Walden more than any other one man who fought through the courts for the Negro's right to vote, fought in the meeting places to get him registered, fought at the polling places to make that vote count.

He was the first great modern organizer of the Negro vote in Atlanta, Georgia and the Deep South, and armed with that weapon he had forged, he fought in the fore of the Negro's march upward toward a more decent life. Often alone, he commanded the formative years, the hard and very dangerous years, of an historic revolution.

He lived to see the day when Negroes did not have to come to him alone any longer. They found many other, younger leaders rising to the breakthroughs. But most important to A. T. Walden—and one of the reasons he wept in Washington—they found themselves. At last the slave's son could fold his steadying hands and go to his rest in peace knowing, in the words of the hymn he loved, Great God, they're moving on.

July 20, 1965
Always Thump a Watermelon

Fifty thousand Georgians went out to the State Farmer's Market here Sunday to get a free slice of 14,000 giveaway watermelons and in view of this show of public interest the record may as well be kept straight.

An accompanying story, or sidebar, in the paper suggested that the old system of thumping a melon "to hear it go 'thunk'" is a poor way to judge its ripeness.

That certainly is so. But the implication is present that some people think a "thunk" is evidence of ripeness. I do not know any such people.

When you thump on an unripe melon, it often goes "thunk," (Really green ones go "theenk.")

But when you thump a ripe melon, it goes "thuk."

And anybody can tell you that "thuk" is a pretty good way to judge its ripeness.

Mr. Roscoe Stewart of Thomasville, who was one of the melon authorities being quoted, quite accurately said, "you have to judge by the whole appearance of the melon" whether it is ripe.

But he is presupposing ideal conditions. He is supposing that you are stepping your way through the flowing vines of a watermelon patch on a nice summer day, examining the dozens of melons that rear their green humps above the foliage.

It is best to look for a big one, of course, for that indicates it is about grown. Next, you ideally bend down and inspect the little curlicue that rises above the stem like a tiny antenna. If it is green, go on. The melon is green. But if the little blossom is brown and withered, the melon is probably ripe. Take no chance.

Roll the melon over gently—don't tear it off the vine yet—and inspect the complexion of the light-colored belly that has rested upon the ground. Gourd-white? The melon may be green. But if it is yellowing ever so nicely, you've got yourself a ripening melon. Yet, is it really ripe? Next comes the final examination.

Springing middle finger smartly off thumb, thump it. If it goes "thuk," and you are a hungry small boy, break the stem loose from the vine right there in the hot field, look all around to be sure no adult is watching the waste, raise the sun-warmed melon surreptitiously and drop it on the ground hard so that it pops open, then reach in to the middle and pull out the cool, red-ripe, super-sweet heart and eat it right there in the sunshine . . .

But what plucked melon, resting in processed perfection in an air-conditioned supermarket, offers the prospector all these clues, these comparisons of melon-bellies and browning curlicues? His options are reduced. All he can really do is reach back into his memory for the tuning-fork accuracy of other days, and thump.

"If it goes "theenk," pass on; "thunk," only maybe; "thuk," take it home. Not to thump at all is unthinkable.

September 3, 1965
Votes Beat Bricks

Out of the confusion at Americus has come the clearest expression of the gain that will last when the tumult is forgotten. A Negro outsider, Dick Gregory, made the phrase on the day when 327 Sumter County Negroes, who weren't outsiders, registered to vote.

Speaking to the Negroes, Gregory said:

"You don't need a brick now. You've got the vote."

That said it very well. Casting votes instead of bricks, Americans have made a pretty good republic work. As the John Birch Society would say in its slogan about republics, let's keep it that way.

As long as some Americans were prevented from casting votes, the system was in jeopardy—a fact to which the Birch Society did not notably address its concern.

But Congress did, and enacted a law to end that danger.

Now Negroes all across the South are guaranteed the vote. The vote will guarantee the representation that no thrown brick can earn.

And so the registration of the 327 Negroes on Friday was symbolic of what will last after the temporary ordeal at Americus fades.

There is roughly one Negro citizen for every white citizen of Sumter County. Yet heretofore there were roughly seven white voters to each Negro voter registered there.

Now, as Gregory said to the Negroes, "You've got the vote."

Congressman Howard Callaway ratified that statement Monday when he assured Atty. Gen. Nicholas Katzenbach that he had reason to believe Sumter County would now readily register all Negro citizens who henceforth apply or reapply for the right to vote.

What this can mean, of course, is the election to office of public servants who will serve the public, not one part of it to the exclusion of another.

And that is a pretty hard system to argue against in a republic that is supposed to derive its powers from the consent of the governed.

This, then, will last. The casting of Negro votes in their just proportions can end much of the injustice where it has pinched most sharply—in the very regions of the South where denial of the voting right has been most flagrant.

Moving now to practice and not simply to profess fidelity to the principle of government by consent of the governed, those regions will be freed of fear and burdened conscience. And the Negro citizen, stepping into a new day at the voting booth, will find votes, not bricks, create just government.

August 22, 1965
Breakfast in Alabama

A part-time deputy sheriff had just killed one man and shotgunned another, authorities said, two counties away in Hayneville, and the Alabama highway east of Montgomery was busy. State trooper cars were out in number. It seemed a good idea to check into a motel and stop for the night at Tuskegee.

The passing traveler who then wants supper finds two restaurants on the main street, Pat's Café and the Lakeview truck stop. I started into the Lakeview. The door was locked, though people were eating inside.

Then I noticed the sign. This was the Lakeview Dining Club—Private: Ring bell. I pushed a doorbell button. Waitresses inside peered out through the glass and examined me but made no immediate move to open the door. A customer was leaving and when he opened the door I went in past him.

"I'm not a member of your club, but I'd like something to eat," I told a waitress.

"Sure," she said. I ordered eggs and bacon. It took a while for them to come. Two state troopers in blue-gray stared steadily at me from the adjoining table. Maybe my necktie marked me as a suspicious stranger. You could almost hear the troopers' mental notes clicking off, teletype style. Too well-fed to be a civil rights worker . . . too out-of-condition to be an FBI man . . . But who?

The troopers left. Before the eggs came, a Macon County deputy sheriff came. He wore a tan pseudo-stetson, brown short-sleeve shirt with a shoulder patch, silver flashlight on left hip and dangling pistol on the right. The pistol kept banging the glass cigar case as he went back and forth conferring with waitresses.

Finally he sat on a stool four feet away and watched me, not casually but deliberately. A waitress came over and whispered in his ear while glancing over her shoulder at me. He went back once to the telephone, banging his pistol on the glass case, and made a call. The waitress went to the door to let in somebody who had buzzed. She elaborately handed the couple a ticket. They handed it back. She put it back inside the cash register.

My appetite wasn't very good. When I paid the check to leave I looked at the worn card beside the cash register. "Guest of the Lakeview Dining Club," it said. "Good for One Day Only." Apparently you don't really have to join. You can be the guest of the truck stop club.

Lawsuits challenging this practice as a patent violation of the public accommodations law are under way. But upon getting up the next morning, Sunday, I wanted some breakfast then, not sometime later. Not wishing to alarm the deputy sheriff again, I skipped the Lakeview and went to Pat's Café. "Breakfast Being Served," said a sidewalk sign. But the place wasn't open. Even if it had been I wouldn't have bothered. "Ring Bell," said a message at the door. Pat's Café was not Pat's Dining Club.

I drove all over downtown Tuskegee but there wasn't any other place to get a cup of coffee.

Glad to be under way with or without breakfast, I headed for Georgia and crossed the Chattahoochee before I got a cup of coffee and a great sense of relief.

September 3, 1965
Whose Law? Whose Order?

Six hundred state troopers moved into Natchez, Miss., Thursday to keep the peace, which is translated by the Negroes and the whites of that unhappy town to mean keeping things the way they've always been—whites up, Negroes down. "Natchez is not going to be another Los Angeles," said Klan Dragon E. L. McDaniel. The point is, Natchez is Natchez.

Let those who were quick to condemn the Negro predators of Los Angeles—and this newspaper unhesitatingly condemned them—let us take a look now at Natchez, and talk more about law, order and peace.

What kind of peace is it that the 600 troops will keep?

The record of Klan terrorism and Negro fear in that river city is a stain on the South.

Earlier this year I had a chance to converse with some citizens of Natchez—the police chief, the sheriff and the mayor as well as some Negro citizens of that place.

The police chief confided that he had been "impressed" with the quality of people he observed at an open Klan rally in the ball park.

The sheriff, admitting Natchez had been having a lot of bombings, was asked if he knew who had been doing the bombings, and he said he thought he did. Then what was he waiting for? He wasn't sure he had enough evidence to make arrests.

The mayor was a pleasant little man of Lebanese extraction, John Nosser. He had hoped to stop the bombings through negotiation and conciliation. So he called in Klan leaders and tried to negotiate and conciliate.

Shortly thereafter the mayor's home was bombed. Damage was estimated at $10,000.

A meek Negro janitor at a Natchez plant displayed both wonderment and puzzlement as he told what had happened to him. He wasn't a civil rights worker of any sort. Yet he was singled out of traffic in the city one day, apparently at random, and taken for a ride by white men into the fastness of a nearby national park. The only reason he could think of to explain what happened then was that he was simply a Negro. His story was supported by medical evidence: He was beaten with whips by the white men until he called out to them that if they beat him any more they would kill him. They stopped beating him and made him drink a bottle of castor oil. Then they told him to run and fired a shotgun blast at him as he ran for his life through the forest.

The terrorism has not been stopped. Last Friday a Negro NAACP official, George Metcalfe, was severely wounded when his booby-trapped car blew up. Subsequent Negro demands include such a simple one as asking that the city at least denounce the Ku Klux Klan.

Instead of that, Klan Dragon McDaniel has openly announced that the Klan is armed. The governor has sent the troops to keep the Natchez peace. To the Negroes of Natchez, that is some peace.

Of all men who demand law and order in Los Angeles, it must be asked what kind of law, what kind of order, they are for in Natchez.

October 9, 1965
The Face Behind the Bus Window

"The picture on the front page of the Thursday *Constitution* tells a sad story," says a letter from a wise and distinguished educator, who has devoted a valuable lifetime to the college education of Georgia's young.

The picture was the one that showed state troopers dragging a white youth and a civil rights worker apart in Taliaferro County. In the background, behind the violently struggling figures, is a school bus, and from the windows stare the uncomprehending faces of many little children.

"What are these children at the bus windows thinking?" writes the educator.

"How will their future be shaped by what they saw?

"What did they think about at school Thursday when some very fine lady tried to teach them to read, spell and learn the principles of United States history?"

Any Georgia teacher can answer those questions. It was not a good school day for the children. Could anyone expect them to keep their minds on studying a civics which holds it self-evident that all Americans are created equal when through the bus window they had just seen force and violence used in an effort to perpetuate inequality?

"We ask ourselves, what does the future hold," writes the wise professor.

"Some things impress one person, some another. But nothing printed recently has held more tragic consequences." The children's faces at the bus window should haunt us all.

"Maybe it is because I am about ready to retire. But it came to me that maybe one of these young faces would be on this campus in 10 to 15 years from now," the educator said.

And by the time those young people enter the college class of 1975, they will be looking back over a long decade at the positions they are now seeing their parents take.

Will they be proud of the stand their parents took in this time of transition, when courage and humane judgment were the qualities most needed to help the Negro race through its ordeal of change?

Or will some of them look back over this decade, after segregation has become as unworthy an anachronism as slavery, and find the stand their parents took a source of shame to them?

The wide-eyed faces at the school bus window were very young. Time had marked little upon them. But it will write rapidly, as the educator knows. By the time they are old enough to understand the terrible scene they saw last week, they will be living in an era when unequal treatment of Negro school children is remembered as an indefensible curiosity. And in that light they will pass judgment on what their parents are saying now.

Julian Bond sits as other Georgia state legislators are sworn in. By permission of the *Atlanta Journal and Constitution*.

1966

The Savage Difference

January   The Georgia legislature refuses to seat newly elected state senator Julian Bond, a black SNCC activist.

March   Major demonstrations protesting American military actions in Vietnam are held in Chicago, Boston, San Francisco, and other American cities.

April   The SCLC board calls for American withdrawal from Vietnam.

May   Radical activist Stokely Carmichael becomes chairman of SNCC.

June   In *Miranda v. Arizona,* the U.S. Supreme Court rules that accused criminal suspects must be apprised of their legal rights before interrogation. The United States begins bombing raids on the North Vietnamese cities of Hanoi and Haiphong. James Meredith's one-man civil rights march through Mississippi ends when he is shot on the second day; the march is completed by SNCC, SCLC, and CORE activists, some of whom voice the slogan "Black Power."

July   Major racial disturbances break out in Chicago and six other American cities. CORE officially endorses Black Power.

September   After several days of interracial violence in Atlanta, Black Power activist Stokely Carmichael is arrested for inciting a riot.

October   Congress passes the Model Cities Act, a major piece of President Johnson's Great Society legislative plan.

November   President Johnson signs the Clean Waters Restoration Act. In the midterm elections, the Republican Party gains three seats in the Senate and forty-seven in the House of Representatives. Republican Edward Brooke of Massachusetts becomes the first black U.S. senator since Reconstruction. In Georgia, the ultrasegregationist

Lester Maddox is elected governor. In California, conservative
Ronald Reagan is elected governor.

December   The U.S. Supreme Court overrules Georgia legislators who had prohibited black civil rights activist Julian Bond from taking his seat in
the state senate.

January 14, 1966
An Admission of Prejudice

Some new growth may yet sprout out of the devastation of last Monday's Julian Bond blowup. In the calm aftermath, many legislators are
bound to have second thoughts about the justice of throwing the young
radical out of a seat he had won simply because they objected to things
he had said.

That's pretty hard for an elected official to justify in this country of
free speech. If they acted out of fidelity to the country's institutions,
what about that institution? There will be long thoughts.

Among Negroes, too, there are signs already that SNCC has over-
stepped. In the distant past there used to be cynical statements among
white politicians that if you ain't for stealing, you ain't for segregation.
SNCC's effort to tell Negroes that if they ain't against the Vietnam war,
they ain't for integration makes just about as much sense.

While condemning the motives of this country is one thing, dissent is
another, and dissent with U.S. policy in Vietnam is entirely legitimate. I
simply dissent with the dissenters, and most emphatically with those
who seem to feel there's a valid connection between defense of Negroes
at home and surrender of peasants in South Vietnam.

Some of the U.S. military units that shielded Negroes against Klan-
type violence in Little Rock and Oxford are now shielding South Vietnamese from Klan-type violence of the Viet Cong in Da Nang and
Pleiku.

The American government that determined long ago to defend Negroes against intimidation and forcible subjugation in this country is the
same American government that is telling North Vietnam it cannot and
will not be permitted to forcibly subjugate the South Vietnamese
people.

U.S. policy is to give South Vietnamese their freedom to lead the lives they wish. Viet Cong policy is to inflict upon them the life the Viet Cong wishes to impose, and to do it in ways familiar to the night-riding bullies who imposed their will on frightened Negroes until the United States government said stop.

I do not expect SNCC to see it this way, or try to. But I suspect a majority of Negroes in this country do, and that they aren't going to buy the SNCC propaganda that if they ain't for surrendering Vietnam to forcible seizure, they ain't for Negro freedom. In my view, it doesn't make sense.

I will readily admit that my view is colored by the fact that when I was in Vietnam, seeing hospitals and schools and medicines this nation was providing, in villages where Viet Cong terrorists were killing women and children with grenades, one of the U.S. officers I met was training village militia in how to defend themselves against the terrorists, and he believed deeply in the worth of what he was doing, and he was a Negro.

And the morning when a helicopter dropped me and a bunch of little yellow South Vietnamese infantrymen into a valley west of Hue, where the Viet Cong immediately shot at us, the left door gunner who did a great job of beating up our landing zone ahead of us, with an M-50 machine gun bucking in his lap, was a welcome, wide-shouldered Negro.

So yes, I am prejudiced when anybody tries to tell me Negroes don't understand or won't fight that war. SNCC is wrong.

February 12, 1966
The Negro People Thought It Out

Net yield of the Legislature's refusal to seat Julian Bond is bitter fruit. Bond's dubious views are generally overlooked and he is hailed as a martyr throughout the world. Georgia's progressive efforts are overshadowed and the state is widely stigmatized as a political primitive.

For the first time in the nation's history the judiciary has asserted the right to judge a legislature's decisions with respect to its membership qualifications.

Racial divisions are widened.

Confusion of issues is deepened.

Demagoguery is loose again, renewing its erosion of respect for American institutions. (There wasn't much difference in the degree of contempt Bond showed Thursday for the federal judges, when he suggested they were "unwilling" to protect the democratic process, and that shown by Lt. Gov. Peter Zack Geer, when he said he was heartened to find the judiciary following the law "for a change." Demagoguery, separate but equal.)

Most of this mess would not exist if the Legislature had censured Bond to its heart's content but then had defended his right to be wrongheaded and put him in his seat.

Instead the legislators drove him from the field and "t'was a famous victory."

"Another such victory over the Romans," said Pyrrhus, "and we are undone."

One impressive and hopeful fact does seem to be emerging, however, due to the continued assertion of the great good sense of most American Negro citizens.

They have energetically defended Bond's right to be wrong, and his claim to his seat in the chamber to which he was elected.

But they have not, in any appreciable mass, bought the curious goods SNCC tried to sell through him—that if they weren't against U.S. foreign policy, they weren't for civil rights.

That hasn't caught on, in spite of the impetus the Legislature contributed to the SNCC effort.

Bond is famous now, but famous primarily as a victim of expulsion from a Southern legislature, not as a sensible commentator on the Vietnam War.

So the victory—and it is about the only plus to come out of this damaging episode—belongs to the Negro people of the country who refused to be rattled off balance by the demagoguery of segregationists or SNCC.

This quiet fact, I expect, will encourage Secretary of State Dean Rusk as much as today's open demonstration in Atlanta Stadium in support of U.S. efforts in Vietnam.

May 2, 1966
"What Will They Think of Me?"

She had the kind, intelligent face of a good schoolteacher. A woman of middle years, she had risen before daylight on Saturday morning and ridden the Greyhound bus a long way to shop in Atlanta. "I tell my pupils it's good to start early in the day," she said. "It's the quiet and pretty time."

In her shopping bag she had a French textbook and a long-playing instructional record in French. "I want to take the National Teacher Examination and I have to review my French," she said. She teaches high school English. She is a graduate of Clark College.

Casual conversation indicated she was one of those quietly conservative persons who disliked the rancor of civil rights demonstrations. She worried that colonialism might have ended too soon, leaving immature societies without security.

Since she was a Negro teacher, it seemed logical to ask her how she felt desegregation was going to work out in the schools of her small Georgia city.

A look of uncertainty crossed her face. "It will work out well—is working out well—for the children," she said. "But . . ."

But what?

"There is talk," she said, "that the last teachers hired in our school may be asked to teach in white schools this fall, and I'm one of the newest on our faculty."

"I don't know," she said. "I guess I'm afraid. What will the white children think of me?"

Wasn't she a good teacher?

"Yes," she said quietly, "I am a good English teacher. But when I wonder what the white children might think, looking at me, I feel very timid."

Wouldn't white teachers feel the same timidity about facing Negro children?

"Oh, no, they should not," she exclaimed. "Our children want them. They've heard white teachers are better than we. They tell us so. White teachers would know they were wanted."

Wasn't her own doubt based more in her own mind than it would be in the minds of white children?

"I suppose so," she said. "I suppose that if I showed them I loved them, and taught them well, they would respond as children. And I would love them—I love every child. Still, I would feel very timid the first day."

Would she set aside her fears and try, if so assigned?

"Yes," she said.

She added: "But if I'm not assigned to a white school, and a white teacher instead comes on the faculty of my school, I will tell you this. I am going to welcome her, and guide her, and help her, and offer her my friendship and my prayers from the very first day."

May 3, 1966
The Faculties Hold the Key

As forced exclusion of Negro children from white schools ends in Georgia, a harder problem remains. How can children who exercise their freedom of choice to stay in inferior schools be given educational quality?

To say that all predominantly Negro schools are inferior to all predominantly white schools would be a misstatement of fact. But to say that, in general, most of them are, is simply to state an assumption on which the primary argument for desegregation has turned.

And since a de facto dual school system will remain physically for a long time after a racially segregated school system is dead legally, the problem has to be examined.

For all Negro children in the state cannot transfer into white schools. Not even the bulk of them can; there isn't physical room to hold them. Nor can the state afford simply to vacate the Negro school plant, which in many places is on par with the white plant.

To say this problem can be resolved by arbitrarily forcing a quota of white children into swapping over from a *superior* white school into an *inferior* Negro school violates the very precept that the white South has spent nearly three centuries coming to accept, namely, that one element of society cannot lift itself up by pulling another element down.

It was unfair for white children to be pulled up during all these years at the expense of Negro children being pulled down. It would be equally unfair for Negro children to be pulled up at the expense of white children being pulled down in their educational chance.

Desegregation is working beneficially precisely because it offers every child now the prospect of going upward. Arbitrary assignment of some children to go downward in order to make room for others to go upward would raise an entirely new question, of severe implications.

What, then, can be done to raise up the inferior schools to a superior status, so that no children assigned to them, regardless of race, will be relegated downward to educational inferiority?

That seems to be the logical next step. If the proposition is accepted that most (though not all) of the presently inferior schools are predominantly Negro schools, then the primary need will be to upgrade these schools.

In many places that is primarily a matter of improving poor teaching, so as to break the cycle that produced the poor teacher.

Some Negro teachers, it goes without saying, are excellent teachers. But many have not had the chance, the education or the experience to be, and aren't. Only recently have Negro teachers been permitted to attend teachers' meetings with white teachers; only now can they even observe the patterns and techniques common in white schools. Federal aid, to buy materials and pay remedial specialists, is vitally important. And against this background the overriding importance of faculty desegregation, with finest teachers going to inferior schools, can be seen clearly. That is the point at which the true drive for educational equality most practically begins, after the present racial equality struggle ends in gains for only a few.

May 7, 1966
Can a Skyline Be Segregated?

Word that yet another new office building may be added to Atlanta's skyline—this one built by the big Negro-operated Atlanta Life Insurance Co.—tells its own story. Negro entrepreneurs are an integral part of Southern business, and they share in the new problems as well as the new opportunities in the region.

Urban renewal, for instance, has redistributed a substantial portion of the Negro population in Atlanta's center. This process has disarranged the customer patterns on which Auburn Avenue's Negro businessmen depended in the old, set day of segregation.

What should these businessmen do—desert the downtown to follow their old customers? Or stay downtown, renovate Auburn Avenue, expand service and bid for a share of the general trade of both races?

Is there any long-term reason why the substantial Negro-owned bank, Citizens Trust Co., should attract white borrowers and depositors to Auburn Avenue? Paschal's Restaurant has long since attracted white diners to Hunter Street.

What about the professional buildings? "Negroes in the South have lacked risk capital," says the Urban League's Clarence Coleman. "You find doctors and dentists operating out of old nickel and dime structures built a long time ago by Elks or Masons. When the risk capital is put together for multi-story buildings, where should the Negro investor build—back on old Negro Street, or downtown?

Atlanta Life's consideration of Auburn Avenue for its new building site gives one answer to Mr. Coleman's question.

But there are many questions. Negro businessmen all over the South are approaching a time of basic decision—shall they follow the trade of a shifting Negro population or strike out now into the general competition for the customer's dollar—any customer?

The National Urban League, together with the National Business League, recognizes the crisis that social change has bought for Negro entrepreneurs. Here in Atlanta they are calling together Negro businessmen, deans of business schools and students from all over the South for an Economic Development Institute May 18–20.

Assistant Secretary of Commerce Eugene P. Foley will speak. Panels will explore sources of capital, business education techniques, business opportunity in the wake of urban renewal, and the rest.

Not only will Mayor Allen address the institute, but the executive vice president of the Atlanta Chamber of Commerce, Opie Shelton, will introduce the keynote speaker, National Urban League Director Whitney Young, which indicates pretty clearly one attitude that helps make this a booming town for businessmen—any businessmen.

June 7, 1966
Part of It Could Happen Anywhere

"Oh!" cried James Meredith, as the gunshots beat him down to the Mississippi pavement. "Oh!" Cry it for the white South, bleeding brother. You can only die with a torn body. The white South must live with its sick soul.

"We're no different," the white Southerner wants to say.

Aren't we?

The savage difference is there to look at. See whose face is reflected in the puddle of blood.

"But people get shot anywhere," we want to say. Yes, the president himself was shot by a madman.

But the savage difference that does still shamefully separate the South from other regions is that nobody expected the president to be shot.

Meredith expected he would be.

The president went to Dallas, confident that he would live. Meredith walked into Mississippi fearing he would be killed.

That is the fear Negro Southerners must always remember, and a fact the white South has tried to forget. It will not be forgotten.

What a terrible weight rests on this land. Not primarily because some weak, inflamed mind turned murderous. That can happen anywhere.

What does not happen anywhere else but in the South is the sustained inflammation of those weak, uncomprehending minds by men who know better.

That is the savage difference. That is the unspeakable unconcern.

Every Negro in the South has had to live like Meredith, day in, day out, with knowledge of the danger those weak minds present to his life.

When Negroes have turned to the strong white minds of the South for safety, what have those minds offered? Have they reduced the inflammation with calm counsel, powerful example, concerned votes?

No. The majority have not. They have listened when racists orate, be they parlor brand or stump; they have used power and substance to install emotion-searing demagogues in office; they have closed their own doors to Negroes instead of setting examples of open minds; they have conversed agreeably about conservatism and the Constitution while the Negro has run for his life.

That was the point of Meredith's walk into Mississippi. He was angry with himself for being afraid. He felt less than a man. So he walked down the road and presented his life. His safety at the moment passed into the keeping of the strong white mind of the South.

That mind had shirked its duty. Not just to Meredith. To itself. It had evaded, alibied, caviled and quit; it had sought to justify, not rectify, the fearful plight of the Negro. And by the power of its honored example, it had loaded the weak man's gun.

The gunman pulled the trigger. That much could have happened anywhere. The savage difference lies in the rest of us, and we won't even be arrested. We only have to live with the knowledge until, in God's own time, we assume responsibility.

June 30, 1966
"Thank God for Dr. King"

A reporter returning from the strange civil rights march through Mississippi offered a sober comment. "You've heard it said that the day would come when white Southerners would be saying 'Thank God for Martin Luther King,'" he said. "Well, you'd better believe it, that time is now."

Dr. King spoke sharply in Mississippi with the radical "black power" fringe roughly grouped around the Student Nonviolent Coordinating Committee. The ensuing contest for leadership of civil rights activists will set a fateful course in the nation.

The new management of SNCC indicated in Mississippi that it is out to detonate the explosive that has been compounded of racial ills. Members of the group desecrated the American flag, incited violence and counter-violence, chanted "black power" in the Klan context of "white supremacy," and heedlessly obscured or even ruined the effect of a march that otherwise would have been certain to advance civil rights following the shooting of James Meredith.

The display "helped Mississippi get off the hook," as Dr. King said. Suddenly it was white Mississippi that was winning points for passivity and restraint in the face of Negro taunts and ugliness, instead of vice versa. The very rules under which the civil rights movement took its effect seemed to have reversed sides.

But it does not appear that Dr. King proposes to stand idly by and see his dream of integrated Americanism shattered by the divisive folly of black nationalism.

He understands the Negro impulses of frustration and desperation which the bitter leaders seek to exploit. But he also comprehends the harvest of bitterness, which is, as the segregationist South learned, self-defeat.

His own way is direct—his courage and credentials are beyond question—but it is effective because he operates from a deep faith in his fellow man and in the American system.

Whether his appeal to faith and reason, in addition to courage and nonviolent action, will now be adequate to sustain his leadership in the face of the heedless and embittered exponents of chaos will determine much of what is to happen next in the troubled cities of the nation.

Dr. King has drawn the line for American Negroes between great hope and grave folly. But American whites will determine whether he succeeds or fails in standing that ground. Only they can fulfill the hope he promises.

July 15, 1966
"Black Power" Is Weakness

Accounts of the Spelman College speech by the "black power" man, Stokely Carmichael, report his saying to Negroes, "I think you can't speak from weakness," and that is right.

Labor had to organize in this country, Jews and Catholics had to organize. Nationality groupings had to organize their strength, and Negroes are having to do the same in order to gain their rights. They cannot speak from weakness.

But Carmichael does.

His prescription for getting "white people off our backs" is a weak one. If Negroes were weak-minded enough to follow his anti-white racism, as some Southern whites have been so long misled by anti-Negro racists to do, such weakness of logic would produce the same result it produced for white Southern segregationists. It would get more people on their backs, and off their side.

Carmichael's addled idea of how "black power" might be exercised politically is summed up in his quotation:

"You go to the man in power and say, 'Look, baby, I got 5,000 votes and either you pave this road—or else.'"

In Alabama recently, where Negroes tried using their voting power in polarization, polarized whites replied, "Look, baby, I got 50,000 votes," and elected Lurleen Wallace. Some black power. And the implication of everything Carmichael says is that he would be content to polarize Negroes and pit them in a power struggle with the white race.

To polarize the Negro vote is political weakness, not power. It is a minority vote. Like labor and the rest of the power groupings in America, the Negro vote must work in concert with other groupings to achieve any power at all. A minority can't secede and expect to impose its will on the majority; the white South learned that some time ago.

Moreover, before men in political power can be told look, baby, anything, the fellow doing the talking has got to have the votes. Negro voter registration in Georgia is lagging dismally with only 10 days remaining to register for anyone who intends to vote for a candidate for governor in the Democratic primary.

Yet very little is being done to truly organize a registration drive that would give form and substance to black power. Trading on emotion, the Carmichael set is instead trying to sell to unknowing Negroes the illusion of power from a position of weakness. The white South has heard a lot of this from its segregationist politicians. Remember when we were assured we had the power to defy the Supreme Court? We didn't have it. We had the same windy weakness Carmichael has. The fact that his worthy end is to improve the lot of Negroes, in place of the Southern Klansman's unworthy goal of repressing them, is bound to be obscured and lost if the Klansman's means of hatred, viciousness and violence are adopted.

Violence . . . nonviolence. "It's irrelevant," Carmichael said. Violence is not irrelevant. It brings repression, not reward. It will not be accepted in this country. It is, as the example of violent Southern whites should have taught Carmichael by now, a foredoomed weakness.

September 7, 1966
A Day to Forget

A fume of tear gas still stung the eye occasionally. It made Ivan Allen look as if he had been weeping.

The mayor stood in a pool of glass fragments in the middle of Capitol Avenue with his shoulders slumped wearily. A police car with blue light flashing passed on one side of him, and a Grady Hospital ambulance with a red light passed on the other.

He lifted his reddened eyes to the porches and looked at the Negro men, women and children whose rights he had long fought for at the risk of his own political life. They looked back at him.

On the upstairs balcony of a bleak apartment house—"four rooms, will redecorate, $59.50"—a girl of about 15 jerked and shook idly in a silent dance.

"They don't know," Mayor Allen said gently. "They just don't know."

But the SNCC leaders knew. When Stokely Carmichael's crowd finally got a police shooting to play with, they stirred up those men, women and children as skillfully as white demagogues used to get a night ride going.

Like the old white mobs, the rock-throwing Negroes didn't have a very clear idea what had hold of them Tuesday. Demagogues had hold of them. SNCC was in charge.

SNCC comes in on a scene of trouble like an ambulance. But not to heal any fractures. It has been a long, chilly summer in Vine City's slum. SNCC's sound trucks had failed to stir riots. Maybe Vine City residents got toughened to the black power demagoguery and immune to it. Here, almost in the shadow of Atlanta's new stadium, was a fresh neighborhood with a built-in incident. And here was SNCC.

As Allen said, the people just didn't know. But SNCC did. To say past white injustices to Negroes was fair provocation for what the black power zealots did to Atlanta Tuesday is about like justifying white bombers and burners on grounds some Negroes are criminals.

The mayor understood what was going on even while the Negro rock throwers who literally threatened his life did not. He gave them their target. He walked in the open down the middle of the street while some policemen were taking cover behind an armored car under the hail of stones. His courage was remarked by every tough cop present. He acted like a man who didn't want to be safe if his city wasn't.

Almost—but Not Quite

For a while it looked as if the mayor might pull it off. He waded into the middle of the riotous crowd at Capitol and Ormond (you go past the stadium on Capitol, and across Georgia, and across Little and Love— that's right, Love—and there's Ormond) and tried to lead them out to the stadium. They followed him for a block. Then SNCC got hold of the thing again, yelling black power.

They weren't gonna go to any white man's stadium. Pretty soon they had the crowd back at Ormond and Capitol. Allen got up on a police car and tried to talk to them. Demagogues knew what to do about that.

They rocked the car violently until he was shaken off it. Encircled and shoved, he simply bored deeper into the black crowd, demanding order, exhorting peace.

Rocks flew. Windshields and windows crashed in. Police cars had their glasses smashed. A white woman's car was hit; she paused at the stadium parking lot to shake the glass out of her hair. People were getting hurt. While Allen stood between them, Negroes threw rocks and policemen fired into the air.

Tear gas finally broke that one up. The police ran out of tear gas. But they stood on the street corners with their gas guns at the ready and nobody knew they were empty until new supplies came.

Policemen are always targets in mobs like these. The strain showed in their faces and you couldn't blame them. Shotguns, pistols, gas guns, billies—the tense brandishing of so much hardware was imposing. They had seen too many cars smashed, too much anger, to be easy. They were as tight as coiled springs, looking all about. There in the middle of them, unarmed and unrattled, was Mayor Allen.

"I wish I could slow that guy down," said Capt. George Royall, his police aide and bodyguard, sprinting up Little Street. The mayor had suddenly walked up there to insist that a crowd of Negroes disperse and go to their homes. The crowd moved slowly.

Two policemen were assigned to herd the crowd back up that side street. They were white, though many of the policemen on the scene were Negro. The two white policemen had company. "This is the Rev. Sam Williams," Capt. Royall told the pair of policemen. "He is going with you and he is going to ask the people to go to their homes peacefully."

The Rev. Williams did. A tough, smart NAACP militant, the Baptist minister and college professor had been fighting for his people against white oppressors all his life and he did not hesitate to go to the scene Tuesday and fight against their being hurt by SNCC. It took great courage. He went up the street with the policemen, commanding respect.

Like Sam Williams, the Rev. Martin Luther King, Sr. was there, deploring violence and laying the blame on those who incited it. "We have got to have law," the old man said. "If I only had my strength, I would tell these people we have got to have law. Else we have no protection."

"You've got your strength, old friend," Ivan Allen said, taking his hand in the street.

Negro Leaders Came

Negro politicians like Q. V. Williams and John Hood were there, laboring to lead their people out of folly. Clergymen like the Rev. William Holmes Borders were there, and leaders like Jesse Hill. The Negro leadership turned out to do what it could, just as staunchly as the white leadership used to do when the Klan mentalities threatened violence. But the violent and the disorderly always have an advantage in seizing leadership of a crowd. They are unhampered by responsibility and they have emotion going when responsible leaders, rational men, often look vulnerable and even futile in such a setting. But they have to go.

Dusk was falling. "Are you hurt? Did any of the rocks hit you?" Allen was asked in the lull. He looked at his friend Sam Williams there in the street and laughed. "Man," he kidded, "you know they can't throw anything as fast as I can run.

"I've got great peripheral vision. Blind to color, blind to class. I've got to be blind, haven't I, Sam?"

The Rev. Williams smiled. "That's right," he said quietly. The two strong men, one white, one black, looked at each other for a second in the gathering night, then moved off to see if they could calm and disperse some more of the silent, staring spectators.

Walking along the center of the Capitol Avenue sidewalk, a tall, thin Negro man wearing a striped sport shirt and a wisp of beard met a policeman and deliberately confronted him head-on, refusing to yield room for him to pass. The policeman held a shotgun at port arms and stood there for a minute. He jerked his thumb to the side but the Negro did not move.

Blind hatred contorted his face into a furious mask.

The policeman shrugged and walked on around him. The thin, goateed Negro walked on, muttering, looking over his shoulder and hating the white man with a passion that seemed to be consuming him like some foul, fatal fever.

Shattered glass lay in the street. Flickering lights glinted on the police guns. Night was falling and the mayor was thinking about opening up the schoolhouse at the corner of Capitol and Little and inviting everybody in to talk instead of fight, burn, stone and shoot.

It was almost as if the mayor, after half a day of presenting his body in the street, was as intent on willing peace and a return to normality as he was in building up his forces of police to crush any renewed disorder.

In the gathering darkness, somebody said to the tired mayor, as he stood there in the street, that he ought to go on home and leave the night peril to his policemen and the people on the porches.

"Listen," he snapped, "if anything is going to happen here tonight, it's going to happen over me."

September 29, 1966
Lillian Smith, Southerner

Lillian Smith was a beautiful woman—sensitive, fragile, gifted. She knew one love, in her youth, and he broke her heart. She tried to tell truths of value about the South, in her writing, and Southerners tried to break her spirit.

She ran away to a China mission for years after her disappointment in love. But she did not run away from the South; her spirit was not breakable.

"Was it something in the land that made us different?" she asked softly from her hospital bed, a few days ago when she could still fight back the illness.

She was talking about the sandbeds and pine barrens of south Georgia and north Florida (she was born in Jasper, Fla.) and the way the people who are born there seem to know no in-between; they tend either to extend to the Negro the hand of understanding or else raise the fist of violence, one or the other, utterly. Hers was a gentle hand. It never trembled.

She recalled her own early childhood when her family was comfortably well off. She remembered being pillowed in the lap of a Negro mammy whom she loved, and of recoiling from the sight of one human being mistreating another. From earliest remembrance she felt the Southern white must change and put right the wrongs done the Negro. But she was not a writer at first. She was a musician.

A family conference was called when the girl asked if she might go to Baltimore to study at the conservatory. A brother made the point that she was very young and inexperienced to be left alone in that great city. Her father replied with words that warmed her heart until her death:

"Lillian is a good girl. She has learned the values we have taught her. So if there is ever trouble it will not be your sister's fault, but ours."

She studied music professionally, and remarked with wonder, in the days before her death, that she became a writer only by chance. Her father fell on hard times. The Jasper place was lost. The family retreated to north Georgia's Rabun County. Her father opened a mountain camp for young people, tried vainly to operate it, and finally sent for her. She had to give up her career in music. But her father had given up much for her. She quickly organized and for a long time operated the camp for girls. As an incidental result of the ruin of her musical career, she turned to writing.

The novel *Strange Fruit*, in 1944, established her as a writer of top rank and extraordinary courage. Its racial theme also brought down upon her a storm of rage in the South. Never shaken, she wrote with blazing eloquence, and worked untiringly for civil rights, through years when she was not simply the focus of controversy but of hatred. Ironically, at the end she had to break with SNCC and CORE, and turn upon violent Negroes the same dissent she had directed at violent whites all of her life.

She was an artist, however, not a sociologist. Her art, being real, simply required of her that she address herself to the reality of conflict around her, and in the South that happened to be race. Because she was an artist, she told the truth. In telling it she never despaired of the human condition; she always believed in the power of the human heart. Her own is silent now. But the life she lived made hers the death of a very beautiful woman.

October 17, 1966
Letter to a Troubled Child

Dear little girl: You always have opposed cruelty toward other people. So I was pleased when you asked, "You can't be for Lester Maddox for governor, can you?" That is right, you were told. Never, under any circumstances, could I be for Mr. Maddox.

"Then why haven't you come out for Bo Callaway?" you asked. Because you are little, you are not yet aware that hurt can be caused by a strong man with the wrong idea just as surely as cruelty can be inflicted by an unknowing man.

You can't know better; you might say Mr. Callaway gives me pause because he should know better.

He is a strong man. He believes his idea of what our state needs is right. I am afraid it is wrong.

It is a very old idea in Georgia, not a new one. Mr. Maddox shares it with Mr. Callaway now. They say they want us to help ourselves, and not to lean on the government to do things for us. As far as it goes, this is a very good aim. I hope you will live by it all of your life.

But even if your own self-reliance is sufficient to meet your needs, there are others who simply may not be able to meet theirs. What bothers me most about Mr. Callaway is his willingness to leave so many of these unhelped. Who are some of these?

Negro families who traveled along our roads were not even sure where they would be permitted to buy supper for their children or rent a motel room in which to sleep for the night until the government passed a law requiring us to stop this cruelty. I am glad the government finally gave this help to those people who could not help themselves. But when Mr. Callaway went to Congress he said he wanted to undo that law. Threatening a Negro with an ax handle is obvious cruelty. What is it when we, who are comfortable, close our eyes to his need for food and shelter?

Georgia's schools are among the poorest in the nation largely because so many Georgians are poor and can't pay enough in taxes to make them into good schools. So the federal government has passed an aid-to-education law. It is sending Georgia millions of dollars to help us lift our children toward an education as good as children get in richer states. I believe this is needed; otherwise, how can our children ever compete with other American children on even terms? Yet Mr. Callaway interrupted his campaign and flew to Washington the other day to vote in Congress against this help.

I believe our elderly people needed the Medicare law. Under it, the government now helps those over 65 to pay their hospital bills in their closing years when most of them are no longer able to earn enough money to pay those bills without hardship. Mr. Callaway was against that, too.

He voted this year against an increase in the minimum wage. This is a bottom amount which the government requires employers to pay their lowest workers all over the nation. Without it, unskilled workers in the poorer states like Georgia would have to take a much smaller wage than they now make in order to get work. I'd rather we go back to plowing a mule than see Georgia solicit cheap industries by deliberately keeping its workers poor.

So you see, my dear, Mr. Callaway and I hold fundamentally different views about the needs of Negroes, school children, the elderly, working men and many, many others. He may honestly feel his timeworn way will lead somehow to a new kind of future; I feel it would condemn us to the failures and injustices of a better-forgotten past.

Because he is a strong man, his election might fasten his old idea anew on Georgia for countless years to come, with the supporters of a defeated Maddox returning to Mr. Callaway and reinforcing his numbers. I am not sure when we then could work our way back to the moderate and progressive kind of government we have known in your lifetime under Governors Vandiver and Sanders. And because I so strongly feel Mr. Callaway's is the wrong idea of our people's real and desperate needs, I cannot change.

A man is arrested by Atlanta policemen during a disturbance on Broad Street. By permission of the *Atlanta Journal and Constitution*.

10

1967

Hooked on a Log

January   A fire on the *Apollo I* spacecraft kills three astronauts. In Alabama, Lurleen Wallace succeeds her husband, George, as governor.

March   The House of Representatives votes to expel Adam Clayton Powell Jr., a black congressman from Harlem accused of misusing government funds.

May   National Guardsmen open fire on black students at Jackson State College in Mississippi, killing one.

June   President Johnson and Soviet leader Alexsei Kosygin hold a summit meeting in Glassboro, New Jersey. Israel defeats Jordan, Syria, and Egypt in the Six-Day War. Noted civil rights attorney Thurgood Marshall becomes the first black justice appointed to the U.S. Supreme Court; his confirmation is on August 3.

July   Major race riots erupt in Detroit and Newark. SNCC chairman H. Rap Brown is arrested for allegedly inciting racial violence in Cambridge, Maryland. President Johnson creates the National Advisory Commission on Civil Disorders.

October   A massive antiwar demonstration in Washington results in 647 arrests.

November   Mississippi, Louisiana, and Virginia each elect one black state legislator, the first such elections of the twentieth century. Voters elect black mayors in Cleveland, Ohio (Carl Stokes), and Gary, Indiana (Richard Hatcher). Congress passes the Air Quality Act.

December   The Stop the Draft movement holds mass antiwar demonstrations in several cities and college towns; hundreds are arrested, including Dr. Benjamin Spock and poet Allen Ginsberg.

February 1, 1967
A 12-Pound Bass on a Cane Pole?

Mr. Jack Wingate, Wingate's Fish Camp, Lake Seminole, Bainbridge, Ga.

Dear Jack: Some crazy fool took my wife's picture with a 12-pound bass down at your place last weekend and she came home claiming she caught it. Ha.

As you and I know Jack, that is not possible. Sue does not know which end of a spinning reel to tie the plug on. And the only time I ever let her try to cast, she hooked her hat on the back-swing and threw it half way to Spring Creek.

So would you please let me know the straight of this? I have followed your guidance through the years, and I have fished every gallon of Seminole with Imps, Bushwhackers, Divebombers, Lazy Ikes, Rapalas, plastic worms and every other item of expensive hardware you have recommended. And the biggest bass I have boated weighed six pounds (you said five but you're a conservative).

Mary and I have tried to humor her. As Mary said, "If you think you caught that 12-pound fish, Mama, sure you did." But Jack, would *you* believe it if your wife went out on a lake that you and I know like the back of our hands (and into which we have cast thousands of times with hundreds of dollars' worth of equipment) and claimed she had caught this 12-pound bass on a—now get this, Jack—on a cane pole?

"I was fishing for a bream with a little minnow," she says. Ha.

As you know, I haven't let her go fishing with me since she boated two 15-pound cobias at Crystal River while I was catching one six-ounce saltwater cat. She doesn't understand the sport at all. That's why, when the Raymond McKinnons from Adel said come on down to Seminole for the day, I said to her, "You go on."

"How did you keep a fish like that from snapping off the end of your fishing pole?" I asked her, craftily.

"Oh, I thought I was hooked on a log," she says brightly. "So I just wafted it around for a long time, back and forth, trying to get it loose."

She wafted it around.

After a while, she claims, this 12-pound bass just came floating up to the boat, worn out and belly up. Where is the fish, I asked her. "Jack kept it to enter in the boat show," she says. In the boat show.

What's the straight of it, Jack? I'm trying not to hurt her feelings by asking too many questions. But she's beginning to hurt mine, the way she keeps sticking to this ridiculous story.

March 1, 1967
First Man Lays an Egg

"The Atlanta papers," George Wallace told the Georgia Legislature, "have a hard time understanding plain English." He managed to make himself clear. Peddling shopworn goods with a snake oil pitch, he was beneath his audience.

He got good applause from admirers in the gallery. Members on the floor of the Georgia Legislature were a good deal more restrained. And the harder he harangued Georgians to do as he said and defy school guidelines, the deeper the silence grew among the representatives of Georgians who are trying to do things their own way. He finally skipped some of those pages about the federal government "trifling with your children" when it became uncomfortably clear that it was he who was here trifling with our children, and his conclusion was rather plaintive ("Read what Harold Howe said about God is Dead!").

To plenty of those present he was still the hero from Montgomery, come to stand in our schoolhouse door. They'll vote for him for president next year. But to plenty of others George Wallace was nothing more than that little surrender-hell Confederate dressed up in a blue serge suit. He flashed a stump-speaker's wit in the early going, but it was brittle and edged with meanness—unlike the easy and earthy non sequiturs that Lester Maddox employs so naturally to coat his shirtless impossibilities.

Gov. Maddox couldn't resist introducing the Alabama governor's husband as "the first man of Alabama," and he avoided solemnity when he thanked Wallace for being the only governor who sent him encouragement in those Pickrick days "when I was under invasion."

Wallace returned the compliment solemnly, and caused Maddox a little squirm, by announcing that Maddox had raised more money for his 1964 presidential campaign than any other American.

Then Wallace proceeded to make the speech most Southerners were raised on, and which would best be forgotten. There was one key difference. Ole Gene, Ole Marvin, and even the old Lester, rang a lot truer because they came right out in favor of keeping the Negro, by name, in his place. There was at least a gritty honesty about the thing in those days. Wallace was just slippery. He has switched to constitutional government, states' rights and free enterprise from the horse everybody knows he is really riding. And while he pitched and paced his singsong very skillfully, the content was pretty patchy.

There were our forefathers, "walking back from Appomattox." There were the good Southerners who flung off the yoke of discriminatory freight rates in the absence of "some of those who holler loudest now about discrimination"—a construction of history that overlooked Georgia's liberal Ellis Arnall, who led the freight rate fight. There was the usual denigration of federal judges—"one might be standing in your midst right now." It took as many policemen to guard Wallace in New York, Wallace said with a curious pride, as it took to guard Khrushchev.

But his announced main mission was to tell Georgians about how to run their schools (he interspersed the instruction with "You-know-how-to-run-your-schools-of-course") and in laying this egg before the eyes of the General Assembly he appeared to be an outsider agitator trifling with our state's children.

April 1, 1967
Dr. King Crosses the Mekong

Dr. Martin Luther King, Jr., has now chosen to turn away from the course of Sen. Edward Brooke and toward the path of Stokely Carmichael on Vietnam. To those Americans who have looked to Dr. King to keep the domestic civil rights movement on a clear track, unen-cumbered by dubious detours into foreign policy, his decision is disap-pointing.

His Southern Christian Leadership Conference resolved Thursday "to do everything in our power to end the war" in Vietnam. This is pre-cisely the goal of President Johnson's policy, so that statement is unex-ceptionable.

But the statement leading up to it—"at home we fight a war on pov-erty, abroad we fight a war against the poor"—misrepresents the United States' aim so badly that it can only divide Dr. King's friends, sustain his enemies and require rejoinder.

The motive of United States policy is to fight for the South Vietnam-ese poor, not against them, as every U.S. policy statement and every action on the ground has made clear. If some Americans disagree with the means being employed, this gives them no rational cause to impugn the motive. Far too much of this kind of sloppy conformity was taking hold among liberals even before Dr. King permitted his name to be added to the obedient list. The contradiction between the war on pov-erty at home and the war on poverty, and against the violent exploitation of it, in South Vietnam, can occur only in minds that are closed more tightly than Sen. Brooke's.

The SCLC did not believe it could "long tell Americans to practice nonviolence at home while our nation is practicing the very essence of violence abroad." Such a statement came after Presidents Eisenhower, Kennedy and Johnson had deployed the armed forces of this nation to shield the rights of Negroes in Arkansas, Alabama and Mississippi with-out being accused of practicing the essence of violence, as they are now accused when it is the rights of the South Vietnamese they are shielding.

What is it in the SCLC mind that draws a distinction between fight-ing for the rights of a colored people at home and the rights of a colored people abroad? Turned around, the statement would not differ greatly from the charges Faubus, Barnett and Wallace once flung at the U.S. government.

If the fight were being made to subdue, mistreat or exploit an Asian people, it certainly would deserve the SCLC label as a "morally and po-litically unjust war."

But the point of the spending and the dying, as the government sees it, is to stop the practice of externally precipitated violence against an Asian people and to assure them the right of self-determination. If crit-ics see the effect of the government's policy as differing from this inten-tion, the criticism certainly ought to be freely stated. But to characterize the intention itself as being to make "war against the poor" is going to sit wrong with a lot of people who approved of U.S. force when it was used to shield the rights of Dr. King.

May 11, 1967
Is Maddox Chasing Rabbits?

One of the nicest things I ever called Gov. Lester Maddox was a "coun-try governor" who outslickered the *Meet the Press* reporters, and now he has even jumped on me for that. I don't think he really meant to throw off on me because of my rural background.

But the fact remains he told the board of the Atlanta Chamber of Commerce, with a certain urbane flourish, that he reckoned "a man who came to Atlanta from Adel, Ga., has every right to call a native Atlantan a 'country boy.'"

Since I actually grew up three miles out from Adel, on the dirt road east from Sparks toward Chaserville, while the governor-to-be was learning city ways, I am chagrined to find he might think my use of the term "country boy" could convey anything less than admiration.

Being one, and proud of it, I just thought I might share the mantle with him. He seemed to me to be getting the image of a high-handed city slicker who needed a little help in straightening himself out, after he threw those country boys from Carroll County out of his office for not letting him tell them how to run their schools.

He sure wasn't thinking like a country boy when he decided the state school-building authority had the right to block a local school board, which is answerable to its local people, from consolidating local schools;

if that were the case, then the state government could become an octopus that could tell every local district where it had to have its schools. No country boy would take to that.

And even though Gov. Maddox did go on to tell the Atlanta Chamber that he would like to be both a country and a city governor, his throwing it up to me that I'm country and he's city hurt deep down, since I was only trying to accord him honorary rural status so as to broaden his urban background.

But that's water down the millrace now. I may even have to take back his honorary title if he persists in his interference from Atlanta with the way country school districts run their business. The way he goes along pretty well for a while, and then runs right off the track, reminds me of a story that Aubrey Bates, who lives out from Adel, once told me about the quail-hunting grandpa.

Some hunters from up north went to South Georgia to hunt, and instead of dogs the guide used his grandpa to point birds. Grandpa could find them, too, and he froze on covey after covey. The hunters were surprised but greatly pleased.

They returned the next year and the guide met them with dogs. "Where's that fellow who found the birds last year?" the disappointed hunters asked. "Aw," said the guide, "grandpa got to chasing rabbits and we had to shoot him."

May 30, 1967
Many Screens Have Fallen

A man who couldn't even get a hamburger downtown when I first met him will receive a testimonial banquet in the Grand Ballroom of the Marriott Hotel tomorrow night. He was a Phi Beta Kappa from Bates College, but he couldn't get a seat in a first-run movie house in Atlanta.

He took his master's degree and his doctorate from the University of Chicago, but he couldn't have gotten a teaching job in most of the city's grammar schools back them.

He was to receive a total of 17 honorary degrees, write five books, advise presidents, help found the Peace Corps and represent the United States at the funeral of Pope John XXIII in Rome, but when I first met him 10 years ago, Dr. Benjamin E. Mays couldn't check into a first-class hotel in Atlanta, or attend a concert at the city auditorium, or ride in the front of a bus.

Looking back across this one brief decade during which these indignities were removed, one by one, most white Southerners can only wince that a way of life they once defended could have inflicted such treatment on a man who must be counted as one of the outstanding citizens of the United States.

It was Dr. Mays, 10 years ago, who gave me an early look into the deepness of Negro feeling in the South. We were walking together under the trees of the Morehouse College campus. In his 27 years as the 100-year-old college's president, a post from which he is now retiring, Dr. Mays has nearly doubled the size of that campus, doubled its enrollment, quadrupled its endowment, raised some $15 million for it, added 18 buildings and built a faculty from one that had only two Ph.D.s in 1940 to more than 50 percent Ph.D.s now. A tall, reserved and dignified man of striking presence, he spoke quietly as we walked, but with great force.

He foresaw the forces that would require fairer treatment for the Negro and spoke gently of the need for me and other Southern whites to understand why—to understand the effect our complacent segregation was truly having upon Negroes. He spoke of having had to sit behind a screen in order to eat in the dining car on a train on his frequent trips to Washington, as if his blackness of which he was proud had been some kind of shamefulness to be hidden from others. But Pullman diners had been desegregated 10 years ago, and he had experienced for the first time the same service as white diners, without the screen.

"I had not known until that moment," he said quietly, "just how much resentment had grown in me. As I sat there among the others, being served the same as the others and able to *see* those white people without a screen between us, a thought overwhelmed me and I almost wanted to say it out loud to them: 'I don't hate you any more.'"

He looked at me keenly to see if his meaning had sunk in. It had. Across these turbulent 10 years, many more causes for resentment and hatred have diminished as old screens of fear have fallen. And while building a great college and giving distinguished service to his country, Dr. Mays has placed his wisdom at the leading edge of the change through these years. Tomorrow night proper honor will be paid him in a region he has taught. Some of his most needful students were white.

August 6, 1967
How to Hurt

At Least She Taught the Children

On the first day of federally financed summer school in a small Georgia city which will not be named, a white father brought his eight-year-old child to school early and learned the child's teacher was to be a Negro. He announced out loud that he would quit paying taxes to a government that would put his child under a Negro teacher.

Recently the same man came to the Negro teacher (she teaches reading) at the end of the term and said to her: "You're the first teacher my child has ever had."

The teacher talked quietly about her ups and downs this summer. Well-spoken but retiring by nature, she is a graduate of Spelman and is now working on her master's thesis. That first day of school frightened her, she said—until she entered the classroom.

She was the first Negro teacher to be summoned to the white school, and "I thought there might be a riot." There wasn't. And once she joined the children in her room—12 were white, two were Negro—her nervousness vanished. "They never did seem to notice my color," she said. They didn't mention it the first day, or ever.

Tests showed progress of the class under her was excellent.

"The Negro children were behind," she said matter-of-factly. "We must do a better job of teaching them."

She has taught for 19 years, most of them in the small Georgia city which is her hometown. Her neighbors, incidentally, have always been white. The school officials told her she had been requested to teach in the white school because she was one of the Negro school's best teachers.

"But if I am a good teacher," she said, "and I believe that I am, shouldn't good teachers be in the Negro school where the Negro children need help most?"

But there is another reason, too, why this excellent Negro teacher is considering a return to the Negro school in the fall. Instead of accepting an offer to stay in the white school where she did such a splendid summer job, and where she could serve as an example to lead whites and Negroes alike toward an end to fear of desegregation.

It has nothing to do with the parents. She was gratified to find this summer that the white parents, like the white children, were courteous to her and often cordial. None offended her. "They looked at me," she said.

One younger white teacher finally made it a point to eat lunch with her, for which she was grateful. But there was no closeness with the other white teachers. She noticed they did not look at her when they spoke to her. "But there were no insults," she quickly explained. Then she added, "Well, none until the other day."

She had read a letter to the editor in the *Atlanta Constitution* at breakfast, so she knew its position on the editorial page. It was a vicious letter from a writer who was not especially well educated, and who wanted to know why white children had to be subjected to "substandard teaching" by Negro teachers in Georgia. The letter had troubled her, and had been on her mind all morning.

So when she saw some white teachers handing around the newspaper, folded to the place where she knew that letter was printed, she thought she knew what they were saying to each other about her even though their faces showed nothing as they read it, one by one.

Maybe women have some special deftness at cruelty. Anyway, they hurt her, and she said she had never been one to take quick offense at anything. Quickly, without anger, she said she thought then she might better just go on back to the Negro school.

Dr. Martin Luther King Jr.'s funeral procession passes in front of Atlanta's City Hall near the Georgia State Capitol. By permission of the *Atlanta Journal and Constitution*.

11

1968

A Thousand Times
Unafraid

January	North Vietnamese regulars and Viet Cong guerrillas launch the Tet Offensive in South Vietnam. North Korean patrol boats seize the U.S. Navy intelligence vessel *Pueblo* and its crew of eighty-three.
February	Sanitation workers go on strike in Memphis, Tennessee.
March	Antiwar candidate Senator Eugene McCarthy wins 42 percent of the vote in the New Hampshire Democratic presidential primary. Senator Robert F. Kennedy of New York enters the race for the Democratic presidential nomination. President Lyndon Johnson announces his withdrawal from the presidential race and calls a halt to American bombing campaigns north of the twenty-first parallel.
April	The Reverend Martin Luther King Jr. is assassinated in Memphis, provoking major racial disturbances in Washington, Baltimore, Chicago, and scores of other American cities. Members of the Students for a Democratic Society and other student antiwar protesters at Columbia University seize five buildings. Similar takeovers occur at Boston University and other college campuses. Congress passes a Civil Rights Act aimed at racial discrimination in housing.
May	Peace talks between the United States and North Vietnam begin in Paris. The SCLC-sponsored Poor People's Campaign begins in Washington, D.C.
June	Robert Kennedy is assassinated in Los Angeles. Washington police close down Resurrection City, a protest village sponsored by SCLC's Poor People's Campaign.

August	Richard M. Nixon wins the Republican Party presidential nomination and selects Governor Spiro T. Agnew of Maryland as his running mate. A massive antiwar protest challenges the legitimacy of the Democratic National Convention in Chicago, leading to police violence and mass arrests. Vice President Hubert H. Humphrey of Minnesota wins the Democratic presidential nomination and selects Senator Edmund Muskie of Maine as his running mate.
October	President Johnson withdraws the nomination of Associate Justice Abe Fortas to be chief justice of the U.S. Supreme Court. In an effort to break a stalemate at the Paris peace talks, Johnson announces a halt to the aerial bombing of North Vietnam.
November	Richard Nixon defeats Hubert Humphrey and third-party candidate George Wallace of Alabama for the presidency.

January 13, 1968
The Life and Death of a Judge

J. Waties Waring should have been at home in the red azalea gardens of South Carolina's low country and the stately drawing rooms of Charleston. He was a 10th-generation Waring in that old city, son of a Confederate veteran—a courtly and mannered man of the law and a respected federal judge, though he did marry a woman from Detroit.

But he died in exile in New York this week, a Southerner without a home.

He committed, in 1947, what he called the South's "unforgivable sin." He ruled that the Negro was a full citizen of his state; he struck down the Democratic party's "white primary" in South Carolina, a state that had tried to defy 1944 court rulings to that effect.

As a reporter in South Carolina during the period, I was shocked at the virulence of the hatred directed at the judge for daring to say "niggers" should vote. His name was blackened. His home was pelted with bricks. His "traitorous" act was denounced by bellowing politicians on every stump from Jolly Street to the sea. He was ostracized socially, and finally withdrew from his Charleston clubs and organizations. Old associates cut him off. He did receive a few sympathetic letters marked "confidential."

"But no one would dare back me openly because he would have been ruined socially and possibly financially," Judge Waring said later.

South Carolina congressmen received petitions signed by more than 20,000 South Carolinians demanding his impeachment.

Saddened but unmoved, he went on issuing racial rulings according to the law and his judgment until he retired in 1952. As early as 1951—three years ahead of the U.S. Supreme Court—Judge Waring held, in a dissenting opinion, that segregated schools were inherently unequal.

When he retired from the bench the next year—an old man without friends, cursed by his kin—he sold the Charleston home where he had lived for 35 years and took a train for New York. There he lived out his life. He had known in advance that "if you deny white supremacy, you're damned." He was prepared to pay the Southern price rather than stultify his conscience and the law.

"We don't have a Negro problem in the South," he said 18 years ago. "We have a white problem. The white men in my part of the country are obsessed with false doctrines." As a judge with power to act, he did not temporize. "You can't cure racial prejudice with reasoning and talk," he said. His rulings stuck. So did the unreasoning hatred he received in return.

But even in retirement and exile, he continued to speak his mind. In 1954, when James F. Byrnes and Herman Talmadge were speaking defiantly of the Supreme Court's desegregation ruling, he charged them with "trying to lead ignorant but decent people into doing wrong."

The Southern judge, at peace with himself, composed his own obituary. "I would like nothing better than to be remembered in the type of tribute paid President Cleveland, about whom someone said 'We love him for the enemies he made.'"

February 4, 1968
Voting Power

Glimmerings of a New Politics

The Voting Rights Act of 1965 is taking on political meaning in Southern politics now. Negro registration is more than 50 percent of the voting age Negro population in every Southern state. Before the law was passed, this was true only of Florida, Tennessee, and Texas.

In Georgia, the percentage has risen from 27 percent to 52 percent. But the biggest gain has been in Mississippi, where Negro registration has shot from 7 percent to 60 percent of the Negro citizens of voting age.

Not all of the registered Negroes vote, nor do all registered whites. In some elections, the Negro doesn't have much choice and therefore doesn't have much interest, as some recent Georgia elections showed.

Elsewhere, as in Alabama in 1966, as many as 74 percent of the registered Negroes voted for a gubernatorial candidate who was friendly to them, but because the issues polarized the races, he lost overwhelmingly to a white supremacist.

A Negro registration, which now may run as high as 300,000 in Georgia, will not long be neutralized, however. Only 150,000 voted in 1966, according to the voter education project of the Southern Regional Council.

But that was in the Maddox-Callaway race.

Glimmerings of a new politics distinguished by moderation are a natural outcropping of the large new factor which the Southern Negro now presents.

This ought to be a source of satisfaction to all who believe in the fundamentals of democracy, which is based on government by consent of the governed—all of them not some.

Negroes themselves have not hesitated to enter politics as candidates. The number of Negro officeholders in the 11 Southern states is now twice the number serving when the Voting Rights Act of 1965 was passed.

Again, Georgia can take pride that more Negroes have been fairly elected to its state legislature than have been elected in any other Southern state. Eleven Negroes now sit in the Georgia House and Senate. Tennessee has 6, Texas 3.

The self-adjusting mechanisms of democratic government should eventually absorb the Southern Negro vote in a fairly balanced proportion. But the day of perfection hasn't quite dawned.

In many cases, particularly in Alabama and Mississippi, new efforts have been made to dilute large Negro votes by such obvious gerrymandering that the federal courts have had to throw out the procedures as being the rankest form of discrimination.

In the Negro strike for urban power, there also have been some instances of self-dilution. Many Negro politicians made common cause with segregationist whites to fragment Atlanta into more than a score of districts where the legislators would be elected by the vote of the district only, as opposed to countywide voting. As a result, several Negroes sit in the legislative seats representing Negro districts, but they are outnumbered by white legislators who are no longer answerable to Negro voters as they were in the time when countywide voting made them responsive to the Negro swing vote.

It is a time of continuing adjustment toward a new Southern politics. The only certainty is that the vast new freedom of the ballot which the Voting Rights Act opened up to Negro citizens will have its effect forever.

April 5, 1968
A Tale of Two Southerners

(After writing today's page one editorial on the death of Dr. Martin Luther King, I started to remove this column also and substitute one about him. Then I thought, no, Dr. King understood this South and its different kinds of Southerners, and he would have wanted these things said.)

As Georgia's old familiar white supremacists gathered in Atlanta Thursday to tub-thump coarsely for George Wallace's presidential candidacy, the plight of being Southern seemed personified suddenly in Wallace and Lyndon Johnson.

Both sprang from the Southern body of people containing the virtues and the vices which W. J. Cash listed: "Proud, brave, honorable by its lights, courteous, personally generous, loyal, swift to act, often too swift, but signally effective, sometimes terrible, in its action—such was the South at its best. (Its characteristic vices were) violence, intolerance, aversion and suspicion toward new ideas, an incapacity for analysis, an inclination to act from feeling rather than from thought, an exaggerated individualism and a too narrow concept of social responsibility, attachment to fictions and false values, above all too great attachment to racial values and a tendency to justify cruelty and injustice in the name of those values."

Like any people, Cash wrote, in his *Mind of the South*, Southerners "preferred the comforts of complacency and illusion to facing highly unpleasant facts for which the remedy was far from being obvious." But more than most, Southerners were "trained to believing what they liked to believe," Cash thought.

Lyndon Johnson, a Southern president, tried to turn away from the ancestral vices. He strove toward remedies for the unpleasant facts, though certainly few were obvious. Yet his efforts were not credited. Southerners who believed what they liked to believe called him a turncoat. And although he may not have expected the viciousness of the assaults, Johnson was a realist who always knew he would not be appreciated in the North either.

As early as April, 1964, riding to the White House through the dark streets of Washington, he leaned his head in his hands wearily and predicted in a quiet voice that the Eastern press and intellectuals would not rest until they had ruined him.

He had just handled the Guantanamo and Panama crises well. No criticism of him had then begun. I suggested he was hypersensitive and mistaken—that he should concentrate on continuing to make the right decisions and he could then count on being treated fairly.

He raised his head, looked out the window of the moving car, and said thoughtfully, "No, you're wrong. Just wait until I make one mistake—or what they think is a mistake. Then you'll see how they're going to go after me."

Lyndon Johnson read the patronizers who sneered at his Southernism better than they read him. He knew he would be hated.

George Wallace, of course, is taking the other, easier road of telling them what they want to believe—a course that has bound down the South in the ignominy of its vices instead of giving free run to its virtues as Johnson tried to do. "Wallace states it in his own language," Roy Harris, his Georgia backer, has explained. "It's going to be states' rights and the right to run your own schools. But when you get right down to it, there's really going to be only one issue, and you spell it n-i-g-g-e-r."

April 5, 1968
An Editorial

"Free at last, free at last, Lord God Almighty, I am free at last!"

Yes, Dr. Martin Luther King, Jr. is free. The lesson of his life is written large. Let every man of every race search his heart now, as the president asked, and face the enduring truth.

No white American can fail to find there a deep and terrible shame. This was a believing and gentle man who said to his people that violence is not the way. To his death he strove to lead them in the path of gentleness. Vengeance was not in him. Love them, he said. And they killed him.

Every white American must face that lesson, as old as the Cross, and guide himself. Let the voice and the hand of the decent white South be raised at last in speaking and voting an end to the poisonous politics of hatred that turns sick minds to murder. Dr. King was reviled from an Atlanta platform on the very day of his death. Let the white man say, "No more of this, ever," and put an end to it—if not for the sake of the Negro, for the sake of his own immortal soul.

No Negro American can respond to this man's death with vengeance without destroying the meaning of his life. Dr. King based his life on the lesson of the Crucifixion, and he would caution now, "Forgive them, for they know not what they do." If his brethren for whom he died fail now to honor the cause of non-violence for which he lived, his years will have been wasted, his memory dishonored and his grave a tomb of sorrow. He trusted his people to follow his dream of brotherhood through gentleness, not vengeance.

He faced death a thousand times unafraid in his faith that they would believe and bear witness. Now the meaning of his life is in their hands, to honor and not despoil. Every Negro who truly mourns him will realize it was through love and faith and forgiveness that he taught them to overcome. To the end of his days he opposed the violent men and called his people back to the lesson of the Cross.

It is now that he must depend on the people he loved and died for to honor his life by living its lesson and not forsaking him for the violent men he fought. That is the great memorial Dr. Martin Luther King, Jr. most wanted his people to raise. Let him not have lived in vain.

April 6, 1968
Dr. King's Hand Is Gone Now

Martin Luther King, Jr. is home now, forever. There will not be another King. If his truth is to march on, it must have taken fire now in the heart of the human family. The one new leader who is capable of replacing him is the American white.

He introduced us whites to our consciences. Then he paid with his life and left us here. Gone now is the convenience of being pressed by him to do what is right. If his life and death failed to move us to take our own worst natures in hand, to forswear the cruelty and complacency of the past, and to build here one nation in brotherhood because we believe in it, then he failed. He could do no more in his 39 years than show us the way. But he believed in us, believed we would follow awakened consciences.

We, American whites, alone have the power to finish the tasks he could only show us—to enable an American man of any race to get work, to shelter his family decently, to educate his children well, and above all, to be treated as a neighbor according to his character and not his color.

We can no longer draw back from the accusations of our own hearts and wait resentfully to hear them spoken by a Martin Luther King. He is gone. There will not be another like him. He has left it to us. And the burden passes now to the white American spirit in which he deeply believed, to the end.

Negro Americans must choose a course too while the white man looks inward for the decisions of conscience now due. False leaders are telling the Negro that Dr. King's life was a lie.

He said love; they say hate. He preached nonviolence; they seek blood. He had a dream for America; they have contempt. He raised his mighty voice in the name of God and in appeal to that better part of the human spirit which quests for the noble and divine; they pander to the base and criminal instincts, to the beast that sleeps in man. Love thy white neighbor, he is your brother, Dr. King preached. Hate him, they said.

Martin Luther King, Jr. fought these violent men, wrestled with them for the soul of black America, and went to his death in the process of proving—as, with time, he would have proved—that nonviolence and love and appeals to conscience are the only levers that move mountains. "The plain, inexorable fact is that any attempt of the American Negro to overthrow his oppressor with violence will not work," he wrote. Only nonviolence and love in its commanding sense could rid the white man of the fear-hate in himself, he said.

But before this brave and good man was in his grave the false leaders, no longer stayed by his powerful hand, were upon the Negro people like carrion. They defiled his memory with mad cries for retribution, calling for violence in the name of a nonviolent man. They hated and fought him in life but they could not bring him down. If the Negro people desert him in death to follow the vicious false leaders who seek to undo his work, it will be as if the Apostles had turned from the Cross and said, "He is only a dead man. His life meant nothing. Let us join his enemies."

His life meant only what we, who heard him, do now. On the white man, his death imposes a duty. On the Negro, it places a test.

April 10, 1968
A Memorial for Dr. King

Television doesn't quite close the distance. You've got to be inside the Ebenezer Baptist Church, among this intensely human family called the Negro people, as they sing, "Softly and tenderly, Jesus is calling" over the body of their dead brother—among them in the heat of the little church where tears mingle with perspiration and the lips of the choir singers tremble.

You've got to sit between the mourners and touch shoulders with them in the crowd and feel the heat come up through your shoes from the hot pavement as you march with them behind the casket drawn, with perfect fitness, by a two-mule wagon.

TV doesn't catch it at all. On the contrary I think it symbolizes what the trouble is. You look at them from a distance. They are just a picture then. It gives you the illusion of knowing them. You do not know them until you join them, and look them in the face, and white Americans have not done that yet.

You have to be there in the pews for the funeral of Martin Luther King, Jr. to know the full truth—that we whites have committed the monstrous wrong of thrusting away a people we do not even know, and hurting them out of our fear born of our ignorance. It is absurd to have been afraid of them.

Surely these are the gentlest of people, the most loving of people, the people of deepest forgiveness and faith in all of this land. And they have had so little, these worshipers whose humble red brick church is bare of all elegance, its planked-in staircases looking homemade though painted to a loving neatness.

We have treated them as if they were somehow dangerous—these loyal, warm, large-hearted, vulnerable neighbors of ours who have asked so little of America, and received so much less. The demagogues have slandered them until we have somehow blinded ourselves to the humble gift of friendship they have been offering. Their hateful, violent underclass, which is only a counterpart to the white violent underclass, has been seized upon by us as an unworthy excuse to libel their color.

You have to be among them to receive the full impact of the stupid wrongs we have committed in our hearts and in our acts. Suddenly you realize these gentle folk were not eager to press demands for rights; they were afraid. As an act of will they still must quell fears we whites do not even comprehend before they can bring themselves to make challenges to the white man. And we, who do not even know them, dared to be outraged when Dr. King gave them courage by accepting our punishments, and finally our death. All of us, in one degree or another, belabored him for disordering our lives with bus boycotts and sit-ins, freedom rides and marches. But now that these good and gentle people we mistreated can vote, and sit in waiting rooms, and eat lunch where they are hungry, and seat their children with dignity anywhere on the bus, we ought to be overcome with bitter remorse that we would not see the justice of these things until he showed us.

We will not even now see the overwhelming injustice we continue to visit upon these people who still believe in us unless Dr. King's death teaches us that we must hereafter be among them, and know them, and take their hands and walk with them as men whose friendship will ennoble us. Their faith in us runs deeper than the faith we have shown in ourselves, and we ought to be deeply ashamed of the cruelties we offered in return for such trust and love. Jobs, housing, education are only programs. Knowing and loving our neighbors is the needed memorial to Dr. King. And that is so easy, when you are among them.

Three

Reflections

12

Forged in Battle

The Formative
Experience of War
June 5, 1994

Eugene Patterson

I did not want to kill the two German officers when we met by mistake in the middle of the main street of Gera Bronn.

They somersaulted from their motorcycle when it rounded a corner directly ahead of my column of light armor. They scrambled to their feet, facing me 20 yards in front of the cannon and machine gun muzzles of my lead armored car, and stood momentarily still as deer. The front wheel of their flattened motorcycle spun on in the silence.

Months earlier, in 1944, I had framed my selfish principle of war: that you live longer yourself if, wherever possible, you shout instead of shoot. So I slapped the turret of the six-wheeled M-8, beckoned with my hand, and bellowed, "Kommen sie hier mit deinen händen höch! Mach schnelle!"

The two big men neither came forward nor raised their hands. That defiance fed my prickling fear that they were the point of an oncoming German column which was about to collide with mine. Before I could raise my M-1 rifle, the biggest one bolted five yards to his right and vanished behind the corner of a building. The other's eyes darted in the same direction.

"Nein!" I cried, and aimed the M-1. "Nein!" He was proud and shamed. He ran for it, too. My tracking bullet nicked masonry dust from the corner of the building just as he reached its cover.

Alarmed at what might be bearing down, I hurried the column of iron vehicles forward into an apple orchard on the edge of town where we found room to make a U-turn and backtrack out of Gera Bronn. We were the rear guard of an American force retreating from Crailsheim. We were scouting the flanks behind the pullout and trying to ward off, not wade into, a fight. As my M-8 pulled even with the bullet-nicked corner of the building, I could see that the first German officer had gotten away.

The second one lay crumpled like a pile of garments.

In my turret, Sgt. Grant Turner said, "Nice shooting, Lieutenant." I felt sick. In one accidental instant that neither of us had wanted, my .30-caliber bullet had torn life from that still being. I was the squeamish Georgia farm kid who'd never liked to shoot quail or rabbits and who'd insisted my older brother be the one to wring the chicken's neck for Sunday dinner. Now here, much nearer than the cannon's reach, lay a man dead at my feet. I wished I had missed him.

Justice Oliver Wendell Holmes Jr. orated to some federal veterans long after he was shot at Antietam that by great good fortune, when they were young, "our hearts were touched with fire."

War seized mine with dread.

Holmes did admit "the reality was to pass a night on the ground in the rain with your bowels out of order, and after no particular breakfast to attack the enemy."

Two generations after Holmes spoke, as you lay on the ground of France or Germany beside your tank in an ice-crusted sleeping bag, you rated the hollow tenor pounding of the outgoing rounds against the ragged bass crash of the incoming shells and ranked the mutual artilleries, even in exhaustion, into the bearable and the unacceptable.

When the sleeper was tired enough and had heard those detonations long enough to gauge them, he could sleep while listening. When he finally had to wake, he sank into the day, hardening his readiness to do without a tomorrow. Over months, this exponential likelihood of finality lay under each waking moment like a small nausea. One started the day steeling the body to die and arrived at evening faintly surprised and cumulatively less hopeful of making it through one more. Nevertheless, about dawn or before, you and your bonded brothers-in-dread moved on up the road and into the woods again. These were strange matins, when your procession solemnly marched out into the morning in search of human beings to convert to death, with prayers that they not kill you first.

Like Holmes, I did find in the terrible gantlet of war a formative force of my life. Leading men in combat remains the most selfless work I ever did. Given the daily prospect of dying young, it was also the most demanding.

Its small and sole reward came when word got back to me 12 years after the war that former Cpl. Herbert Biles of my platoon had volunteered to a person, who passed it on to me, that "Lt. Patterson never said, 'You go.' He said, 'Let's go.'" If the curse of war bestows any meager blessing, I would settle for that remembrance.

A Man of the 20th Century

Nor would I swap a life that bridged most of the 20th century for existence in any other time. Calvin Coolidge's permissive years cast my boyhood into the desperate scrabbling of Herbert Hoover's Great Depression. War thrust me to graduation from the University of Georgia and enrollment in officer candidate school at age 19, and placed my 21st birthday in Normandy. I emerged alive at the end of that one in time to enter the unrelieved stress of a near-half century of atomic showdown, which abruptly eased about the time I retired from 41 years as a reporter and editor; the Cold War and I had run our course together.

At last, I leaned back.

Let the new generation test itself against the 21st century. Mine was the millennial 20th. It swept me from farm boy to soldier to journalist living across the world, in New York, London, Washington. It stationed me for 12 climactic years at the editorial helm of the *Atlanta Constitution* at the moment when my Georgia kinsmen and I had to repudiate our

Confederate great grandfathers' futile cause and develop a just regard for every American's civil rights. The emotional editorial conflict with southern traditionalists, who were my family, engendered stresses that rivaled the shooting war's intensity. This time also was, of course, the high point of my professional life. The time had come to decide. One cannot hide in the editor's chair. Alone, if necessary, one had to speak what southern generations had dared not think.

Lead with the Heaviest Punch

The accident at Gera Bronn in March of 1944 had begun a few shattering days earlier when Pfc. Amory Speight asked me to explain one more time why we had to go to Crailsheim.

The question irritated me because I had just finished explaining the mission to the shivering men huddled around my rain-proofed map case propped on the front slope plate of an M-24 light tank. The 30 men of my cavalry reconnaissance platoon stood there in the morning fog on a road south of Bad Mergentheim, along with 20 crewmen of our four attached light tanks.

I felt like snapping back at Speight with an angry thought that lay often on my mind when I was tired and scared: that we were going to lead an armored column 35 kilometers southward through God-knew-what to Crailsheim because some staff officer safe and warm at a higher headquarters had made a slash with a wax pencil on the acetate cover of some big wall map and airily ordered us vulnerable human beings to follow that arrow on the unforgiving ground.

But I stayed as proper as I thought a second lieutenant was supposed to be. On a larger map I showed where, far to the southwest, a part of our 10th Armored Division was locked in a battle for Heilbronn. Our own combat command had sprung loose and driven eastward toward Nuremburg across the face of the German line which fronted north along the Jagst River. Suddenly one of our task forces had swung south, crossed the Jagst and broken into Crailsheim. From there it was turning back west toward Heilbronn behind the German front and threatening to roll up their whole line defending Baden-Wurttemberg.

Predictably the German generals had counterattacked. They had surrounded the first intruding Americans in Crailsheim and cut the road behind them. So our orders were to lead a miles-long armored column down that road and reopen it.

One of the M-24 tanks would lead, followed by the three other tanks, three armored cars and six jeeps of my point platoon. I had learned early to ignore the Fort Knox reconnaissance doctrine that you led with a couple of jeeps. They drew fire. You led with the heaviest punch you had. Tanks scared Germans. I would ride on the rear deck of the lead tank and communicate over its radio. I rode exposed, both to share the vulnerability of the men like Speight in the following unarmored vehicles and to respect the place in the turret of the tank platoon sergeant whose attached crew I had ordered to be my platoon's point.

The guy with the wax pencil had seldom handed us one as nasty as this. Even if we could ram through, Crailsheim was besieged. Previously unheard-of German aircraft with incredible speed, called jets, were burning up our C-47 supply planes on the airfield. If we lived to get to Crailsheim, then what?

The time had come to mount up and go see. Pfc. Speight was pale, and so was I. Speight had joined our platoon just a couple of months earlier as a replacement for one of the casualties we'd taken in the Battle of the Bulge. So he lacked long combat experience. But he'd shown courage and coolness. And he possessed a noticeable maturity because he had a wife and two children back home in Unadilla, Ga.

As we moved out in a thunder of engines, I wondered if Speight might have had a premonition.

From the Georgia soil

Amory Speight and I grew up in Georgia about 75 miles apart during the Depression 1930s, he at Unadilla, south of Macon, and I at Adel, farther south in the piney woods near the Florida line.

At least he'd lived in town. His father ran a wholesale grocery warehouse. I toiled as a boy behind a plow drawn by two mules across 50 acres of isolation on the farm where my father and mother had to move us when the bank that employed him closed its doors in 1930.

That had been a jolting comedown for my parents. We would no longer live in the gray and white two-story house with awnings and French doors on Sellars Street in the pretty town of Douglas. Abruptly our furniture, including my mother's new Brambach baby grand piano, was loaded on a flatbed truck and hauled 60 miles over dirt roads to a small frame farm house she had built for tenants. The tenants had to move on because the landlord had to move in. My mother recalled our family could muster a total of $36 in cash at that point. And my father owed depositors of the busted bank twice the value of the stock he'd held in it. He paid off every nickel of it over the coming years. He never considered bankruptcy.

For the rest of his life my father, a mild, upright, unlucky man, remained crushed by the economic ruin of his time. He traveled Georgia, working at jobs that ranged from liquidating agent for the state banking department to cashier of small-town banks that survived. He lived in boarding houses during the week and rode the Greyhound bus home for weekends on the farm with his family.

My undefeatable, red-haired spitfire of a mother vowed never again to move the family away from the security of the land. To help anchor us on her few acres near Adel, she returned to full-time school teaching for the next 36 years. The county paid her $60 a month in scrip. Luckily she had used money her father had left her to buy—from her husband's parents—what came to be 50 acres of cleared land. Adjoining those fields stood some 300 acres of slash pine timber that she thought might someday be worth something as lumber if the nation ever started building anything again. In the meantime, our razorback rooters and lean range cows grazed scrub grasses there. And my older brother, Bill, and my younger sister, Anne, and I grew up hard there. We milked cows, butchered hogs and steers, hoed peanuts and pulled corn and picked cotton and cropped tobacco. School and then college offered the only escape.

My adolescent insistence on becoming a line officer and getting into combat terrified my mother. Her bridegroom had marched off to World War I in France with the 82nd Division leaving her "petrified." My father's olive drab sergeant's uniform still lay trim in her cedar chest when I sailed for France just 26 years after he'd come home. On the little single sheet V-mail stationery of the time, she wrote me a letter every day I was abroad in World War II. I knew that a full-time teacher who was running a farm and a family had to draw deep on a well of fatigue to write so faithfully. I also knew the frequency betrayed her fear that I would not hear from home on the day I died.

What I did not know until I came home was the diagnosis her doctor had made in 1945, when I was 21 and fighting the war: She was 55, and fighting uterine cancer.

Senseless Dying

Amory Speight was riding in the middle of the front seat of his mortar jeep, driven by Cecil Burnett of Lexington, Mo., and flanked on the outside by Andy Popkie of Dunglen, Ohio, when we blasted into the darkness of the deep pine forest near Blaufelden, two-thirds of the way to Crailsheim, with all machine guns firing.

We went into the forest very fast. We knew it was full of Germans because I had stopped the miles-long column of armor behind me to survey the woods line with binoculars and had seen, to my amazement, an American Army jeep rocketing out of the trees toward us. A tank company captain named O'Grady, whom I knew, huddled low in the jeep alongside a dazed driver as they screeched to a stop in front of my tank. Their windshield was shot to pieces. Both had ducked and somehow neither had been hit. "Those goddam woods are full of Germans," O'Grady yelled, looked blank, and sped on.

The shattered windshield, the shouting captain, the fear of the black woods ahead, sent my eyes on a frantic search of the map. Sure enough, a cow path marked by dotted lines skirted the woods. Yet I had seen whole columns of tanks mired on just such dotted-line lanes that turned to mud. Dare I? Suddenly officers a mile behind my lead tank were radioing that they were drawing flank fire from enemy artillery. "Move this goddamn column" was the basic entreaty. That cleared my mind.

We hadn't come this far to skirt the Germans in the woods ahead. I radioed the reinforced platoon to follow me through the woods with all bow, coaxial and pedestal machine guns to alternate continuous fire, one vehicle's guns directed to one side of the road and the next vehicle's to the other, as each closed on the woods. My tank hit the dark pine tunnel at near 30 miles an hour with our three deafening machine guns unfolding a bright fan of tracer bullets ahead. A red blizzard of ricochets from guns opening up behind us swept in front of the lead tank, enfolding us in fire. Crouched in the open on the tank's rocking rear deck, I clung to the turret ring with one hand and fired my M-1 with the other at an occasional green-clad figure I could see scuttling through the thick trees beyond the ditches. It was a terrifying bedlam at desperate speed. The thought has occurred to me that the German who had shot up O'Grady's jeep must have marveled at how ridiculously excessive was the wrath of God that so swiftly descended upon him. For whatever moments he still had to live, he would see mile after bellowing mile of armor approach and batter past in explosive retribution.

Once out of the woods I jumped down from the tank to count noses in my platoon's passing vehicles. Burnett's mortar jeep swerved to a stop. On his far right, Andy Popkie had taken a German bullet through both thighs. In the center seat, the same bullet had gone on to sever the femoral artery in Amory Speight's right groin.

Speight's whitening face watched me in silence as I tore away his combat suit. My compress was useless. Within a minute or two a medical half-track swung out of the column. Capt. Ronald Martin of Eden, N.Y., jumped down and took over. As the doctor went to work I squeezed Speight's shoulder and told him I'd see him in Crailsheim. All he had was a leg wound and the doc would fix it up.

Ronnie Martin came to my command post as soon as he got into Crailsheim. "I'm sorry, Pat," he said. "I couldn't get hold of the artery. Your man died."

The attack we'd pressed southward was fruitless. We angled back west of Crailsheim only as far as the village of Ilshofen before the German counterattacks caused our generals to fold their hand. They ordered us to fight our way back out to the north, past Gera Bronn, just as we'd fought our way south on the parallel route to Crailsheim. We came. We saw. We retreated. So much of the dying in war is senseless.

Two Certainties about War

Soon after my Japan-bound troopship rerouted me to Norfolk, by grace of President Truman's use of the atom bombs on Hiroshima and Nagasaki, I got on a Greyhound bus to Unadilla and went to see Amory Speight's family. His strong, accepting parents and his pretty young widow, Janie, and his two small sons, Roy and Jack, seemed to like me. I wanted to apologize. But they did not blame me. It was they who took pains to comfort me. Their forgiveness made my throat hurt.

Twenty years later the two brothers dropped by my office at the *Atlanta Constitution* where I had become the editor. We'd stayed in touch. Roy was finishing in business administration at the University of Georgia. Jack was studying biology at Emory and considering a career in public health. I'd just returned from a December 1964 reporting trip to the battle fronts in Vietnam. The fighting was low grade then. But the Speight brothers' eyes sparkled as they told me they were joining the air force together.

Don't do that, I told them. Your father has paid your family's dues. He fought the big one to spare you this. Vietnam is as minor as it is dangerous. He would want you to go on with your educations and your lives. I do not think you ought to join the air force, I said.

"We already have," they said. The flag was there. Their father went. They would.

Roy rose to the top management of the vast U.S. military commissary system in Western Europe during the Cold War. Jack became a top gun jet fighter pilot who volunteered for extended missions in the flak-thick skies over North Vietnam, and when he came home he qualified as a test pilot for the air force at Eglin Air Force Base in Florida. Upon retirement, they became achievers in the private sector.

Their father didn't make it out of World War II. My mother did. A brilliant young oncologist at Emory University Hospital named Dr. Elliott Scarborough stopped her cancer in its tracks with only the primitive radium and X-ray tools of 1945. Later he died of pancreatic cancer in his 60s. She lived to be 88.

The German officer who died young at Gera Bronn missed the half century that I have had. I went back to that village in 1989 and walked the street. No bullet nick remains visible in the edge of the aging building. The apple orchard where our column made the U-turn still stands. I remembered the young German and wished my aim had missed. The road stopped short near Crailsheim for him and the young American,

Amory Speight. Luck left long avenues of life ahead for me. I have walked them with the memories of those two men present in my heart, and with two certainties about war lodged firmly in my mind.

First, there is my certainty that war is the ultimate obscenity. I came away from the terror convinced that it is the antithesis of civilization for human beings to organize the killing of one another when, unlike animals, they aren't even hungry. Civilized ways simply must be found to settle man's post-jungle conflicts.

Second, I am certain that pending the discovery of these civilized ways to deter violence, decency requires peaceful people to stand up and stop human predators from savaging the helpless when conscience is called to meet brute force with just strength. Shrinking from that duty has ill served peace, I think.

I see a sadness in this paradox, but not a contradiction; just a logical duty to act as conscience compels until intelligence can elevate the animalism that coarsened the history of my century.

My postwar calling as a newspaper editor never seemed to lift my battle-battered being very far above the combat, either.

But I keep hoping.

In the meantime, my wife and I have decided we will be buried, when this shortening life is done, in Arlington National Cemetery. She is a native Virginian. And a lot of the soldiers who rest there are friends of mine.

The Long Road Back to Georgia

January 9, 2001

Eugene Patterson

So this is how it ends for me. This white Georgia farm boy, who studied at a racially segregated University of Georgia and then came to fight southern segregation through the central years of a journalistic life, returns today to the same wintry campus to celebrate, with old white governors and affectionate black friends, the fortieth anniversary of the desegregation of the university and so much more.

The hard path to real integration of America's society runs on into deep woods ahead. At age seventy-seven, I can walk it not much farther. Yet today my soul is rested as I regard the distance we have come.

Charlayne Hunter is here and so is the widow of Hamilton Holmes, who along with Charlayne risked physical harm and emotional ruin that January 9, 1961, when a federal court order freed them to walk under the black iron arch onto main campus and register in the ancient Academic Building, the first African Americans ever to attend a white public school in post-Reconstruction Georgia.

Our *Atlanta Constitution* reporters told of the jeering chants they faced and the sheets they saw lettered "Nigger Go Home." Two nights later Ku Klux Klan–led student rioters shattered dozens of windows in Charlayne's dormitory, Myers Hall. A rock and a bottle sprayed broken glass over her clothes in a not yet unpacked suitcase. By the time Athens police tear gas and fire hoses and a tough old dean named Bill Tate had forcibly dispersed the mob, another dean had suspended Charlayne and Hamilton "for their own safety" and Governor Ernest Vandiver had ordered the state patrol to return them to their homes in Atlanta.

I stand today beside Isabella Holmes, Hamilton's dignified mother, looking at a photograph in an exhibit. It shows Charlayne leaving the campus that night. She was only eighteen. She was holding a hand to her face. "Look," I said, "she's crying." Very softly, Mrs. Holmes said to me, "It was cryin' time."

Old federal judge William Bootle, who's not here, promptly ordered Governor Vandiver to put the two brave kids back into the university. "The university suspended the wrong students," I wrote in the next morning's *Constitution*. "They need not have surrendered (to the mob) if the state had sent the troopers needed for protection."

Vandiver is here, gray and on a cane. He remembers the call he made to me at dusk of that January day forty years ago. I can recall it almost verbatim. "Gene," he'd said, in his deep bass, "I'm sitting out here by myself in the governor's mansion. Fifty of my legislative leaders and closest advisors have just left. I'm by myself."

He told today's gathering what he'd gone on to tell me that evening. "I went around the room and asked each one of the fifty, 'Do you think I should close the university and the public schools, or obey the courts and integrate them?' and every one of them said close them, except for two—Carl Sanders and Frank Twitty."

On that long-ago evening I'd told him, "Governor, I know what you're going to do."

"You do?" he'd said.

"Yes," I'd responded. "You're going to remember the state constitution makes you conservator of the peace and you're going to send in the state patrol and protect those children when you put them back in and I know you're going to obey the law and put them back in."

"I'm out here thinking about it," he'd said. That decent man did what I knew he would do the next day, and the crisis ended.

Now there sits old Vandiver on the stage of the university's Hodgson Hall this morning, with two other snowy-haired white men on his left. They are the Senate president pro tem of the time, Carl Sanders, who went on to succeed Vandiver as a progressive governor, and George T. Smith, whom Sanders appointed speaker of the House and who later got elected lieutenant governor before going on the state supreme court when he realized, as Vandiver and Sanders were to find out, that their courage to lead the state into racial change had sacrificed any elective future for them in the Georgia of that time.

"I expected to run for the U.S. Senate," Vandiver confides to today's crowd, "but I found I had no support." He returned for keeps to his law practice in Lavonia.

Sanders makes the same report. He'd supported Lyndon Johnson for the presidency in 1964, the year Johnson had rammed through Congress the Civil Rights Act opening public accommodations to black Americans, and the voters were ready to punish him. Sanders tells today's audience how he'd also blocked efforts by segregationists to invite Alabama's segregationist governor George Wallace to address the Georgia legislature. So when he'd run for governor again in 1970, he'd been plowed under by a candidate who'd made a campaign promise to invite Wallace to Georgia to address the legislature. Sanders names the name, with sharp asperity. "He was Jimmy Carter, your future president."

Sanders never ran for anything again. Neither did Justice Smith, who left politics and served out his career in the judiciary. Their elective careers were finished like Vandiver's and those of other southern whites who dared to lead responsibly on racial change, from Florida's gallant governor LeRoy Collins, who was defeated for the U.S. Senate in 1970 by a forgotten Republican whose campaign distributed pictures of Collins alongside Martin Luther King Jr., to President Johnson, who knew when he engineered his civil rights acts that he was committing political suicide and losing the South for the Democratic Party.

Leadership isn't always about winning for oneself.

The governors who won brief popularity by pandering to white segregationist passions in the 1950s and '60s swiftly vanished into richly earned oblivion. Mouthing about states' rights, Governor Faubus of Arkansas left it to elements of the 101st U.S. Airborne Division to safe-guard the children desegregating Little Rock's Central High School. Louisiana's Governor Davis gave the nation the televised spectacle of white mothers spitting on Negro children trying to go to school. Mississippi's Governor Barnett abdicated his state's responsibility for public order and left it to federal marshals and ultimately federal troops to stop the shooting at the University of Mississippi. Alabama's Wallace, the ultimate demagogue of that shameful era, stood in the schoolhouse door. And windy gentlemen in South Carolina and Virginia prated about their states' right to interpose state preferences and nullify re-quirements of the U.S. Constitution as if John C. Calhoun had pre-vailed and Appomattox had crowned Lee victor.

Only in Terry Sanford's North Carolina and LeRoy Collins's Florida had citizens of the old Confederacy seen leadership worthy of the name, until Vandiver of Georgia stopped dancing the tortured old adagios and arabesques of segregation politics and told his legislature in January of 1961, "We cannot abandon public education," and "I will not be a party to defiance of law." Those simple words lost him any future public office but gained him a place of honor in history.

Today the Georgia governor of a new generation and a new century, Roy Barnes, tells this interracial gathering on the campus of the state's flagship university that Georgia and Atlanta owe their position of lead-ership in the South to the decision forty years ago to desegregate their schools peacefully and with grace. He reminds that Atlanta had no heavy industry at midcentury, as Birmingham did with its steel mills. Charlotte's geographic positioning rivaled Atlanta's. This city and state pulled ahead of the pack because leaders of both races chose to make progress together.

If not for the courage of Charlayne Hunter and Hamilton Holmes, and the leadership of a state that finally supported them, says Michael Adams, president of the University of Georgia, "UGA today wouldn't be one of the top twenty public universities in the country."

Enough of the old. New history is evident on this January 9, 2001, in the friendly and, yes, affectionate celebration of races come together. Seated onstage with the gray old governors are the three main black lawyers who obtained the federal court orders requiring them to admit

Hunter and Holmes to this university. Their white thatches show their ages too—Donald Hollowell, whose Atlanta firm won these and so many other cases for African Americans in Georgia; Constance Baker Motley, longtime lawyer for the NAACP Legal Defense and Educational Fund, now a federal judge; and Horace Ward, another federal judge, who tried vainly in the 1950s to gain admission to the University of Georgia law school and finally studied law at Northwestern University.

"I may have been the most experienced lawyer around," Judge Ward jokes. "I tried seven years to get into one law school and three years to get out of another one." With another young attorney in Hollowell's law firm, Vernon Jordan, he accompanied Holmes and Hunter to Athens for their enrollment.

Judge Motley is a formidable figure of a no-nonsense judge. She tells with zest of her days of litigation before federal judges in the South. "We knew the ones who were plain segregationists," she said. She maneuvered constantly to get her cases before federal district judges such as William Bootle in Georgia and Frank Johnson in Alabama, and circuit court of appeals judges such as John Robert Brown in Texas, John Minor Wisdom in Louisiana, Richard Rives in Alabama, and, champion of all the hardnoses, Chief Judge Elbert Tuttle in Atlanta. "We went through some turbulent times in the twentieth century," she said. "But the work is far from over. I must tell you I expect more turbulent times in the twenty-first."

Then suddenly, Charlayne Hunter-Gault is at the lectern, just off the plane from Johannesburg where she is CNN bureau chief, and she is a star. Freed of the PBS TelePrompTer that often seemed to hobble her television delivery on the *MacNeil-Lehrer News Hour,* she instantly captures the large crowd and turns it rapt.

Calling Hamilton Holmes "Hamp," she alludes to the extended Holmes family members who have flocked here in his memory by saying she and her daughter and husband can't match "the 9,000 of Hamp's relatives who have turned out here."

More than I have ever seen these qualities on television, she is witty and warm, graciously conversational, sweetly eloquent. She's self-deprecating and funny and makes no pretense of heroism in her role. She didn't really recognize the situation enough to be afraid when the rocks started hitting her dormitory windows. Only later, when she and Holmes were suspended and preparing to return to Atlanta late that night, did she give way to her perquisite as an adolescent and pitch a temper tantrum at Hamp because he wanted to drive her in his car through all those little towns to Atlanta. She demanded he join her in a state patrol car for the trip and he did.

She feels she had it easier than Hamp because she lived in a dormitory with other students around, a few of them nice to her, while he lived with a private family in an off-campus home. She remembers white students letting the air out of his car tires, nevertheless. (I remember him visiting me at the *Atlanta Constitution* on a trip home. "How's it going?" I asked the former football star and student leader at Morehouse. "Not so good," the nineteen-year-old replied. "You got any friends over there?" I asked. "No," he said. "What do you do for relaxation?" I asked. "I shoot some baskets in the back yard," he said. "I study a lot.") He studied enough to make Phi Beta Kappa at Georgia and gain admission to the Emory University medical school. He became a distinguished orthopedic surgeon and medical director of Grady Memorial Hospital in Atlanta. He died at fifty-four after coronary bypass surgery. In his later years he embraced the university and served on the board of the University of Georgia Foundation.

Charlayne discloses offhandedly that her dormitory life wasn't all nice. For a while, when she was studying at night, some white girls took turns stamping on the floor above her room. But hers is a high-spirited message of affectionate remembrance of classmates who befriended her. In Johannesburg she'd met a fellow UGA graduate and they'd traded a high five and a "Go Dawgs!"

In a serious moment, Charlayne says, "If Hamp and I had known that forty years later only 6 percent of the thirty-four thousand students at our university would be African Americans, I think instead of walking through the arch to register we'd have sat down on the curb and cried."

At the conclusion of her affecting speech she dispenses with a standard peroration and instead, with a sparkling grin, brings the crowd to its feet by bursting into the civil rights anthem "Ain't Gonna Let Nobody Turn Me Roun'." Suddenly her strong soprano and clapping hands have us all clapping and singing . . . "Gonna keep on walkin', gonna keep on talkin' . . . ain't gonna let nobody turn me roun'." She sings her way off the stage and back to her seat and leaves a smile on our faces all through lunch.

In the old university chapel that afternoon, President Adams speaks again—"It is time to come together"—and Governor Barnes delivers a dedication speech full of praise for African-American contributions to Georgia.

Then we walk next door in the freezing afternoon light to the Academic Building where all students enroll. With Charlayne standing by Hamilton Holmes's pretty schoolteacher widow, Marilyn, and the two of them flanked by President Adams and Governor Barnes, a red silk covering is whisked from a black iron marker with raised gold letters, the permanent kind of sign that bears the names of buildings around the campus, and this one proclaims the new name of the old building. It is, of course, the Holmes-Hunter Academic Building

In her remarks, Marilyn Holmes says she wishes Hamp could be here because "he would have a big smile on his face—no, he'd be laughing out loud—at the irony of this building they tried to keep him out of now bearing his name!"

This day has been one that will leave a warmth in my heart always. The friendliness and ready wit and firm handshakes and unreserved acceptance of us whites by these extraordinarily kind black companions in our common land remind me yet again how fortunate we southern whites have always been to have offered this race mistreatment and received forgiveness, to have slighted them and had politeness returned, to have hurt their pride and been given their blessings, to have tested their patience and found their forbearance unending, to have cruelly withheld our love and found theirs constantly present for us.

How very overdue we are finally to acknowledge such friends and commit ourselves at last to rectify, not justify, unworthy aspects of our past conduct.

Yes, Judge Motley is right. More turbulence lies ahead in race relations in America. All is not well. At least we are at the end of a beginning. Civil war ended slavery in the nineteenth century. Moved by brave black protests, white America struck segregation laws from all states' law books in the twentieth.

More important, political, social, and economic shifts changed the mind of the South. Politically today, Governor Roy Barnes is openly and eagerly courting the black vote, which no statewide politician dared do forty years ago. Economically, the dollars of the growing black middle class are essential for any successful business to value and pursue, whereas forty years ago restaurants and department stores and motels and movie houses insultingly turned away nonwhite customers. Socially, the gentle and cultivated people on this campus today are delightful friends to talk and laugh and join and eat with, and indeed it marks a white person as ignorant and oafish to treat them with less than respect, whereas in the mid-twentieth century whites invited peer censure if they addressed blacks as Mr. or Mrs. (lawyers like Donald Hollowell were called "colonel" to skirt the issue). The directional change over these forty years on the social, political, and economic compass of the South has been just about 180 degrees.

So in the twentieth century, whether we jumped or were pushed, white southerners did turn out to be better than we were. May America hold to that true bearing in the twenty-first.

A Postscript
St. Petersburg, Florida
June 2001

If I were able to start another life as a southern editor in this new century, I think I know what I would say to this strong and decent nation that still is not comfortable with itself.

I would recall unsparingly the fact that enslavement of captive Africans placed upon America's history from the eighteenth century a stain that we have not yet cleansed. White Americans, mainly, fought in the nineteenth century the bloodiest civil war that the world has ever seen on this issue and emancipated the slaves, while my father's grandfather and four of his great-uncles bravely died in Confederate uniforms on the wrong side of a moral cause. Emotion drove narrow pride ahead of broad common sense and inflamed our history as hot temper will. Then in the twentieth—my century—we southern whites meanly fastened racial segregation laws on supposedly freed black Americans sufficient to hold them in social and educational and economic bondage comparable to the chains of slavery. Yet after midcentury, history drew again from the wells of American decency the sweet waters of justice under the leadership of two new Lincolns, these from the South. Martin Luther King Jr. went willingly to his physical death for marching his people to freedom from segregation laws, and Lyndon B. Johnson readily accepted his political death to emancipate his white southern kinsmen from wronging their fellow Americans with those laws any longer.

In the twenty-first century, the work is not finished, though I am grown old, but what might I say if I could go on? I do believe I would editorially encourage the brave politicians—the ones like Lincoln and Johnson who would lead, no matter the cost—to strike forward as boldly as America advanced in the two centuries past: to lift up the people we held down for so long, to pay wages for the forced labor whose sweat let us prosper, to cleanse from American history the stain of past wrongs by rising to repay the debt that we owe. We should choose to extend now to black Americans the national investment we offered after 1945 to 16 million surviving war veterans who gave up the best years of their lives for our country. Congress called it the GI Bill of Rights then, and it offered to pay for the higher education of veterans who had been deprived of it, to guarantee them low-interest loans to buy decent houses they'd had no way to save up for, to subsidize employers who would offer on-the-job training for citizens whose sacrifices had left them lacking skills. That program transformed a postwar generation of Americans in the twentieth century and may have been the most profitable investment this nation ever made. If we try it again for African Americans in the twenty-first, a Free America Act, it might generate a great national thrust toward the final redemption America has searched for and reached for and marched toward, at our worthiest, for a very long time now.

Left: Gene Patterson in 1925 at the age of two, then living in the little town of Nicholls, Georgia. Photo courtesy of Gene Patterson.

Below: An early love of language is revealed in the name on young Gene's soapbox derby rig. The other kids did not grasp that Percy Veer was a pun on "persevere." They just called him Percy. Photo courtesy of Gene Patterson.

Lieutenant Patterson atop one of the M-8 armored cars he commanded in 1944. Photo courtesy of Gene Patterson.

As a journalist Gene was always a hard charger. ROTC cavalry training, on his horse Ike, helped. Photo courtesy of Gene Patterson.

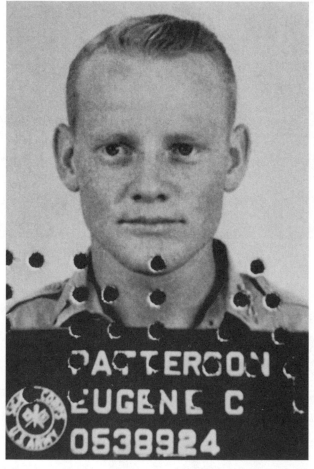

Lieutenant Patterson's 1944 military photograph, complete with ID number and filing perforation. Photo courtesy of Gene Patterson.

Gene with his father, William, in front of the family home in Adel, Georgia. Photo courtesy of Gene Patterson.

Gene poses for a formal portrait in 1946 at Fort Sill, Oklahoma, while still in the army. Evidence of his true calling is in his hands: an autobiography of famous editor William Allen White. Photo courtesy of Gene Patterson.

Above: Gene strides along the street in Atlanta with his father and his brother Bill, who became a surgeon. Photo courtesy of Gene Patterson.

Left: For his first day on the job as a cub reporter for the *Daily Telegram* in Temple, Texas, in 1947, Gene bought a new suit. Photo courtesy of Gene Patterson.

Gene became editor of the *Atlanta Constitution* in 1960. He is pictured here at a Labor Day union barbecue next to his daughter, Mary, and wife, Sue. Photo courtesy of Gene Patterson.

Gene Patterson called Ralph McGill "Pappy." McGill was Gene's inspiration, mentor, and best friend. Photo courtesy of Gene Patterson.

A harmonic trio of journalists, Ralph McGill (left), Gene Patterson (center), and Harold Martin patrol Forsyth Street in Atlanta, circa 1965. Photo courtesy of Gene Patterson.

A prominent Texan takes the hesitant arm of Sue Patterson while assuring Gene that he's devoted to the first lady. Photo courtesy of Gene Patterson.

Gene stands beside the formative influence of his life, his mother, Annabel Corbett Patterson, at the family farm in Adel, Georgia. Along with
running the farm, Gene's mother taught for forty years in the public
schools. Photo courtesy of Gene Patterson.

Gene is greeted in 1984 by his good friend Katharine Graham, publisher of the *Washington Post*. Gene served as her managing editor from 1968 to 1971 and persuaded her to publish the Pentagon Papers. Photo courtesy of Gene Patterson.

Gene Patterson with Nelson Poynter, the man who hired him as editor of
the *St. Petersburg Times*, 1973. Photo courtesy of Gene Patterson.

Gene Patterson

An Appreciation

Howell Raines,
executive editor,
New York Times

Howell Raines follows the tradition of great southern journalists who have become executive editor of the *New York Times*. Born in Alabama, he worked at newspapers in Tuscaloosa, Birmingham, Atlanta, and St. Petersburg, where he was hired as political editor by
Gene Patterson.

There was a time when I feared I would never get to work for Gene
Patterson. In 1968, I was the city hall reporter at the *Tuscaloosa News*,
and like most young southern liberals, I looked to Patterson and Ralph
McGill at the *Atlanta Constitution* as the South's most heroic voices on
civil rights and race. Then in the fall of that tumultuous year, the news
magazines reported that Gene had resigned from the *Constitution* in a
dispute with its conservative management and moved on to the *Washington Post*. By the time I finally reached the *Constitution* in 1971, McGill
was gone, too. Newsroom veterans told stories about them, of course,
but the stories made me sad. I had missed the days of legend.

I finally met Gene in 1976. I had left the *Constitution* to work on a
book, *My Soul Is Rested*, an oral history of the civil rights movement.
Gene was coming to Atlanta to give a speech, and I contacted him in
advance about an interview for the book. Since he knew the neighbor-

hood, he said that he would swing by my house and we would talk there. I remember the day with such clarity—because of what Gene Patterson said and because our meeting in a sunny den strewn with my young sons' toys turned out to be a pivot point in my career and, indeed, in the way I thought about newspapering.

In his introduction to the present collection, Roy Clark quotes from that interview to show Gene's principled resistance to J. Edgar Hoover's attempt to smear the reputation of Dr. Martin Luther King. From a news standpoint, that interview was important to the book because it was hard in those days to find people who had firsthand knowledge they were willing to share about the FBI's attempts to undermine the civil rights movement and its greatest leader. Even so, it was the eloquence with which Gene spoke of our homeland and the sealed world of segregation in which he and I had grown up that most moved me. It has lingered in my memory as the most eloquent description I've ever heard of the intellectual paralysis that gripped the South in the 1950s and '60s.

"To know that period of the South is to know that it was frozen in silence," he said. "People were not discussing the issue. Neighbor and neighbor were afraid of each other. Conformity was established by precedent. And for a man who might doubt the wisdom of segregation to sit down with his neighbor and say, 'Hey, I'm not sure we're right' could have ruined that man in most Southern states. And it could have in Georgia. Therefore nobody discussed the issue. Only the politicians, who were aggravating emotions, were discussing it. McGill suddenly and boldly on the front page of the *Constitution* began to talk openly about the rights and wrongs of segregation, and this led people to be emboldened to talk about it even if all they did was cuss McGill."

Typically, Gene praised McGill in that interview and underplayed the importance of his own columns, including those that won the Pulitzer Prize for condemning the Georgia legislature's refusal to seat Julian Bond because of his opposition to the Vietnam War. But I think Gene had greater direct impact on many journalists of my age because of the way he demonstrated that one could combine stainless-steel principles and a wide-ranging career at a variety of major newspapers. His continuing vigor and commitment also conveyed a vision of how journalism could be a force in a South that was no longer frozen in silence but was still discovering the transforming potential of biracial politics.

As it turned out, Gene's most immediate impact on me was financial. I was as broke as I have ever been while I was finishing *My Soul Is Rested*. Not long after our interview, I wrote to tell Gene that the book was substantially done and I was looking to get back into newspapers. As I recall, I wrote on a Tuesday, and Gene called two days later to invite me down for an interview. (The mail worked fast in those days, at least between Atlanta and St. Petersburg.) In less than a week, I was employed as political editor of the *St. Petersburg Times*. Gene offered a decent salary and a direct challenge—to bring his readers a more vivid style of political reporting and writing. Thus began one of the great learning experiences of my life. I think of it now as my personal graduate school in journalism.

I learned what "command presence" really meant by watching Gene operate in a newsroom. Much has been made of Gene's erect, chestforward posture and his purposeful, military stride. Sometimes reporters, talking among themselves, called him "Treads," in reference to his days as a tank commander. Certainly, World War II had put its stamp on Gene. But so had his years at United Press, the *Constitution*, and the *Washington Post*. He was a man of the world, who forced our reporting vision beyond the county courthouse and the state capitol. And if you watched Gene closely, you could see that he led by being authoritative, not authoritarian. He had the kind of guts essential to great editors—that is to say, he demanded the highest standards of fairness and accuracy and then defended his staff with a fierce, but measured, determination when the community didn't like the truths revealed by that style of journalism.

The *St. Petersburg Times* was my fifth newspaper, but the first in my experience where the top editors let folks on the newsroom floor see how important decisions were made. In other words, Gene taught the same way he led—by example. He was also a strong believer in incentives. Given the pinchpennies I had encountered in other venues, I was nearly speechless when Gene called me at home one Sunday morning and said he thought my article that day was so good he was giving me a fifty-dollar-a-week raise. That was a big raise in those days. As Roy Clark notes, Gene was a pioneer in emphasizing the movement to improve the quality of writing in American newspapers. The impulse grew from the fact that he himself was a formidable stylist, both on paper and in conversation. He was well read in history and literature. But Gene also grasped earlier than most editors the implications of the changing educational demographics of postwar America and of the economic growth of the New South he helped create. As the educational level of our readers went up and the mass audience drained away to television, Gene realized that the intellectual and literary quality of newspapers had to improve if we wanted to hold the more sophisticated readers who had become our main audience.

I was Gene Patterson's political editor for two years. I think I did some of my best writing in his newspaper. He remains a friend, adviser, and sometimes fishing buddy. But the most important thing I carried away from him was a method for finding my way through the professional and ethical dilemmas that confront every writer and editor on every newspaper, regardless of size. It has been more than two decades since I worked for the man, but when I'm confronted with a particularly knotty problem about how to deal with a story, a colleague, or a reader, I simply say to myself, "What would Gene do?"

The Legacy of
Gene Patterson

An Interview with
Cynthia Tucker

Cynthia Tucker holds what has historically been one of the most influential jobs in American journalism, that of editorial page editor of the *Atlanta Constitution*. In effect, she inherited the mantle of Ralph McGill and Eugene Patterson. She is African American. Interviewing her is Roy Peter Clark.

Clark: Gene Patterson left Atlanta in 1968. How is the city different in 2001 than it was in 1968?

Tucker: I think that the city of Atlanta, and I use that term broadly to reflect the close-in suburbs as well, has changed to become very close to what Ralph McGill and Gene Patterson would have liked. And that may be more true in 2001 than it was in 1990. The 2000 census shows that for the first time since 1970 the city of Atlanta has enjoyed a net influx of whites, and I happen to find that well worth celebrating for a couple of reasons. One, I believe in diversity. Period. Because it brings many values of its own. Second, I think that reflects the fact that Atlanta is now finally past the pitched battles of race.

Shortly after Gene Patterson left in 1968, the first black mayor of Atlanta was elected in 1973, Mayor Maynard Jackson. And while that definitely reflected progress, it was not progress of an easy nature. Many whites responded with fear and anxiety and many of them pulled up stakes and left. They didn't even give it a chance to see if this would work, if a black mayor could govern the city efficiently and represent white Atlantans as well as blacks. They just left. As white flight picked up, Atlanta was left with the increasing urban problems that came to mar many major cities in the country. Part of it was because the flight of white middle-class residents left the city poor. That meant a smaller tax base, rising crime, rising unemployment. That in turn made the whites who had left feel justified in their decision to leave: "See, I told you so."

I am happy to say, however, that there were enough citizens of good-will left, black and white, that the city not only persevered; it got through that period and is now turning around, and it may be a better place than it was economically in 1960. It is certainly a better place po-litically than it was in 1960. You now have whites, blacks, an increasing population of Latinos and Asians, something that Ralph McGill would be surprised to see and that was not the case when Gene left in '68. You have a city that is economically much stronger. You have increasing ac-tivism from Atlanta's gay residents. We have the possibility of the first openly gay city council president being elected in November [2001], and so I believe that the city of Atlanta is much the place now that McGill and Patterson would have hoped for.

Clark: Did I understand something Gene told me, that not only are whites moving back into the city, but the black middle class has been extending itself into the white suburbs?

Tucker: Absolutely. One of Atlanta's strengths going back to the for-ties has been the presence of an educated and significant black middle class. It is that group out of which Martin Luther King Jr. came. It is that group that white businessmen and politicians were used to negoti-ating with in the forties and fifties, before blacks had any real voting strength. It's also part of the secret as to why the city of Atlanta did not erupt as some other cities did. You know, it is absolutely true that this city was blessed with some far-sighted white political and business lead-ership. But I think part of the story that has been overlooked is that they had to have a constituency to address. They needed to have black middle-class residents with whom they could sit down and talk and ne-gotiate. That has always been part of Atlanta's strength.

Well now, this black middle class has gotten bigger and bigger and bigger, and they are now going to the suburbs for some of the same reasons that whites went. I have to say whites didn't go just because they feared black political leadership, but because housing was cheaper and schools were better and crime was lower and all that. And so now, especially if you look out through DeKalb County, you see a huge black middle class. In fact, here's a funny thing. I don't know if you know anything about the history of Stone Mountain, Georgia.

Clark: Gene told me that's where the Klan used to meet.

Tucker: Right. Stone Mountain has an unfortunate history. First of all, the stone mountain itself is carved with the visages of all of these Confederate generals. Perhaps because it seemed a friendly place then, it traditionally was the place the Ku Klux Klan held its big meetings. Well now, Stone Mountain is heavily black, it's home to these subdivisions of $400,000 homes that black folk live in, and it has a black mayor. So how's that for change in the South?

Clark: Cynthia, help me understand the difference between the white editorialists in the fifties and sixties who were moderates, as opposed to those who were liberals. The reason I mention that is because Dr. King is very critical of the moderates. How did Patterson and McGill differ from those white moderates whom Dr. King seems to revile?

Tucker: It's funny. I reread the letter from the Birmingham jail not that long ago, and I think it was a reflection of Martin Luther King Jr.'s increasing frustration at that point—there were so many whites who believed themselves progressive and right thinking and people of goodwill, who kept cautioning that Negroes were in too big a hurry: "You need to wait." And indeed, I think he believed that when a white moderate leader, be it a politician or a newspaper editor, wrote something like that, it just gave cover to those whites of goodwill who were still unsettled by the demands for social change, and it gave them an excuse to move slowly, if at all. And so I think I can understand his frustration.

On the flip side of it, however, I have to say that I'm one of those people who understands the history of the South enough—I was born after all in 1955 in Monroeville, Alabama, a year after *Brown v. Board of Education.* My parents were married in '54. And my mother says that after that Supreme Court ruling she assumed her children would never attend segregated schools. I want you to know that it was 1970 before schools in Monroeville, Alabama, fully integrated. I remember the segregated South, and I remember white resistance very well. It's not something I've read in history books. I remember it.

And so I don't have any trouble placing Patterson's writing in the context of the times. You see him moving. And by the early to mid-sixties, he was well out ahead of his readership. Many of them did not believe there was such a thing as a moderate. Those who resisted segregation believed you were either with them or against them, and as far as they were concerned, Patterson was against them. In the context of the times, I see his work as not only progressive but courageous, but I also see him struggling.

That's one of the interesting things if you read some of his earliest stuff. You see him struggling. You know, he was not only a southerner; he grew up poor. He didn't grow up wealthy, well educated, sophisticated. He was learning to accept the idea that black Georgians, too, were due full citizenship. And the only thing that he had to guide him was his own moral compass. There wasn't a whole lot of that around among Gene Patterson's peers.

Clark: What do you think of the idea of a daily column?

Tucker: I am completely overwhelmed by it. I simply cannot imagine that. I know that Gene did a lot of reporting, which then makes it even more awe-inspiring. He went over to the legislature, he hung out with those guys, and I do mean guys. He must have been working day and night. Now he also had range.

There is something else that I have learned from both McGill and Patterson, and I won't claim to have done it nearly as well as they. But one of their tricks, if you will, was to constantly remind their readers that they were southerners. And obviously I'm not a white southerner, but I'm a southerner, and not only that—I love the South. I mean despite all of its history and its difficulties, I love the South. And so every now and then I try to reflect that.

During the controversy about Thomas Jefferson's ancestors, I wrote a piece about family reunions. Well, this is something almost every southerner understands—the notion of family and how even a family gathering can be a little bit difficult. You know, all of us have relatives we don't get along with that well. And so every now and then I try to do something like that. I don't have hunting dogs, but I do remember that you have to every now and then remind your readers that "I am not apart from you."

Clark: Let me use here the metaphor of the photographic image and negative. Excuse me for it, but what I'm seeing is Patterson talking to his kinfolk and writing for his kinfolk and telling them some things that they may not want to hear and trying to nudge them and persuade them and cajole them and humor them, and I see you doing the same thing with your kinfolk, but yours just don't happen to be white.

Tucker: If I take any lesson from Patterson and McGill, it's that one. This idea of courage and trying to speak directly to your peers for me is far less about talking to my white readers than talking to my black readers. I am certainly going to be vigilant against racism. I mean, racism continues to exist throughout America and certainly in the South. There is much about the South that still needs to change. But let's face it, for an African-American female editor in Atlanta in the year 2001, denouncing racism doesn't take much courage.

But it's a bit more of a challenge for me to help my black readers understand when they, too, are narrow-minded, guilty of bigotry, playing the race card. In fact, for Monday we are addressing the changing face of Atlanta in terms of political redistricting. I talked to you earlier about the new census, which I happen to be very excited about. Again, for me, diversity is a core value. I just accept that diversity is a good in its own right. But for many of my African-American readers, diversity is a really good thing when you're talking about including more black folk in the process. But it is not as easy to take when you're talking about including more Latinos or whites in the process.

I had to write an editorial chiding some African-American legislators just a few months ago because a bill came up during the session to broaden the state's legal definition of minority so that Latino business owners could be included in the state's set-aside program. African-American legislators resisted, and I had to write an editorial reminding them, "Hey, you can't do this." Not only are they legitimately a minority group that has also struggled, but you just proved the point. If you want to say they have not faced prejudice, they're now facing yours. In Monday's editorial we've got some black city council members who don't want their districts redrawn to become more white, and we have to remind them that diversity is a good thing and that if you now have to go beyond your traditional black base and appeal to whites and Latinos, too, that's a good thing, not a bad thing.

And so that is perhaps the greatest lesson I draw from the legacy of McGill and Patterson. Let me also say, however, that there's another important component of this. It is because they campaigned relentlessly to make Atlanta the city it is today that it is possible for me to do this. I understand that if African Americans in Atlanta were still struggling for political and economic justice, it would be much more difficult for me to find acceptance chiding black leaders. In cities where African-American leaders feel less secure, it would be very difficult for a black columnist to chide the few black leaders who were around, because blacks would feel that it was a betrayal and that the cost was too high. But because Atlanta has changed as much as it has, Atlanta has an economically secure, politically active African-American middle class that is not that easily threatened. And so I have a foundation from which to remind them to do the right thing.

Cast of Characters

Ivan Allen Jr. (1911–92), prominent Atlanta businessman and politician; after serving as chairman of the Atlanta Chamber of Commerce, he became the mayor of Atlanta in 1962; during his eight years as mayor, he earned a reputation for pragmatic liberalism and racial moderation.

Ross Barnett (1898–1988), militant white supremacist attorney and governor of Mississippi, 1960–64; defeated in the 1951 and 1955 Democratic gubernatorial primaries, he was elected in 1959 by running as the candidate of the White Citizens Councils; during the Freedom Rides of 1961 and the University of Mississippi desegregation crisis of 1962, he emerged as a regional symbol of massive resistance and Deep South intransigence.

Julian Bond (1940–), Atlanta-based black civil rights activist and leader of the Student Nonviolent Coordinating Committee; elected to the Georgia House of Representatives in 1965 but not seated until a U.S. Supreme Court decision in 1967 upheld his right to serve in the legislature despite his opposition to the Vietnam War; antiwar delegates to the 1968 Democratic National Convention nominated him for the vice presidency.

Howard "Bo" Callaway (1927–), corporate executive (president of Callaway Gardens) and one-term Republican Georgia congressman (1965–67);

native of La Grange, Georgia; as the Republican candidate for governor in 1966, he lost to Democrat Lester Maddox in a close election that marked the first serious Republican challenge in Georgia gubernatorial politics since Reconstruction; he served as a Republican National Committeeman from Georgia from 1968 to 1973 and as secretary of the army from 1973 to 1975.

Stokely Carmichael (1941–98), radical civil rights activist, Pan Africanist, and SNCC field secretary; born in New York City and educated at Howard University; popularized the term *Black Power* during the 1966 Meredith March through Mississippi; he joined the Black Panther Party in 1967 and two years later helped organize Kwame Nkrumah's All-Africa People's Revolutionary Party; he moved to the African nation of Guinea in 1969.

Wilbur J. Cash (1900–1941), journalist born in South Carolina; reporter for the *Charlotte News*; author of the classic and highly influential regional study *The Mind of the South* (1941); while on a Guggenheim Fellowship in Mexico City in 1941, he committed suicide.

LeRoy Collins (1909–91), moderate governor of Florida, 1955–61; president of the National Association of Broadcasters, 1961–64; director of the U.S. Community Relations Service, 1964–65; undersecretary of the U.S. Department of Commerce, 1965–67; unsuccessful candidate for the U.S. Senate in 1968.

Eugene "Bull" Connor (1897–1973), militant white supremacist and commissioner of public safety in Birmingham, Alabama, 1937–54, 1958–63; he received international attention in 1961, when he failed to protect visiting Freedom Riders from a white mob, and again in 1963, when he ordered police to use fire hoses and attack dogs to quell civil rights demonstrations.

Orval Faubus (1910–94), Arkansas governor elected as a moderate in 1954; he later became a militant segregationist who defied the authority of the federal government during the attempt to desegregate Little

Rock's Central High School in 1957; he served six consecutive terms (1955–67) as governor.

Barry Goldwater (1909–98), conservative and libertarian five-term U.S. senator from Arizona (1952–64, 1969–87); as the Republican Party presidential candidate in 1964, he carried the Deep South states of Georgia, Louisiana, Mississippi, Alabama, and South Carolina, but overall he was soundly defeated by President Lyndon Johnson; author of *Conscience of a Conservative* (1960), opponent of the 1964 Civil Rights Act.

Dick Gregory (1932–), popular black comedian, campus lecturer, and militant social activist; born in St. Louis, Missouri; author of *From the Back of the Bus* (1962) and *Nigger* (1964); he fasted for forty days in 1967 to protest the Vietnam War and ran for mayor of Chicago the same year; in 1968 he ran for president on the U.S. Freedom and Peace Party ticket.

Roy V. Harris (1895–1985), arch-conservative attorney, legislator, and self-proclaimed "kingmaker" of Georgia gubernatorial politics; as a longtime state representative (1932–46) and lobbyist from Richmond County, he wielded enormous power from the 1930s to the 1960s; an ally of Senator Herman Talmadge and Governor Marvin Griffin during the 1950s, he became increasingly reactionary on matters of race, editing the white supremacist *Augusta Courier*, serving as president of the Citizens Councils of America, and interjecting himself into the 1957 desegregation crisis in Little Rock, Arkansas; he later allied himself with segregationist Lester Maddox during the 1966 gubernatorial campaign.

William B. Hartsfield (1890–1971), progressive Atlanta lawyer and politician; member of Atlanta City Council, 1923–28; Georgia state legislator, 1933–36; mayor of Atlanta, 1937–61; he coined the slogan, "Atlanta, a city too busy to hate" in 1961.

Hamilton Holmes (1941–95), academically talented black student from Atlanta, who, along with Charlayne Hunter, desegregated the University of Georgia in January 1961; after submitting his application to the

University of Georgia in 1959, he spent one year at Morehouse College; selected for Phi Beta Kappa, he graduated from the University of Georgia in 1963; in the fall of 1963 he became the first black student to enroll at Emory University Medical School; he went on to become a distinguished orthopedic surgeon, a lecturer at Emory, the medical director of Henry Grady Hospital, and a member of the University of Georgia foundation's board of trustees.

Charlayne Hunter (1942–), born in South Carolina, daughter of an army chaplain; along with Hamilton Holmes, she desegregated the University of Georgia in January 1961; her marriage to white classmate Walter Stovall ended in divorce; following her graduation from the University of Georgia in 1963, she was a columnist and reporter for *New Yorker* magazine (1964–67) and the *New York Times* (1968–78); in the 1980s, working under her married name, Charlayne Hunter-Gault, she became a successful award-winning television news reporter and analyst for the PBS network.

Lester Maddox (1915–), ultra-conservative Atlanta restaurateur and notorious advocate of armed resistance to desegregation; he first entered politics in 1957, unsuccessfully challenging Atlanta Mayor William Hartsfield; as the leader of the segregationist organization GUTS (Georgians Unwilling to Surrender), he finished second to Ivan Allen Jr. in Atlanta's mayoral race in 1961; in 1966 he was elected governor of Georgia, defeating Republican candidate Howard "Bo" Callaway; after four years as governor (1967–71), he served one term (1971–75) as lieutenant governor.

Malcolm X (1925–65), charismatic black nationalist leader; born Malcolm Little in Omaha, Nebraska, he joined the Nation of Islam and changed his name to Al Hajj Malik Shabazz; also known as Malcolm X, he left the Nation of Islam in 1964 to found the Organization for Afro-American Unity; after coauthoring (with Alex Haley) a best-selling memoir, *The Autobiography of Malcolm X* (1964) and making a pilgrimage to Mecca, he was assassinated in New York City in February 1965.

Harold H. Martin (1910–94), journalist, magazine writer, and biographer of Ralph McGill and John F. Kennedy; born in Commerce, Georgia, he worked as a columnist for the *Atlanta Constitution* (1938–43, 1946–66) and as a contributing editor for the *Saturday Evening Post* (1951–53, 1958–69).

Benjamin Mays (1894–1984), noted black educator; born in Epworth, South Carolina; dean of the Howard University School of Religion, 1934–40; president of Atlanta's Morehouse College, 1940–67; mentor of the Reverend Martin Luther King Jr.; longtime president of the United Negro College Fund.

Ralph McGill (1898–1969), noted liberal southern journalist; born in Tennessee, he worked as a reporter for the *Nashville Banner* before moving to the *Atlanta Constitution* in 1929; during his forty years as a *Constitution* reporter and editor, he championed educational and political reform, racial tolerance, and gradual social change; a founding member of the Southern Regional Council (1944), he won a Pulitzer Prize in 1959 for his editorials condemning the bombing of an Atlanta synagogue.

James Meredith (1933–), Mississippi-born black civil rights activist and U.S. Air Force veteran (1951–60), who braved angry white mobs during his attempt to desegregate the University of Mississippi in 1962; following his graduation from the University of Mississippi in 1963, he studied in Nigeria (1964–65) before enrolling at Columbia University Law School; while at Columbia, he wrote and published the memoir *Three Years in Mississippi* (1966) and attempted a lone freedom march through Mississippi that ended when he was shot by a white supremacist; surviving the attempted assassination, he graduated from Columbia in 1968.

Reg Murphy (1934–), Georgia-born journalist; after eight years with the *Macon Telegraph and News* (1953–60), he served as the political editor of the *Atlanta Constitution* (1961–65) and managing editor of *Atlanta Magazine* (1965–68); in 1968 he returned to the *Constitution* as a general editor.

Dean Rusk (1909–94), Georgia-born diplomat; president of the Rocke-feller Foundation, 1952–60; secretary of state under Presidents Kennedy and Johnson, 1961–69; stalwart defender of America's interventionist policy in Vietnam; in 1970 he became a professor of law at the University of Georgia.

Carl Sanders (1925–), Georgia-born attorney and legislator; widely regarded as a racial moderate, he served as president pro tem of the Georgia state senate (1960–62) before winning the governorship over archsegregationist and ex-governor Marvin Griffin in 1962; he served as governor from 1963 to 1967.

John A. Sibley (1888–1986), prominent Atlanta financier and corporate attorney who presided over the 1961 Sibley Commission; created by a legislative resolution, its nineteen members conducted twelve public hearings on attitudes toward school desegregation; held in ten congressional districts across the state, the hearings revealed a wide range of opinion on the advisability and practicality of school desegregation.

Lillian Smith (1897–1966), Florida-born teacher, magazine editor, novelist, and social critic; author of the controversial novel *Strange Fruit* (1944), an influential study of southern race relations, *Killers of the Dream* (1949), and *Our Faces, Our Words* (1964), a reflection on civil rights activism; a staunch defender of racial justice and women's rights, she edited *South Today*, which provided a forum for southern liberalism, and served on the national board of CORE in the 1940s.

Herman Talmadge (1913–2002), son and political heir of controversial Georgia governor Eugene Talmadge; as a two-term Democratic governor (1948–55) and four-term U.S. senator (1957–81), he was a consistent advocate of racial segregation and political conservatism; a University of Georgia Law School graduate and former naval officer, he was more polished and less bombastic than his demagogic father but no less committed to the politics of sectionalism.

Ernest Vandiver (1918–), Democratic governor of Georgia (1957–61); a firm advocate of segregation and political ally of Herman Talmadge, he nonetheless came to recognize the futility and economic liability of an intransigent defense of the racial and political status quo; in January 1961 he incurred the wrath of Roy Harris and other extremists for refusing to defy a federal court order desegregating the University of Georgia.

Carl Vinson (1883–1981), conservative Georgia Democrat; born in Milledgeville, Georgia, he served four years in the state legislature (1909–12) and forty-two years (1914–65) in the U.S. House of Representatives; in the later stages of his long congressional career, he chaired the House Committee on Naval Affairs and the House Armed Services Committee.

George C. Wallace (1919–98), populistic and demagogic state legislator (1951–55) and circuit judge (1955–63), elected governor of Alabama in 1962 as an ultra-segregationist Democrat; after symbolically "standing in the schoolhouse door" in 1963, he offered himself as a pro-segregation and pro–states rights presidential candidate in 1964, 1968, 1972, and 1976; though seriously wounded in a 1972 assassination attempt, he ultimately served four four-year terms (elected 1962, 1970, 1974, and 1982) as governor.

Lurleen Wallace (1926–68), first wife of George Wallace, whom she succeeded as governor of Alabama in 1966; with her husband acting as "no. 1 advisor," she served as governor until her death in May 1968.

Julius Waties Waring (1880–1968), racially liberal jurist of Charleston, South Carolina; serving as judge of the U.S. District Court for Eastern South Carolina (1942–52), he issued a series of pro–civil rights rulings; ostracized by many of his fellow white South Carolinians, he moved to New York City in 1952.

Whitney M. Young (1921–71), Kentucky-born black civil rights activist and executive director of the National Urban League, 1961–71; from 1954 to 1961 he was dean of the Atlanta University School of Social Work.

Selected Bibliography

Anderson, William. *The Wild Man from Sugar Creek: The Political Career of Eugene Talmadge*. Baton Rouge: Louisiana State University Press, 1975.

Arnall, Ellis. *The Shore Dimly Seen*. Philadelphia: J. B. Lippincott, 1946.

Arsenault, Raymond. "Civil Rights Movement." In *The Oxford Companion to United States History*, edited by Paul S. Boyer, 126–28. New York: Oxford University Press, 2001.

———. "The Folklore of Southern Demagoguery." In *Is There a Southern Political Tradition?* edited by Charles Eagles, 79–132. Jackson: University Press of Mississippi, 1996.

Ashmore, Harry S. *An Epitaph for Dixie*. New York: W. W. Norton, 1958.

———. *Civil Rights and Wrongs: A Memoir of Race and Politics, 1944–1994*. New York: Pantheon, 1994.

———. *Hearts and Minds: The Anatomy of Racism from Roosevelt to Reagan*. New York: McGraw-Hill, 1982.

Bartley, Numan V. *From Thurmond to Wallace: Political Tendencies in Georgia, 1948–1968*. Baltimore: Johns Hopkins University Press, 1970.

———. *The Creation of Modern Georgia*. Athens: University of Georgia Press, 1983.

———. *The New South, 1945–1980*. Baton Rouge: Louisiana State University Press, 1995.

Bayor, Ronald. *Race and the Shaping of Twentieth-Century Atlanta*. Chapel Hill: University of North Carolina Press, 1996.

Black, Creed C. "Presidential Profile." *The Bulletin*, American Society of Newspaper Editors (April 1977): 22–25.

Blackwell, Louise, and Francis Clay. *Lillian Smith*. New York: Twayne, 1971.

Branch, Taylor. *Parting the Waters: America in the King Years, 1954–1963*. New York: Simon and Schuster, 1988.

———. *Pillar of Fire: America in the King Years, 1963–1965*. New York: Simon and Schuster, 1998.

Carson, Clayborne. *In Struggle: SNCC and the Black Awakening of the 1960s*. Cambridge: Harvard University Press, 1981.

Carter, Dan T. *The Politics of Rage: George Wallace, the Origins of the New Conservatism, and the Transformation of American Politics*. New York: Simon and Schuster, 1995.

Carter, Hodding. *Southern Legacy*. Baton Rouge: Louisiana State University Press, 1950.

Carter, Jimmy. *Turning Point: A Candidate, a State, and a Nation Come of Age*. New York: Times Books, 1992.

Cash, Wilbur J. *The Mind of the South*. New York: Knopf, 1941.

Cason, Clarence. *90 Degrees in the Shade*. Chapel Hill: University of North Carolina Press, 1935.

Chappell, David. *Inside Agitators: White Southerners in the Civil Rights Movement*. Baltimore: Johns Hopkins University Press, 1994.

Clayton, Bruce. *W. J. Cash: A Life*. Baton Rouge: Louisiana State University Press, 1991.

Clowse, Barbara B. *Ralph McGill: A Biography*. Macon: Mercer University Press, 1998.

Cook, James Graham. *The Segregationists*. New York: Appleton-Century-Crofts, 1962.

Curry, Constance, et al. *Deep in Our Hearts: Nine White Women in the Freedom Movement*. Athens: University of Georgia Press, 2000.

Dabney, Virginius. *Below the Potomac: A Book about the New South*. New York: D. Appleton Century, 1942.

———. *Liberalism in the South*. Chapel Hill: University of North Carolina Press, 1932.

Dabbs, James McBride. *Who Speaks for the South?* New York: Funk and Wagnalls, 1964.

Daniels, Jonathan. *A Southerner Discovers the South*. New York: Macmillan, 1938.

Dudziak, Mary L. *Cold War Civil Rights: Race and the Image of American Democracy*. Princeton: Princeton University Press, 2000.

Dunbar, Anthony P. *Against the Grain: Southern Radicals and Prophets, 1929–1959*. Charlottesville: University of Virginia Press, 1981.

Eagles, Charles, ed. *Is There a Southern Political Tradition?* Jackson: University Press of Mississippi, 1996.

————. *Jonathan Daniels and Race Relations: The Evolution of a Southern Liberal.* Knoxville: University of Tennessee Press, 1982.

East, P. D. *The Magnolia Jungle: The Life, Times, and Education of a Southern Editor.* New York: Simon and Schuster, 1960.

Egerton, John. *Speak Now Against the Day: The Generation Before the Civil Rights Movement in the South.* New York: Knopf, 1994.

————. *The Americanization of Dixie: The Southernization of America.* New York: Harper's Magazine Press, 1974.

Escott, Paul D. *W. J. Cash and the Minds of the South.* Baton Rouge: Louisiana State University Press, 1992.

Fairclough, Adam. *To Redeem the Soul of America: The Southern Christian Leadership Conference and Martin Luther King, Jr.* Athens: University of Georgia Press, 1987.

Fitzpatrick, Vincent. *Gerald W. Johnson: From Southern Liberal to National Conscience.* Baton Rouge: Louisiana State University Press, 2002.

Galphin, Bruce. *The Riddle of Lester Maddox.* Atlanta: Camelot, 1968.

Garrow, David J. *Bearing the Cross: Martin Luther King, Jr. and the Southern Christian Leadership Conference.* New York: William Morrow, 1986.

Gaston, Paul M. *The New South Creed: A Study in Southern Mythmaking.* New York: Knopf, 1970.

Grantham, Dewey. *Southern Progressivism: The Reconciliation of Progress and Tradition.* Knoxville: University of Tennessee Press, 1983.

Graves, John Temple. *The Fighting South.* New York: G. P. Putnam's Sons, 1943.

Greenberg, Cheryl, ed. *A Circle of Trust: Remembering SNCC.* New Brunswick, N.J.: Rutgers University Press, 1998.

Hays, Brooks. *A Southern Moderate Speaks.* Chapel Hill: University of North Carolina Press, 1959.

Henderson, Harold P. *The Politics of Change in Georgia: A Political Biography of Ellis Arnall.* Athens: University of Georgia Press, 1991.

————. *Ernest Vandiver: Governor of Georgia.* Athens: University of Georgia Press, 2000.

Hill, William I. "ASNE Presidential Profile: Eugene C. Patterson." *Editor and Publisher*, April 30, 1977, 7.

Hobson, Fred. *A Serpent in Eden: H. L. Mencken and the South.* Chapel Hill: University of North Carolina Press, 1974.

————. *South-Watching: Selected Essays by Gerald W. Johnson.* Chapel Hill: University of North Carolina Press, 1983.

————. *Tell About the South: The Southern Rage to Explain.* Baton Rouge: Louisiana State University Press, 1983.

Hunter-Gault, Charlayne. *In My Place*. New York: Farrar, Straus, and Giroux, 1992.

Isserman, Maurice, and Michael Kazin. *America Divided: The Civil War of the 1960s*. New York: Oxford University Press, 2000.

Kennedy, Stetson. *Southern Exposure*. New York: Doubleday, 1946.

Key, V. O., Jr. *Southern Politics in State and Nation*. New York: Knopf, 1949.

Kilpatrick, James J. *The Southern Case for School Segregation*. New York: Crowell-Collier, 1962.

King, Richard. *A Southern Renaissance: The Cultural Awakening of the American South, 1930–1955*. New York: Oxford University Press, 1980.

Kirby, Jack Temple. *Rural Worlds Lost: The American South, 1920–1960*. Baton Rouge: Louisiana State University Press, 1987.

Kneebone, John T. *Southern Liberal Journalists and the Issue of Race, 1920–1944*. Chapel Hill: University of North Carolina Press, 1985.

Leidholdt, Alexander S. *Editor for Justice: The Life of Lovis I. Jaffé*. Baton Rouge: Louisiana State University Press, 2002.

Lewis, Anthony, and the *New York Times*. *Portrait of a Decade: The Second American Revolution*. New York: Random House, 1964.

Lewis, John, with Michael D'Orso. *Walking with the Wind: A Memoir of the Civil Rights Movement*. New York: Simon and Schuster, 1998.

Loveland, Anne C. *Lillian Smith: A Southerner Confronts the South*. Baton Rouge: Louisiana State University Press, 1986.

Martin, Harold H. *Ralph McGill, Reporter*. Boston: Little, Brown, 1973.

Mays, Benjamin F. *Born to Rebel*. New York: Charles Scribner's Sons, 1971.

McGill, Ralph. *The South and the Southerner*. Boston: Little, Brown, 1963.

McWhorter, Diane. *Carry Me Home: Birmingham, Alabama: The Climactic Battle of the Civil Rights Revolution*. New York: Simon and Schuster, 2001.

Mims, Edwin. *The Advancing South: Stories of Progress and Reaction*. Garden City, N.Y.: Doubleday, Page, 1926.

Morris, Willie. *North Toward Home*. Boston: Houghton Mifflin, 1967.

Morrison, Joseph L. *W. J. Cash: Southern Prophet*. New York: Knopf, 1967.

Mullane, Deirdre, ed. *Crossing the Danger Water*. New York: Anchor, 1993.

Myrdal, Gunnar. *An American Dilemma: The Negro Problem and American Democracy*. 2 vols. New York: Harper Brothers, 1944.

Norris, Hoke, ed. *We Dissent*. New York: St. Martin's, 1962.

Oasthaus, Carl R. *Partisans of the Southern Press: Editorial Spokesmen of the Nineteenth Century*. Lexington: University Press of Kentucky, 1994.

Odum, Howard W. *An American Epoch: Southern Portraiture in the National Picture*. New York: Henry H. Holt, 1930.

————. *Race and Rumors of Race: Challenge to American Crisis.* Chapel Hill: University of North Carolina Press, 1943.

Patterson, Eugene C. *The Bridge Beyond: A Family History.* St. Petersburg: E. C. Patterson, 1993.

————. "Great Careers, Modest Beginnings." *Gannett Center Journal* (Spring 1988): 46.

Pierce, Robert N. *A Sacred Trust: Nelson Poynter and the St. Petersburg Times.* Gainesville: University Press of Florida, 1993.

Powledge, Fred. *Free At Last? The Civil Rights Movement and the People Who Made It.* Boston: Little, Brown, 1991.

Pratt, Robert A. *We Shall Not Be Moved: The Desegregation of the University of Georgia.* Athens: University of Georgia Press, 2002.

Pratte, Alf. "Eugene Patterson." In *Dictionary of Literary Biography*, vol. 127, *American Newspaper Publishers, 1950–1990*, 236–40. Detroit: Gale Research, 1993.

Raines, Howell, ed. *My Soul Is Rested: Movement Days in the Deep South Remembered.* New York: G. P. Putnam's Sons, 1977.

Roche, Jeff. *Restructured Resistance: The Sibley Commission and the Politics of Desegregation in Georgia.* Athens: University of Georgia Press, 1998.

Sherrill, Robert. *Gothic Politics in the Deep South.* New York: Ballantine, 1969.

Singal, Daniel Joseph. *The War Within: From Victorian to Modernist Thought in the South, 1919–1945.* Chapel Hill: University of North Carolina Press, 1982.

Smith, Frank E. *Look Away from Dixie.* Baton Rouge: Louisiana University Press, 1965.

Smith, Lillian. *Killers of the Dream.* New York: W. W. Norton, 1949.

Sosna, Morton. *In Search of the Silent South: Southern Liberals and the Race Issue.* New York: Columbia University Press, 1977.

Talmadge, Herman E., with Mark Royden Winchell. *Talmadge: A Political Legacy, A Politician's Life.* Atlanta: Peachtree, 1987.

Teel, Leonard Ray. *Ralph Emerson McGill: Voice of the Southern Conscience.* Knoxville: University of Tennessee Press, 2001.

Tindall, George Brown. *The Emergence of the New South, 1913–1945.* Baton Rouge: Louisiana State University Press, 1967.

Trillin, Calvin. *An Education in Georgia: The Integration of Charlayne Hunter and Hamilton Holmes.* New York: Viking, 1963.

Tuck, Stephen G. N. *Beyond Atlanta: The Struggle for Racial Equality in Georgia, 1940–1980.* Athens: University of Georgia Press, 2001.

Viorst, Milton. *Fire in the Streets: America in the 1960s.* New York: Simon and Schuster, 1979.

Watters, Pat. *Down to Now: Reflections on the Southern Civil Rights Movement.* New York: Pantheon, 1971.

Weltner, Charles. *Southerner.* Philadelphia: J. B. Lippincott, 1966.

Wilkie, Curtis. *Dixie: A Personal Odyssey through Events That Shaped the Modern South.* New York: Scribner, 2001.

Wofford, Harris. *Of Kennedys and Kings: Making Sense of the Sixties.* New York: Farrar, Straus, and Giroux, 1980.

Woodward, C. Vann. *Tom Watson: Agrarian Rebel.* New York: Macmillan, 1938.

Workman, William D. *The Case for the South.* New York: Devin-Adair, 1960.

Wynes, Charles E., ed. *Forgotten Voices: Dissenting Southerners in an Age of Conformity.* Baton Rouge: Louisiana State University Press, 1967.

Zinn, Howard. *SNCC: The New Abolitionists.* Boston: Beacon Press, 1964.

———. *The Southern Mystique.* New York: Knopf, 1964.

Notes on Editors and Contributors

Raymond Arsenault is the John Hope Franklin Professor of Southern History and director of the University Honors College at the University of South Florida, St. Petersburg, where he has taught since 1980. A specialist in the history of civil rights and the American South, he has also taught at the University of Minnesota, Brandeis University, and the Université d'Angers in France, where he was a Fulbright lecturer in 1984–85. His publications include *The Wild Ass of the Ozarks* (1984); "The End of the Long Hot Summer: The Air Conditioner and Southern Culture," *Journal of Southern History* (1984); *St. Petersburg and the Florida Dream, 1888–1950* (1988); and *Crucible of Liberty: 200 Years of the Bill of Rights* (1991), which he edited. In 1986 he was awarded the prestigious Green-Ramsdell Prize by the Southern Historical Association. Since 1996, he has been the co-editor of the University Press of Florida's series Florida History and Culture.

Roy Peter Clark is Senior Scholar at the Poynter Institute, a school for journalists that owns the *St. Petersburg Times*. He has taught writing there since 1977, when he was hired by Gene Patterson, and helped found many of its programs. Among journalists, he is considered one of the nation's most influential writing coaches. He has written or edited more than a dozen books on writing, ethics, and journalism. Clark is founding director of the National Writers' Workshop and was honored as a distinguished service member by the American Society of Newspaper Editors. He can be reached at rclark@poynter.org.

Howell Raines was born in Alabama and developed as a journalist at newspapers in Tuscaloosa, Birmingham, and Atlanta. Gene Patterson hired him to be political editor of the *St. Petersburg Times* in 1976, and he served in that office for two years. From there he joined the staff of the *New York Times*, where he served as a reporter, bureau chief, foreign correspondent, and editor of the editorial page. He won a Pulitzer Prize for feature writing in 1992. Just days before September 11, 2001, he became executive editor of the *Times* and led the paper through coverage of the disaster; this coverage won a record seven Pulitzer Prizes. He is the author of three books, *My Soul Is Rested* (an oral history of the civil rights movement), *Whiskey Man* (a novel), and *Fly Fishing through the Midlife Crisis* (a memoir).

Cynthia Tucker was born in Alabama and now serves as editorial page editor of the *Atlanta Constitution*, a position once held by Gene Patterson. She is a frequent contributor on CNN and on PBS's *NewsHour with Jim Lehrer*. She came to her current position with considerable reporting experience, covering local governments, national politics, crime, and education. Tucker was a Nieman Fellow at Harvard and is a member of the National Association of Black Journalists. She received a distinguished writing award from the American Society of Newspaper Editors in 2000.

Index

Albany protests, 12, 30, 31, 62, 87, 89, 101, 103–5
Allen, Ivan, Jr., 37, 89, 90, 91, 138, 159, 206, 211–14
American Nazi Party, 78–79
Arnall, Ellis, 222
Atlanta as "city too busy to hate," xii, 15, 37, 82

Barnett, Ross, 35, 114, 137, 171, 223, 258
Birmingham church bombing, xiv, 11, 15, 32, 121, 146–48
Black power, 33, 199, 208–10, 211–14
Bond, Julian, xiii, 5, 198, 199, 200, 201–2, 278
Brooke, Sen. Edward, 222, 223
Brown v. Board of Education of Topeka, xii, 11, 28, 29, 35, 37, 283

Callaway, Howard "Bo," 193, 216–17, 234
Carmichael, Stokely, 199, 209–10, 211, 222
Carter, Hodding, 10, 22, 24, 25
Cash, Wilbur J., 22, 24, 149–50, 235–36
Cason, Clarence, 22, 24, 25
Collins, LeRoy, 170, 257, 258
Congress of Racial Equality (CORE), 11, 28, 30, 31, 35, 61, 199, 215

Connor, Eugene "Bull," 32, 35, 96, 121, 130

Dabney, Virginius, 10, 22, 23
Death penalty, 160–62
Desegregation of schools and universities: Atlanta public schools, 79–81, 158; Emory University, 94–95, 133, 158; Little Rock, schools, 11, 30, 57, 257; private schools, 132–33; University of Georgia, 60, 61, 63–64, 158, 255–62

Evers, Medgar, 32, 35, 121

Faubus, Orval, 11, 35, 62, 100, 223, 257
Freedom Rides, 11, 28, 30, 31, 35, 61, 76, 98, 240
Freedom Summer of 1964, 11, 32, 153
Fund to restore burned churches, 108–12, 116–18

Garvey, Marcus, 26
Geer, Peter Zack, 64, 107, 202
Goldwater, Barry, 35, 36, 153, 154
Graham, Billy, 162–63
Greer, John, 53–54

Gregory, Dick, 192

Harris, Roy V., 64, 236
Hartsfield, William B., 37, 82, 89, 90–91
Hemingway, Ernest, 7
Holmes, Hamilton, 60, 61, 127–29, 255–56, 258–61
Hunter, Charlayne, 60, 61, 255–56, 258–61

Johnson, Gerald, 20, 21
Johnson, James Weldon, 26
Johnson, LeRoy, 122, 138
Johnson, Lyndon B., 5, 32, 34, 35, 46, 121, 153, 154, 157, 162–63, 165–66, 170, 175, 181, 199, 219, 223, 231, 232, 235–37, 257, 263

Kennedy, John F., 31, 32, 35, 46, 48, 61, 89, 90, 91, 110–12, 121, 126–27, 132, 135, 137, 151, 154, 157, 223
Kennedy, Robert F., 31, 35, 46, 129–30, 167–68, 175–76, 231
King, Martin Luther, Jr., 5, 8, 11, 12, 29, 30, 31, 32, 45, 46, 89, 98, 101–2, 103, 139, 154, 189, 208–9, 222–24, 230, 231, 239–41, 257, 263, 278, 282, 283; assassination of, 15, 33, 237–38; "I have a dream" speech, 120, 121, 141–42; letter from Birmingham jail, 13, 238
Ku Klux Klan, 12, 13, 20, 35, 195–96, 200, 210, 256, 283

Maddox, Lester, 12, 37, 106–7, 200, 216–17, 221–22, 224–25, 234
Malcolm X, 181, 183–85
March on Washington, 11, 32, 35, 121, 141, 184, 189
Martin, Harold, 7, 9, 124, 186
Mays, Benjamin, 226–27
McGill, Ralph, xi, 3, 5, 7, 8, 10, 12, 13,

15, 19, 22, 24, 38, 40, 41, 93, 104, 186, 277, 278, 281, 282, 283, 284, 285, 286
Meredith, James, 32, 89, 113, 115, 116, 128, 199, 207–8
Murphy, Reg, 171–72
Myrdal, Gunnar, xiii, 18, 19, 27

National Association for the Advancement of Colored People (NAACP), 12, 25, 26, 27, 28, 29, 30, 32, 35, 84, 121, 137, 196, 213, 259
Nixon, Richard, 36, 44, 46, 89, 94, 232

Randolph, A. Philip, 26, 27
Roosevelt, Franklin D., 19, 26, 27, 90, 163–65
Rusk, Dean, 185, 202

Sanders, Carl, 62, 89, 175, 176, 217, 256, 257
Sibley, John A., 56, 65–66, 157
Sibley Commission, 45, 53–54, 56, 58, 61, 65
Smith, Lillian, 214–16
Southern Christian Leadership Conference (SCLC), 30, 31, 32, 35, 37, 45, 89, 199, 223–24, 231
Student Nonviolent Coordinating Committee (SNCC), 11, 30, 31, 35, 37, 45, 142, 159, 199, 200–201, 202, 208, 211–14, 215, 219

Talmadge, Herman, 35, 37, 172, 233
Truman, Harry, 34, 90, 91, 93–94
Twitty, Frank, 62, 256

Vandiver, Ernest, 45, 56, 57, 62, 63, 64, 71, 77, 217, 256–58
Vietnam, 223–24
Vinson, Carl, 157

Wallace, George C., 32, 35, 36, 100–101, 121, 130, 168, 171, 172, 173, 221–22, 223, 224, 232, 235–37, 257, 258

Wallace, Lurleen, 210, 219

Waring, Julius Waties, 232–33

White Citizens Councils, 13, 29, 35, 36, 84

Young, Whitney M., 206